Italian Socialism

ITALIAN SOCIALISM

Between Politics and History

EDITED BY

Spencer M. Di Scala

University of Massachusetts Press
Amherst

Copyright © 1996 by
The University of Massachusetts Press
All rights reserved
Printed in the United States of America
LC 95-38480
ISBN 1-55849-012-4
Designed by Steve Dyer
Set in Janson by dix!
Printed and bound by Braun-Brumfield, Inc.

Library of Congress Cataloging-in-Publication Data
Italian socialism : between politics and history / edited by
    Spencer M. Di Scala.
        p.   cm.
    Includes bibliographical references and index.
    ISBN 1-55849-012-4 (cloth : alk. paper)
    1. Partito socialista italiano—History—Congresses.   2. Socialism—
Italy—History—Congresses.   I. Di Scala, Spencer.
JN5657.S6I73   1996
324.245'072'09—dc20   95-38480
                           CIP

British Library Cataloguing in Publication data are available.

This book is published with the support and cooperation of the
University of Massachusetts Boston.

This book is dedicated to the memory of my brother,

DR. VINCENT A. DI SCALA

CONTENTS

ACKNOWLEDGMENTS

The international symposium on which this book is based, "One Hundred Years of Italian Democratic Socialism, 1892–1992," was held at the John F. Kennedy Library in Boston on 18, 19, and 20 March 1993. Planning for the symposium required several years and the aid of numerous persons and organizations I now acknowledge.

The idea for the symposium originated in a conversation between the Honorable Valdo Spini and me in Rome during the summer of 1990. The Honorable Spini was unstinting in his support and encouragement. Although he was scheduled to attend the symposium and to give a paper, he was named minister for the environment as the sessions began and could not attend. I called upon his father, Professor Giorgio Spini, to substitute for him, taking shameful advantage of his willingness to help. I thank him for the splendid job he did.

Once the idea for the conference germinated, I contacted Chancellor Sherry Penney of the University of Massachusetts at Boston through her faculty liaison, Professor Ann Cordilia. The chancellor's assistant, John Applebee, also facilitated communication. Chancellor Penney was immediately enthusiastic. She helped me with a small seed grant to keep communications with Italy open and put me in touch with Dr. Theresa Mortimer, associate provost for Continuing Education and International Programs at the university. Both Chancellor Penney and Associate Provost Mortimer offered moral and financial support during the planning period, securing several grants that financed released time from teaching and allowed me to continue the planning.

The burden of planning the details of the conference fell upon John Hughes, director of Professional Training Programs of the University's Division of Continuing Education. For a period of three years and the solution of numerous crises that escalated dramatically as the date for the symposium approached, I exploited the expertise of Jack and his staff. Their competence in attending to myriad practical aspects of scheduling a conference of this complexity—from travel to coffee, from hotel to taxis—was matched by their grace under the enormous pressure of doing the job along with their other commitments. Without the support given to me by the university, by the persons already mentioned, and by former Provost Fuad Safwat and Dean (and current Provost) Louis Esposito of the College of Arts and Sciences, this symposium could not have been held.

A co-sponsor of the symposium, with the University of Massachusetts at Boston, was the John F. Kennedy Library, donating the space in the Stephen Smith Center in which the sessions took place. Both participants and audience remarked upon the architectural beauty of the center and on its stunning natural setting. I thank the library staff, in particular, Sheldon Stern, historian, and John Stewart, director of education, for their kind help in facilitating the smooth running of the conference and for arranging a tour of the library for our guests.

The Consulate General of Italy in Boston was an additional co-sponsor. I received the utmost cooperation from Consul General Roberto Falaschi, who was always steady and gracious in his support for the project but magnificent in resolving several crises that, mercifully unbeknown to the participants, loomed menacingly even as they prepared to board airplanes for their journeys to Boston.

I acknowledge as well the help of the Italian Foreign Ministry in Rome, which made the largest financial contribution to the symposium. In this connection, I especially thank Ambassador Guido Martini, now Italian ambassador to South Korea for his efforts, which were essential for the initiation and successful outcome of the conference. Among the institutions contributing financially, the Banca Nazionale del Lavoro (New York) deserves special thanks.

Many individuals made very generous contributions of a different kind. In Italy, Professor Antonio Landolfi was active in keeping contact with persons connected with the conference, listened patiently to my telephoned entreaties, and intervened at strategic times. Professor Luciano Pellicani, editor of *Mondoperaio*, put the review's facilities at my disposal. His staff translated most of the Italian papers into English and handled many other details on the Italian end. I also thank the Honorable Gino Giugni, who agreed to join us and to give a paper on practically a moment's notice and who flew to Boston for one day in order to participate in meetings; he undertook this task despite his crucial role in trying to resolve his county's crisis.

Since some of them are not included in the chapters in this book, I also thank the persons who served as chairs of the sessions: Professors Nunzio Pernicone, Borden Painter, Claudio Segrè, Charles Delzell, and Giorgio Spini. Professor John A. Davis, Emiliana Noether Professor at the University of Connecticut, generously and skillfully intervened at the last moment to edit and read the remarks of the commentator who could not be present. I also thank Francesco Gozzano, editor of *Avanti!* who, while not participating in the symposium, undertook to write an essay especially for this book explaining the genesis of "Tangentopoli" and the likely context of future Italian politics.

The City of Boston cooperated wonderfully in making our Italian and American guests feel at home. Rosemarie Sansone, director of the Mayor's Office of Cultural and Business Affairs, coordinated relations between the City and the symposium organizers with graciousness and efficiency. Mayor Raymond Flynn, who had just been named ambassador to the Vatican, took the time to host a wonderful reception at the Parkman House for the symposium participants, the Italian-American community, and other honored guests. Thomas Menino, president of the Boston City Council and later elected mayor, made the guests particularly welcome and was among the personages who opened the conference.

I thank as well my wife, Laura Clerici Di Scala, for her strong support during a particularly stressful time. Not only did she come up with excellent ideas and skillfully handle relations with the individuals involved in the conference; she bravely confronted her worst fear on behalf of the symposium: a harsh New England winter.

Finally, I thank Kristina Carpine, Carla Bernardes, Meaghan Curley, Elizabeth Cummings, and Brian Purdy, who undertook the demanding task of typing the manuscript. They dealt deftly with difficulties ranging from my handwriting to transcribing some of the chapters directly from the videotape.

The successful outcome of the symposium and publication of this book thus owes a great deal to the cooperation and the coordination of efforts among many individuals and institutions. For all their generous aid, I am more grateful than they can know.

ABBREVIATIONS

ACID	American Committee for Italian Democracy
AD	Alleanza Democratica
CGIL	General Confederation of Italian Labor
CPSU	Communist Party of the Soviet Union
DC	Christian Democratic party
FDIF	International Democratic Federation of Women
IALC	Italian-American Labor Council
IIE	International Institute of Education
ILGWU	International Ladies Garment Workers Union
MSI	Italian Social Movement
OSAR	Organisation Secret d'Action Révolutionnaire Nationale
OVRA	Fascist Secret Police*
PCF	French Communist party
PCI	Italian Communist party
PDS	Democratic Party of the Left
PLI	Italian Liberal party
POI	Italian Workers' party
PRI	Italian Republican party
PSDI	Italian Social Democratic party
PSI	Italian Socialist party
PSIUP	Italian Socialist Party of Proletarian Unity
PSR	Reformist Socialist party
PSU	United Socialist party
SFIO	French Socialist party (1905–71)
SI	Italian Socialists
SIM	Military Information Service
SPD	German Social Democratic party
UDI	Union of Italian Women
UIL	Union of Italian Labor

* There is no agreement on the meaning of this acronym, which some experts believe was made up.

INTRODUCTION

Spencer M. Di Scala

In the summer of 1990, when I originally conceived of the international symposium on Italian democratic socialism on which this book is based, no one imagined the scandalous developments that would revolutionize Italian politics beginning in the winter of 1992. The Berlin Wall had fallen and the international communist movement was in shambles. In Italy, with the Italian Communist party in disarray, the stage seemed set for the triumph of social democracy and probable reversal of the "Italian anomaly": the inconsistency that Italy was the only European country in which a communist party dominated the left while a smaller socialist organization had a secondary role.

Because September 1992 marked the one-hundredth anniversary of the Italian Socialist party's (PSI) foundation, it seemed appropriate around that time to reflect on the crucial, if turbulent, role the party had played in Italy's history. Its creation had signaled the debut of the working class as an active participant in Italian politics, and it spurred important social and economic reforms in the late nineteenth and early twentieth centuries. Benito Mussolini had cut his political teeth as a militant in the organization and as editor of its newspaper, *Avanti!* The party had been an important protagonist in the debate preceding Italy's entrance into World War I and dominated the politics of the country in the first two years following that conflict. After 1920, popular support for Socialist policies and the resulting fear that socialism might take control in Italy stimulated a powerful reaction that contributed to the Fascist rise to power. Fascism's defeat of Italian socialism and the inferiority complex the event engendered in Socialists go a long way to explain the domination of the Italian left by communism, and consequently the destinies of contemporary Italy, and of Socialist party Secretary Bettino Craxi, who had made a career of waging war on the Communists. Paradoxically, the Socialist party itself spawned and influenced other Marxist movements of prime importance in Italian history, including its archrival, communism. Furthermore, the Socialists raised social and political issues that were debated for decades.

The ideological framework shaping the debates on crucial issues in Italy as in the rest of Europe, stemmed from Marxism's dual nature as the underpinning for both reformist and revolutionary movements. Should the Socialist party pursue a "revolutionary" or a "reformist" policy? The left (revolutionary) wing argued that no compromise was possible with the bourgeois order and that the status quo should be overthrown, whereas reformists concluded that socialism could be achieved only gradually as the conditions for it evolved, as described by Karl Marx. Reformists believed that socialism would be born in an increasingly democratic context spurred by accelerating industrialization. They feared that overthrowing the government by violence would produce a dictatorship in which an advance guard of Socialist fanatics would impose their factional view of socialism on society. While for reformists the gradualist concept allowed cooperation with bourgeois democratic factions, revolutionaries viewed such collaboration with the bourgeoisie and the strategic refusal to sanction the proletariat's immediate accession to power as crass betrayal of the working class.

In Italy, this fundamental dispute was more exacerbated than in the rest of Europe because the Socialist left wing was more extreme and more powerful. As a result of revolutionary ascendancy during crucial periods (1903–06, 1911–15, 1919–22, and after World War II, during a time of close Communist alliance) Italian socialism split often and was unable to come to power as a dominant force. With the establishment of the Italian Communist party (PCI) in 1921, the question of an alliance between Socialists and Communists against the reigning order also became paramount. The revolutionaries (now known as "maximalists") sought cooperation with the PCI, and the reformists condemned the communist movement. In effect, the left wing either prevented the reformists from leading the party to power within the government or simply paralyzed the party, with unfortunate consequences for the country.

As the socialist movement entered its second century, questions raised by the evolution of this seminal political force and its influence on the country's most pressing problems thus seemed significant enough to warrant fresh analysis, reexamination, and reinterpretation by historians and social scientists. For that reason, I decided to convene the international symposium entitled "One Hundred Years of Italian Democratic Socialism, 1892–1992." The speakers at that conference (most of whom are included in this book) narrated this essential story from different viewpoints. They included statesmen, scholars, and journalists, many of them important participants in the events they examined and interpreted. It seemed appropriate, moreover, to hold the symposium in the United States; a locale outside of Italy would set the scene for a more serene scholarly reflection on the many and varied vicissitudes of Italian democratic socialism far from the heated atmosphere of Italian politics.

By March 1993, when the symposium took place, all the participants were aware of rapidly unfolding events in Italy. Nevertheless, readers of this book and viewers of the complete videotaped record (preserved at the John F. Kennedy Library and at the Library of the University of Massachusetts at Boston) will notice an important facet of the proceedings. Although the main lines of the "bloodless revolution" were already clear, and the Socialist party had become deeply implicated in the major corruption scandal that precipitated the "revolution," many of the participants were confident that the PSI could be reformed and go on to play, once again, an important role in Italian history. Regrettably the symposium represented a missed opportunity to begin reforming the party; Socialist party Secretary Giorgio Benvenuto failed to encourage the debate opened at the conference and to make it an intellectual springboard for a profound revision of the movement's outlook. Yet the intellectual quality of the participants, of their ideas, and of their criticism (reflected in this book) suggests that the premise for this revision—and perhaps renovation —existed. As time went on, whatever confidence spawned by the symposium disappeared. Bettino Craxi, PSI secretary for sixteen years, was in disgrace; many militants "dropped out" of politics altogether; and it became unclear whether the party would survive. Many political observers predicted the end of the party, and socialism in Italy hovered "between politics and history."

Developments since the symposium's conclusion that unfolded during the editing of this book confirm this ambiguous state of affairs. From 11 November to 13 November 1994, the Italian Socialist party held the forty-seventh congress since its foundation at Genoa in 1892. Before the general elections of March 1994 the party had virtually collapsed; thanks only to its participation in the "Progressive Pole" dominated by the Democratic Party of the Left (PDS)—the successor organization to the Italian Communist party—had it been able to elect some members to Parliament.

At the November 1994 congress, the majority led by former secretary, union leader, and PDS ally Ottaviano Del Turco voted formally to dissolve the Socialist party, the proud creation of such legendary figures of Italian socialism as Filippo Turati, Pietro Nenni, and Sandro Pertini. The majority then constituted an association called Socialisti Italiani (Italian Socialists [SI]) and installed as its secretary a deputy elected within the ranks of the Progressive Pole, Enrico Boselli. This association's goal was to arrange for absorption of the Socialist remnants by small political organizations allied with the PDS.

Another group of Socialist parliamentarians joined with Valdo Spini, a former Socialist minister from Florence (and an influential personage in the planning of the March 1993 symposium), in a new "Labor Federation." Spini believed that both the party form of organization and the term "Socialist" were suspect and would continue to meet rejection at the hands of voters.

A large minority, however, opposed the party's dissolution, arguing that it was an illegitimate and humiliating act for Socialists. This group founded the Partito Socialista Riformista (PSR), intending to continue the historical tradition of Italian socialism while remaining autonomous from other political organizations, especially the PDS. This new party aimed to revive Italian socialism on the basis of clear reformist political and programmatic ideals. The PSR rejected any tendency to revive maximalism or extremism in any form and reconfirmed what it considered the fundamental socialist tradition of liberalism and defense of civil liberties. This last affirmation was directed especially at the magistrates, which, ever since the explosion of Tangentopoli (the "Kickback City" scandal), the adherents of the PSR argued, had been the real rulers of the country and had been guilty—in their investigative zeal—of violating the civil rights of Italian citizens, due process of law, and constitutional guarantees.

Despite its lack of parliamentary representation, because all Socialist parliamentarians were elected within the PDS-dominated Progressive Pole, the PSR has already developed a following in many Italian regions. Many Socialists who had left politics because they disagreed with the pro-PDS policy of Del Turco or who were disgusted by events leading to Tangentopoli have flocked to the new organization. The PSR elected as its provisional secretary Fabrizio Cicchitto, a former Socialist Senator, and as its president the former Socialist deputy Enrico Manca. A Secretariat charged with organizing the new party was also created and included among its members Antonio Landolfi, a former senator (and a contributor to this book). Whether this new political formation will be able to take off in Italy's complex and difficult political situation and whether it will be able to renew the Italian Socialist tradition is an open question. What can be said as this book goes to press is that the odds seem overwhelmingly against such a rebirth of an independent socialist party.

Other small, unstable Socialist groups exist as part of a diaspora. These splinters seem destined to disappear because, despite the present pulverization of political groupings, the tendency appears to be toward separation into two dominant camps: Socialists who wish to be autonomous and reformist; and Socialists who are subordinate to the PDS and do not even wish to have their own party.

Besides addressing specifically Italian concerns, our March 1993 symposium also presented an opportunity to remind people that, during the interwar period, the Italian-American communities in the United States were not hotbeds of fascism, but battlegrounds hotly contested between proponents of Il Duce and antifascist exiles who fled to America. Moreover, as developments after 1943 demonstrated, these exiles and their Italian-Americans allies profoundly influenced the course of Italian history from the vantage of the New World.

Convening the symposium in the City of Boston brought to mind that the New England area was a particularly strong bastion of antifascism centered around Gaetano Salvemini, vocal political exile, sworn enemy of Mussolini, and professor of history at Harvard. From that base, Salvemini directed a multifaceted struggle against Mussolini, not only in the Italian-American communities of the United States and institutions of the United States government but also—and most successfully—within the American intellectual establishment. I can cite one particularly significant example.

During his tenure at Harvard, Salvemini met Arthur M. Schlesinger Jr., son of the history department chairman and destined to become a distinguished historian himself. Salvemini piqued Schlesinger's interest in Italian affairs. In 1961, Schlesinger became special assistant to President John F. Kennedy. In that capacity and recalling his admiration for and links with Salvemini, Schlesinger led the movement within the Kennedy administration encouraging establishment in Italy of the center-left coalition that emerged in the early 1960s. This coalition undid the previous conservative governing alliance and, in one form or another, ran the country until the scandals broke in the 1990s. It was particularly fitting that the symposium's sessions were held at the John F. Kennedy Library and that Arthur Schlesinger could recount this history in person.

The symposium also revealed and emphasized the contribution and increasing importance of American scholars to the study of Italian affairs. Historians from different parts of the United States participated in the debate with lively papers and penetrating comments that illustrated the robustness and quality of Italian studies in the United States. Dialogue is essential to cultural development. I hope that the symposium has initiated continuing and fruitful dialogue between older and younger scholars in both countries.

PART 1
HISTORY

1

BIRTH OF ITALIAN SOCIALISM: REFORM OR REVOLUTION?

Antonio Landolfi

The policy of the Italian Socialist party (PSI) has always been essentially reformist, evolutionary, and gradualistic. Although some individual members, internal groups, and components belonged to a social culture with more revolutionary, extremist connotations, reformist policy, sanctioned by the first Congress of Genoa, has always prevailed. The political and symbolic matrix of the PSI was the split with anarchists, which also marked the definitive abandonment of the various forms of "bakuninism" and insurrection that had characterized its action prior to the foundation of an official socialist party.

"Conceived in the country and born in the city" is how that extraordinary personage, Arturo Labriola, later described the newborn PSI. In fact, the conception, pregnancy, and birth of PSI took fifteen, and possible even twenty years of revolutionary preaching, movements of rebellion, insurrection (planned, organized, and failed), and dreams of revolution and violence dreamt by intellectuals committed to saving society; dreams that inflamed the hearts of hungry, illiterate rural workers, generating fires destined to be extinguished just as suddenly as they had been lit.

This period also saw the expansion, admittedly somewhat laborious, of industry, especially in northern Italy, with the construction of Italy's first major factories and the establishment of many medium-sized enterprises. It was this process that generated the first, still primitive but growing, industrial proletariat and the Italian Workers' party (the POI, the so-called rough hands party), a federation that had sprung up spontaneously here and there, ten years before the foundation of PSI.

The experience of the Workers' party should not be underestimated in terms of its impact on the future PSI: at the founding Congress of Genoa, most of the Workers' party, under the de facto leadership of Costantino Lazzari, joined the Italian Socialist party. During its ten years (1882–92), of existence, the Italian Workers' party had pursued an essentially reformist policy with the social and political-institutional dimensions kept quite separate: absolute independence of the Workers' movement in terms of action and organization, on the one hand, and reforms ranging from extended suffrage to compulsory state education, on the other (both later pursued by the Socialists). The Workers' party even acknowledged the legitimacy of military service and agreed to participate in elections in alliance with other progressive forces.

The anarchists and the antiparliamentary revolutionary, extremist groups of the Workers' party refused to join the new PSI, which was composed in part of members of the former Workers' party and in part of socialist intellectuals, groups first and foremost those belonging to the *Critica Sociale* ("Milan") group.

The evolutionary Marxism pursued by Turati and Kuliscioff, which rejected violence as the matrix of history, met with no obstacles of substance in the social culture that had first consolidated in the Workers' party and then been converted to socialism.

In the last decade of the nineteenth century, the PSI pursued a policy aimed essentially at the national unification of workers' associations, establishing the organizational network necessary for the first modern national party based on mass participation. This led to a profound change in Italy's general political system, previously based on limited suffrage and sporadic, temporary forms of political association spread over the territory, and an electoral system based on a clientelistic relationship. The association between the reformist, gradualistic socialist intellectuals and the pragmatic members of the former Workers' party was also consolidated at the end of the nineteenth century in the fight to combat a new wave of repression.

At the turn of the century, Filippo Turati had already taken a stand on the alliance issue and voiced his disapproval of what he called class intransigence; in early 1894, *Critica Sociale* had cited a letter from the great old man, Engels, inviting comrades not to "disdain" such victories of "bourgeois" democracies, as universal suffrage, freedom of association, and freedom of the press. But it was only after the Congress of Parma

(1895)—when the PSI assumed a real identity and its official title, becoming a party organized according to a system of individual membership—that the Socialist party really became the main mobilizing force against authoritarianism and repression. For six years the Socialists devoted much of their energy to obtaining statutory freedom and defending the rights of workers and of other forces.

Between 1894 and 1900, democracy and liberty had been the leitmotiv of the PSI's clashes with the ruling class that culminated in the repression of 1898. The political battle strengthened the PSI's democratic convictions, increasing its interest in fighting for freedom, not only in relation to workers and class associations, and their freedom to exist and to operate, but also in relation to the press (the first issue of *Avanti!* was published on Christmas Day 1896), to personal liberty, against arbitrary arrests and unfair trials. In this period the PSI also gained electoral experience, participating in the National Parliament and in the municipal and provincial administrations.

Socialist representation in elective bodies, and the socialist electorate, were increasing constantly. At the 1895 Parma congress, the Socialists decided that universal suffrage would be their key objective. They considered this a means of enhancing the social, civil, and political status of workers and, at this time, the institutional role of the PSI.

Undoubtedly, the socialist experience in every aspect of democracy, and in defending democracy and freedom against increasing repression at the end of the decade, strengthened the position of the evolutionary, reformist group of the PSI and weakened that of Costantino Lazzari's "intransigents," who opposed Turati's policy of political alliances. The 26 May–4 June 1896 Florence congress witnessed a serious division between the two positions within PSI that did not, however, reach extreme consequences and was mediated by the unitarian Enrico Ferri.

Reformist policy had already been endorsed by Engels in the letter published two years earlier, showing remarkable foresight in view of subsequent events in Italy. In his letter Engels had referred to the possibility of a bourgeois republic being established in Italy by Italian radicals and republicans, and expressed his support for any action undertaken by these political forces that "would extend further and by much our freedom." According to Engels, Italian Socialists should also support this trend, though remaining completely independent in terms of ideology and organization. Consequently the PSI should "ally for the moment with the radicals and the republicans, but remain completely separate from them."

Events in Italy and the terms of the political struggle drove even those who were ideologically opposed to PSI policy to join the party in the fight to defend freedom and democracy. Consequently the situation in the PSI was highly differentiated, in part also because Italy itself was differentiated in both territorial and socioeconomic terms.

The core of the party, in northern Lombardy and the Po Valley, was reformist but, depending on the circumstances—as, to greater but varying degrees, in other areas and regions—there were "extreme positions that were profoundly anticlerical, against cooperating with the other parties of the Extreme Left, and in favour of militant revolution."

Extremist positions were particularly evident on social issues and in relation to the rural world. The agenda for the 1897 Bologna congress dedicated to socialist initiatives in agriculture was rigidly classist, stating that "small ownership as such" was to be considered "outside the doors of the party." What was actually being advocated was the proletarization of small farmowners with a view to forming a common front with the farm-hands, sharecroppers, and other tenant workers, according to an abstract theory, without taking into account the social network that existed in rural areas already facing a severe crisis.

The 1898 repression also swept away this naive, maximalistic approach, but it was becoming increasingly obvious that the PSI had no alternative but to participate in the fight to preserve liberty and democracy and to rally with the other bourgeois forces in the effort to defeat authoritarianism and guarantee a liberal, democratic order. Events therefore imposed what was referred to by *Avanti!* as the "turning point of the end of the century," marking the success of the reformist policy advocated by Turati, when the Socialists voted in favor of the government.

In 1902, *Avanti!* thus described the Socialist vote in favor of the Zanardelli-Giolitti government: "Until now bourgeois democracy has had to tolerate being weakened by the absence of the proletariat. The reactionaries took advantage of this state of affairs. They were able to grab power and hold onto it undisturbed, using that threat as a lever.

"As soon as the Socialist party successfully abandoned the early period of affirmation and differentiation and responded to the need to be part of democracy, the reactionary parties that had used the discord among the other parties to grab power for themselves, were swept away by the irresistible force of the new civilization" (5 April 1902).

The socialist newspaper placed great emphasis on the parliamentary element, which of course was of great significance: by voting in favor of the Zanardelli government, the socialist members of Parliament launched what proved to be a fruitful, positive, reformist era for PSI. But none of this would have been possible without the events and political initiatives of the previous decade. Moreover, the "turning point" that marked the start of this new reformist era was not without deep contrasts within the party. In the 1890s, Lazzari's "intransigents" had been essentially moderate and Enrico Ferri had pursued a relatively pragmatic policy. By the end of the century, new, extremely militant groups—culturally better equipped to oppose the reformists than Costantino Lazzari had ever been—came onto the scene; among them were the "revolutionary syndicalists," which included figures of the stature of Arturo Labriola and Enrico Leone. Internal opposition soon became particularly animated and was led by men of remarkable cultural and political standing.

It is no coincidence that the original core of the new antireformist faction should have been located in Italy's Mezzogiorno, and especially in Naples. In fact there was increasing divergence between the socialism practiced in the north, where economic and social conditions were relatively more advanced, and the socialism just starting to develop in the poorer south and islands. Initially, ties between the two areas of the movement had been close, in a spirit of true brotherhood and solidarity. The first Socialist conferences organized in the regions of Apulia and Calabria had been attended by Andrea Costa, a friend of Leone Mucci who had launched the movement in Apulia and Enrico Mastracchi from Catanzaro, in Calabria.

The "Fasci siciliani," the Sicilian movement that combined socialist, reformist, anarchic, and corporative features further strengthened solidarity. De Felice Giuffrida and Nicola Barbato, both heroes of the movement, were popular among the Socialists of northern and central Italy, where strikes were organized to express solidarity and protest against the repression of the movement. Its leaders, who had been placed on trial and found guilty, were presented as candidates in the elections held in some northern constituencies.

A young Piedmontese student, Giuseppe Cavallera from Cuneo, who had been among the first to advocate socialism in the region and had presented Barbato as a candidate in his province, was to learn a lot from this experience. Barbato was not elected, but Cavallera became aware of the importance of overcoming the division between socialism in the Mezzogiorno and in the islands and socialism in the north. So much so that, at the end of the century, he chose to go to Sardinia to finish studying medicine and organize some form of political and trade union representation for Sardinian fishermen, miners, and railway workers. Cavallera eventually founded socialism in Sardinia (and became Sardinia's first socialist member of parliament), but always remained in close political contact with his home region.

Despite these noble efforts and expressions of goodwill, the differences between socialism in southern Italy and the islands and socialism in central and northern Italy became increasingly drastic and visible. The degree of development of Italian regions was highly differentiated as was the political context in which the various social and political experiences were developing. In the south and in the islands, economic and cultural conditions were extremely backward. This factor, coupled with the reactionary attitude of the ruling classes, and the fact that the members of Parliament representing the traditional groups, even the more liberal ones, often had dealings with the most backward and even criminal elements, inevitably led to increasing radicalization of the social and political behavior of Socialists in the areas concerned. For the most part, in fact, they sided with the "intransigents."

The Naples and Salerno section produced a group of remarkable young people led by Arturo Labriola, Enrico Leone, and Oreste Longobardi. They managed to recruit followers from the whole region, from Naples to Campania, by waving the banner of antireformism and advocating a policy in favor of the Mezzogiorno. They accused the Socialists of the north of being "regionalistic" and insensitive to the problems of the southern regions. In political terms, the division between northern and southern Socialists had been fueled by the reformist policy of pursuing alliances with other political forces after the repression at the end of the nineteenth century; this policy was embraced by the progressive constitutional party that had always been the main enemy of the Socialists in the south.

However, the strongest opposition to the reformists at the national level was yet to come. In fact the "intransigents" were joined by a particularly vocal group of young southerners who gave Turati and the other reformists plenty to think about at socialist conferences at the turn of the century. These were young men who were firmly opposed to any form of reformism or revisionism, possessing profound political commitment and knowledge. They were almost always loyal opponents in the political battles within the party. Again, two tendencies developed within this same group: a common front of opposition to what they defined as the "right-wing" members of the PSI, but divergence in terms of theoretical approach and political strategy. The two groups were usually referred to as the "intransigent revolutionaries" and "revolutionary syndicalists."

Costantino Lazzari and Enrico Ferri led the intransigent revolutionaries. Lazzari, a former member of the Workers' party, had been one of the first supporters and founding members of the PSI. Though he had a basic theoretical background, he was a man of action rather than a doctrinaire and in favor of a fairly primitive form of Marxism, linked to the interpretation by Marx's early followers from Guesde to Lafarque. Enrico Ferri was a lawyer and a professor. He was renowned for his public speaking and capacity to sway his audience at conferences. He was a man of no great personal constancy (after many political vicissitudes, he ended up becoming senator of the kingdom during Fascism) who tried to achieve a synthesis of Marxism and Spencerian positivism popular in the culture of the period.

This attempted synthesis was the theoretical nucleus of the intransigent revolutionaries, their constant point of reference in the antireformist question and in their propaganda. It was based on the premise of materialism as a philosophical identity and the conception of history and its development as the outcome of solely economic and naturalistic factors. The objective was to provide an explanation of capitalistic society on the basis of an extreme and polar antithesis, "material forces of production" and "legal ownership relations." From this derived the strategy of the revolutionary classes whose objective was to organize and mobilize the proletariat, remaining firmly ensconced in, and opposed to, the fortress of the bourgeois state, while waiting for the automatic and definitive demise of capitalism. At that point working classes would abandon their position and use violence to take over the state, establishing absolute hegemony and socializing all means of production.

On the basis of this theoretical vision, the intransigents categorically refused any social or political alliance, any compromise, any reform. They did agree—by what logic it is not for us to say—to take part in elections, their intention being solely to utilize the institutional bodies as a platform for their permanent state of revolutionary agitation. Although this approach was somewhat primitive even for that time, the leaders of this faction were remarkably successful and even prevailed in some of the socialist conferences. This was in part due to Ferri's tactical ability. Later when he abandoned this extremist position and adopted a more moderate approach, Ferri assumed a major role in the life of the PSI and was also editor of *Avanti!* (Bologna 1904).

Ferri published various books, including *Marxism and Political Science*, that were widely read and popular even in the United States. His proposed Darwin-Spencer-Marx triad was criticized by Antonio Labriola, but aroused considerable interest in Italy and elsewhere, and was closely followed and supported by Veblen. Nonetheless, the intransigents, and in particular Ferri, whose "name was linked to the first major clash to take place within the Socialist party" did not "come . . . [up with] . . . any alternative or critique of substance" to Turati's policy.

The policy pursued by the revolutionary syndicalists was more consistent in both theoretical and political terms. This group, formed just after 1890, was particularly influenced by the works of Georges Sorel who, politically speaking, was to be more popular in Italy than in his native country; indeed, the group counted Arturo Labriola and Enrico Leone among its most prestigious supporters.

Revolutionary syndicalism can be considered a revisionist faction, though in a sense opposite to the revisionism pursued by Bissolati, Bonomi, and Michels. It was a kind of extreme-left "revisionism." Arturo Labriola was a brilliant scholar and, though volatile, a man of great political acumen (in his long political career he supported the extreme socialist left, was labor minister in the Giolitti government, and after the Second World War became an "independent of the left" alongside the Italian Communist party). He wrote many texts analyzing Marxist theory but, as he himself said years later, despite all his efforts, in the end he was left with nothing.

It is beyond the scope of this essay to follow Labriola's complex development through his many works: from *Social Reform and Revolution* to *The Dictatorship of the Bourgeois;* from *The History of Capitalism* to *The Timeliness of Marx* and *The Manual of Political Economy*. It might be pertinent to describe very briefly the main lines of the theoretical and political position of the revolutionary syndicalist faction of which he was a militant member together with Enrico Leone. Enrico Leone was also a prolific writer (his works include *Trade Unionism* and *The Hedonistic Economy*). Like Arturo Labriola, he was a major figure in the PSI and played an important political role, especially in opposing the reformists.

Unlike the revolutionaries led by Lazzari and Ferri, the revolutionary syndicalist faction acknowledged the need for reform, but as a revolutionary conquest and not as a consequence of social and political alliances. Arturo Labriola wittily but unfairly described the contacts between the PSI and democratic forces as an "alliance between the horse and the rider," obviously meaning that PSI was the horse and Giolitti the rider.

Labriola and Leone believed that socialist reformism would never be achieved "by" or "with" the bourgeois government but "against" the government and the bourgeois system. Bourgeois reformism was dangerous precisely because it led the masses to believe (mistakenly) that the existing system was capable of solving the evils of society. Hence, they were against the alliances proposed by the "reformists," which risked being ensnared by bourgeois reformism, placing the masses in a subordinate position vis-à-vis the system.

Thus on the issue of reformism proposed by Turati, the position of the revolutionary syndicalists was no different from that of the extremist groups in the PSI. Their proposals for action were, however, very different. Lazzari and Ferri (before they moved closer to the center), thought it was sufficient to criticize and reject a priori both bourgeois society and the state as the expression of the ruling class while waiting for the catastrophic collapse of capitalism. Arturo Labriola and Enrico Leone instead believed that the proletariat needed to implement an active revolutionary strategy that would destroy capitalism.

The idea led them to oppose political and parliamentary action, or any initiative or alliance, whose objective was to improve the living conditions of the workers, in terms of either legislation or remuneration. In their view this would have allowed capitalism to continue to develop, delaying its demise, dangerously weakening the revolutionary spirit and awareness of the masses. Leftist revisionism was essentially the affirmation of a proletarian voluntarism coupled with a deterministic analysis of economic conditions that would inevitably bring about the demise of capitalism.

This theory was based on Sorel's social philosophy, on the Bergsonian theory of volunteerism, and on Vilfredo Pareto's sociology. A combination of Marxism, volunteeristic and irrationalistic pragmatism, and mysticism of revolutionary action was expressed in a flood of strikes and a proliferation of explosive grassroots movements. In the few years in which revolutionary syndicalism operated within the party, it undoubtedly exercised a hold on the more intolerant workers' groups, on the young and a sizable number of socialist theorists.

Revolutionary syndicalism challenged not only the primacy of the party, but its very role as a political organization representing class movements, giving precedence to direct rather than party organization of the masses. Ironically, Turati's reformists had a stronger impact on the trade union organization, though relations between the trade union and the party were not always smooth or based on a common strategy. In fact, at the time the trade union needed the party in order to be able to implement the legislation necessary to create the conditions that would allow the ascent of the workers' movement and the party needed the trade union as a concrete, organized base in society.

Another factor, peculiar to Italy, was that in this case political experience had preceded the trade union experience: the PSI had been founded in 1892, whereas the General Confederation of Labor (CGL) had only become an organized national body in 1906, despite complex earlier experiences.

The CGL was completely independent of the party and, rightly, was determined to defend this independence. As early as October 1907, an agreement was signed by the PSI and the CGL, clearly defining their respective responsibilities and functions. Essentially, it was a replica of the Resolution of the Seventh Congress of the Second International held in Stuttgart in August 1906, defining the relations between Socialist parties and trade unions.

It was agreed that both the PSI and the CGL would base their activities on socialist principles and pursue a reformist, gradualistic political strategy. The "pact" established that the direction of economic strikes would be the competence of CGL, and that of political events the competence of the party. Decisions in relation to political strikes would be made jointly. This agreement pulled the rug out from under the feet of revolutionary syndicalism. It also ended up removing the platform for exercising concrete influence over the masses from the Bonomi and Bissolati revisionists, who were the upholders of the theory of trade-unionist economism and laborism. The pact with CGL immediately strengthened the Turati faction and the 1906 Rome congress marked the defeat of revolutionary syndicalism, by then a minority. The agreement consolidated reformist control of the PSI for the next six years, but, in one form or another, the reformist-revolutionary battle would continue throughout the party's existence.

2

CHANGING INTERPRETATIONS

Spencer M. Di Scala

Antonio Landolfi's paper is an excellent example of the manner in which historical interpretation changes. Thirty years ago, the suggestion by Luigi Cortesi that reformist head Filippo Turati had been the real founder of the Italian Socialist party caused a row that broke up the editorial board of a journal dedicated to the history of socialism. Ten years ago, it was still commonplace to state that Turati had been a revolutionary until the 1894 repression of the PSI.

As Landolfi points out, under Turati's leadership, the PSI was born reformist, committed to evolutionary socialism of the kind Eduard Bernstein advocated at the end of the century. This is hardly surprising, given that the PSI came into existence as a result of Turati's efforts after a sterile decade-long struggle to create a working-class organization. Indeed, the supposed "svolta" in Turati's ideology—during which Turati supposedly became transformed from a revolutionary into a reformist—never occurred, a fact that would have been immediately obvious to the proponents of the "great change" view had they bothered to read Turati's early writings.

Indeed, one can conduct a simple experiment with regard to this issue; that is, examine Turati's writings and actions around 1892, the year in which the Socialist party was founded. He argued that force degraded the human spirit, killed freedom, and made socialism impossible. To his mind, revolutionary violence indicated that society was not ready for socialism. As he wrote in 1893, "A revolution is not such *because* of violence, but *despite* violence." According to Turati, socialist ideas must be spread peacefully until they so permeated society that people would no longer have the will to resist them. He thus swiftly liquidated the "dictatorship of the proletariat" and emphasized social evolution (which, for the reformists, was synonymous with "revolution"). In short, as true Marxists, the reformists believed that industrial society evolved in a certain direction that would produce socialism; this development would be democratic, a concept that excluded dictatorships of any kind, that of the proletariat included.

Landolfi emphasizes a number of themes, ideological and practical. He did well to stress that, despite the PSI's reformist birth, several extremist variations of Marxism coexisted. In Italy, the reformist victory was incomplete; unlike the situation in other countries, the incomplete victory paralyzed the Socialist party's action. The question may be posed as to why these leftist groups had so much influence.

The reason is usually attributed to the "backward" nature of the Italian working classes, but, while comforting, this standard solution is far from satisfactory. The socialist movement, for example, was concentrated in Milan, where a modern industrial base had taken hold; for some historians, this development neatly explains why the thrust for the party's establishment came from the city and why it was most powerful there. In those areas where modern industry did not take root, the south and the islands, the Socialist party hardly existed. Yet the revolutionary syndicalist theoreticians that Landolfi mentions were southerners. Of course, one can consider revolutionary syndicalism a primitive and backward form of socialism if one wishes to do so, but the fact remains that in seeking to take over the party the revolutionary syndicalists immediately moved to Milan. There they established their headquarters and (with Walter Mocchi's money before he had a chance to run off to Argentina to become a theater impresario) their newspaper, *Avanguardia Socialista*. It was in Milan as well, not the south, that they had their greatest success, taking over the Camera del lavoro (Chamber of Labor) and altering the PSI's direction, at least temporarily.

In other words, this extremist movement succeeded, at least for a short time, in the heart of the "reformist fatherland"—to borrow a term from *Avanguardia Socialista*—and among the most "advanced" workers. The same might be said for the "revolutionaries" of Costantino Lazzari and Enrico Ferri. Although it is fashionable to attribute reformist strength in Milan to the development of industry there and the supposed reformist catering to unions and cooperatives, I would argue that the reformists just proved themselves better organizers than the leftists, as well as better able to bring results.

For example, while the revolutionary syndicalists preached constant strikes, records show that more strikes actually occurred during periods when reformists controlled the labor movement than when the revolutionary syndicalists did so, even though reformists opposed strikes except as a last resort. This development makes sense because it takes organization to conduct strikes, while the left, in practice, did not organize the workers (as the Milanese records also show). At the same time, one might also consider the peasants. In the north these were also organized by the reformists (remember Camillo Prampolini in the Emilia) and constituted a major strength of the Italian Socialist movement, while the leftists wrote the peasants off almost completely.

These last points are significant. Leftists were more interested in their ideological fine points and lost sight of socialism's prime objectives: to confront and resolve the unique problems posed by modern society and organize it in the manner most beneficial to the most people. In fact, we note that Landolfi's paper is most concerned with explaining the ideology of different groups on the Socialist left wing. This is no accident, since left-wing ideology was fragmented and inconsistent. We can cite no dominant ideological figure on the Socialist Left in Italy. Lazzari and the "leftist" Ferri had no ideology beyond unthinking political intransigence, a policy that eventually bore its final bitter fruit after World War I.

The most interesting ideology on the left during this period is no doubt revolutionary syndicalism, as Landolfi indicates. But Arturo Labriola went through so many changes that his comrades nicknamed him "Arturo Capriola" (Arthur Somersault). More than a movement-inspiring ideology, revolutionary syndicalism may be likened to a mystical drug that provides a perpetual high. It will be remembered that the revolutionary syndicalists supported the Libyan War and that they had a major role in convincing Benito Mussolini to come out in favor of Italian intervention in World War I. Ultimately, revolutionary syndicalism flowed easily into war and Fascism.

Unlike the leftist ideologies, reformism was at least consistent and practical; but it was difficult to apply in the context of a divided movement. The temptation to accept parliamentary compromise and to concentrate on electoral maneuvering proved too great; constantly under attacks which they judged unthinking and due to the economic and social backwardness of their country, besieged reformist leaders believed that their country could be rendered responsive to their demands for reform. This action in turn spurred greater attacks on them by self-defined revolutionaries in their own party. The result was paralysis and unresolved continuous conflict. These were the real elements of the reformist-revolutionary debate —and they spelled tragedy for the country.

3

GIOLITTI AND THE SOCIALISTS

Alexander De Grand

Giovanni Giolitti's essential contribution to the Italian political process came in one move when, as interior minister in the Zanardelli government of 1901, he decided to apply a new policy of tolerance to private labor disputes. In so doing he set up a whole new framework for politics. The shift in the attitude of the state toward the peasant and factory worker from hostility to neutrality and even, occasionally, to benevolent mediation during labor strife was greeted by reformist socialist leaders as the dawn of a new age.

A decade later these hopes had largely been disappointed. The new framework for politics remained just that: an empty frame. The disillusionment that marked the end of the Giolittian era was partly the fault of Giolitti, who often promised more than he could or would deliver. But it was also the result of a serious misreading of Giolitti's intentions by leading Socialists. Such a misreading has been perpetuated by later historians who have accepted too easily the definition of Giolitti as a democratic or leftist liberal. Most notably, Hartmut Ullrich in his exhaustive study of the Italian political class from 1909 to the end of Giolitti's last ministry argued for the coherent strategy pursued by Giolitti from 1901 to 1911 that centered around an alliance between the liberal left and the Estrema. In Ullrich's view, Giolitti was at heart always a left liberal. However, to argue this point Ulrich has to devalue the central years of Giolittian politics from 1903 to 1909.[1]

Even if we accept that Giolitti's overall strategy was to enclose the popular parties of the Estrema within the constitutional framework, what did this mean in practice? In 1901 he argued in the Chamber of Deputies that there were only three parties in Italy—the clerical, the socialist, and the constitutional—but Giolitti made it clear that his Liberal party intended to compete with the new parties that were in fundamental ways his opponents.[2] Giolitti believed that the Liberal party was at the center of the political system, not just because the clericals were on his right and the Socialists on the left, but because it represented the only way to govern in Italy.[3]

Giolitti also drew an important lesson from his first government in 1892–93: that it was difficult to maintain a stable power with a ministry drawn exclusively from one part of the chamber. Only briefly during the months before the Libyan War in 1911 did he fall back into this position. For most of his years in power before World War I Giolitti specifically rejected the creation of a two-party system. His governments were open to both sides of the political spectrum. When he moved to the right, there was always a potential opening to the left. Any move to the left, as in 1911, had key figures from the right wing of his majority waiting on the sidelines to rejoin the government. Although in March 1911 Giolitti seemed to believe that a stable majority might be created exclusively by the center-left, when the Libyan War revealed that such a center-left coalition was not possible, he did not resign, but rather tacked to the right. The price for this flexibility was an unsatisfied longing for political clarity.[4] Roberto Vivarelli argued that the problem was with "the very quality of his political faith, which was never profound enough to direct his actions and, within certain limits, bind them, maintaining a certain balance between thought and action and assuring that minimum of coherence, in the absence of which even good programs, that is good intentions, meet the fate we well know."[5]

One of the great illusions of the leading Socialists was a perceived distinction between Giolitti and *giolittismo* which the reformists within the PSI often used to save their relationship with Giolitti. They sought to separate Giolitti from his majority and to split that majority by driving out its right wing by forcing the pace of reforms. Of course, they never succeeded.[6]

Giolitti's view of the Socialist party was coldly realistic. He quite correctly never viewed the PSI as a single political force. He distinguished among the parliamentary party (with which he constantly worked on concrete projects even when relations were most tense), the reformist cooperative and union movements, which he supported, and the revolutionaries, whom he actually repressed.[7]

One must distinguish then between two levels: the administrative or pork-barrel deals that were fundamental to the lives of Socialist municipalities and cooperatives and the area of broad political strategy and legislative agendas. Whereas even Socialist opponents of Giolitti could work with him on the first level, not even the reformists had much input on the second, more important, level.[8] Brunello Vigezzi was absolutely correct when he wrote that "it was better not to speak of a Giolittian-Turatian system." The two men diverged as much as they cooperated on Giolitti's terms.[9] Turati made the fundamental miscalculation to believe that Giolitti would be willing to opt finally for one wing of his coalition.[10]

Several issues drew Giolitti and the reformists within the Socialist party together at the beginning of the 1901–11 period. These were a belief in the fragility of Italian political and social development, faith in gradualism, a preference for negotiation over direct action, agnosticism on free trade, and confidence in the expansion of the state sector. While these important points help explain the degree of cooperation between Giolitti and the PSI, they were eventually outweighed by other, more fundamental, issues that separated Giolitti from the vast majority of socialists: tax reform, the military budgets, limits on unionization in the public sector, a growing belief in the corruption of the Giolittian majority, and, finally, the Libyan War. The rest of this essay will examine these issues to determine the extent and limits of the Giolittian-Socialist relationship.

Both Giolitti and prominent reformists like Turati were firmly gradualist in their approach to Italian development. As early as 1901, Giolitti argued that the better educated and organized the working class, the less likely its recourse to violent strikes. He did not believe that the government could alter the laws of the market. All it could do was help level the playing field.[11] Giolitti argued for a steady pace of reform that would eventually bring the country closer to the more advanced economies.[12]

In 1904 Turati, during the debate over the government's program, also stressed that "one need not be socialist, nor belong to this or that party. It is enough to be modern men to understand that the best way to resolve these disputes consists in raising the level of the masses of workers by getting them used to consider themselves not as subordinates who have everything to fear from the bosses and from the state, but as a collectivity of free and responsible citizens."[13] Again, during a debate on a law regulating labor conditions for female rice workers Turati set forth the difference between revolutionary and reformist socialists in terms quite compatible with Giolittian policies. The reformists, he argued, "think, as do the [revolutionaries], that capitalism is an obsolete, although necessary, social form and that it is necessary to prepare the passage to higher and more evolved social structures . . . but [the reformists], in contrast to the others, think that these transformations, however radical, cannot usefully come except by evolutionary methods of penetration and gradual substitution." [14]

Insofar as they both preferred negotiation to force, Giolitti and the reformist socialists shared an interest in the maintenance of order. Turati was quick to remind Giolitti how much he depended on the reformists during the agricultural strike wave of 1901: "You have up to now maintained order in Italy with a relative economy of disasters and suffering. Do you believe that you can continue to do this much longer remaining within the general policies of the Cabinet? You have maintained order also a bit thanks to us." [15]

But the fundamental disagreement over the meaning of order became more apparent in 1902 and 1903. When Treves asked Giolitti what exactly was public order, the prime minister responded somewhat superficially that it was the opposite of disorder. Treves then shot back that the use of troops against strikers was also disorder. Giolitti rejected this: "The Italian army is composed of all social classes, especially the popular classes, who have a much higher sense of the fatherland than you have." [16]

Giolitti made four fundamental distinctions when dealing with labor unrest: first, between economic and political (especially general) strikes; second, between private-and public-sector strikes; third, between strikes in the north and those in the agrarian south; and fourth, between strikes led by reformists and those sparked by revolutionaries. In the case of a reformist-led economic strike, he would generally instruct the prefect to intervene to help arbitrate a settlement. If the strike were judged to be political, however, it was a different matter. Responding to a question on the 1908 strikes in Emilia, Giolitti noted that they had something in common with contemporary strikes in Puglia "with this difference, however, that in Emilia the workers are organized, but, unfortunately, in many places no longer in the hands of reformists. They have fallen . . . in the hands of revolutionary elements who seek to empty, to eliminate the purely economic profile of the struggles between capital and labor and to give to them a political nature." [17] Giolitti was especially harsh in putting down agricultural leagues in the southern strongholds of his supporters. In doing this he rarely relegated them to violations of criminal laws in part because legislation covering common criminality was often harsher than were the laws dealing with the right to work. [18]

A major area of disappointment for the reformists came over Giolitti's handling of public-sector strikes. Turati publicly identified with the union-ization movement within the state sector and Giolitti just as resolutely worked to combat it.[19] Giolitti also showed himself more than willing to support the harsh disciplinary measures against strikers on railways, even though the reformist socialists intervened to moderate the punishment. He introduced a civil service bill that gave wide latitude to dismiss workers not only for strikes but also for obstructionism.[20] Turati's close identifica-tion with the postal workers' union and his fight against Giolitti's civil service act in 1907 and 1908 had long-term consequences. Turati failed to appreciate how fundamental Giolitti considered the issue, but the re-sulting impasse created an image of a more despotic Giolitti and deepened the futility that gripped both Turati and Anna Kuliscioff between 1908 and 1911. A seething frustration easily came to the surface in his corre-spondence: "The government excludes us from everything. This does not make me unhappy; I don't have time and patience to add more work to what I already have." Then in a somewhat contradictory manner he went on: "In other times the government occasionally let us take part in com-missions. Now one only gets in by a breakdown [in the majority]."[21] Turati's bitterness certainly played a part in the advice given to Bissolati in March 1911 not to enter the government. Giolitti himself, when asked by Bissolati why he did not turn to Turati as he did in 1903, cited Turati's close identification with the unionization of civil servants as one reason for his choice. Turati's ironic comment was "Long live the postal and telegraph workers! And they say that they were to have served as my springboard to office! See how clever I am without intending to be!"[22]

The pace and direction of Giolittian reformism inevitably became an issue between the reformists in the PSI and Giolitti. It was with consider-able satisfaction in 1906 that Giolitti stated in Parliament that "Italy today fortunately finds itself in a position where it can concentrate above all on its internal order, on public services, on questions basically which call for reasoning and not agitation."[23] Far from rejecting the center-right orientation of his long 1906–9 government, Giolitti was quite proud of his achievements. These centered on the completion of the conversion of the national debt, some tax relief, but no overall project for tax reform. Giolitti continued to depend on heavy local taxes and duties on items of basic necessity as sources of revenue. He refused to use the surpluses from the debt conversion for a major restructuring of fiscal burdens. Instead, the gains for the general public came in the form of a shift in spending to public works, especially after the nationalization of the telephone and rail services, and to education. Direct social legislation was undramatic, limited, and fiscally cautious: guaranteed Sunday rest, increased support for old age and pension funds, improvements in legislation on child and female labor.[24]

Two issues exhausted the Socialists' patience with the tempo of the Giolittian program of reform. The first was Giolitti's failure to live up to the promise of fiscal reform. No politician spoke of tax reform so much and over so long a time as Giolitti, but did so little about it once in power. Even when in 1909 he raised the issue just before the fall of his government, tax reform did not then figure in the program of the 1911 ministry. In a letter to Turati in 1903, Anna Kuliscioff noted that fiscal reform was a precondition to any project of major structural reform.[25]

Instead, Giolitti involved different parts of the socialist movement in his system by offering partial, but concrete advantages that cut the parliamentary group off from the masses without any corresponding gain of influence in the formulation of a broad political strategy that Giolitti set alone or within a restricted group of advisers.[26] Although in 1910 and 1911 he actively consulted on his legislative agenda with key leaders of the Estrema, on balance one could not say that the socialists had much influence in shaping broad policies.[27]

To break out of this seemingly vicious circle the PSI at its Florence congress in 1908 called for a series of "great reforms": universal suffrage for both sexes, school reform, tax reform, tax and customs legislation, and the nationalization of public services. Anna Kuliscioff felt that the struggle for these reforms might renew the ties between the reformists and the masses. As the socialists rebuilt their links with the masses and mobilized opinion behind reform, the role of parliament would temporarily become less important.[28]

But the emphasis on major reforms ran into a second obstacle that troubled relations between Giolitti and the Socialists: military spending. Although in absolute terms Italy spent less on the military than the other major powers, the percentage of military expenditures as a part of total expenditures rose from 20.1% in the five-year period from 1897 to 1902 to reach 29.4% in 1913.[29] Given the influence of the king and the military ministers, Giolitti could not radically alter military budgets. Instead he did all he could to draw the PSI into accepting the logic of military expenditures. In 1908 Turati wrote to Kuliscioff that the parliamentary group split on the military budget when the commission on the military came up with revised figures on levels of military expenditures after pressure by the PSI. He wondered how the party could disavow its own work.[30] In fact, Bissolati and Bonomi saw that it was futile to try to work with Giolitti while holding out hope that he would compromise on the military budget. More realistically but in the end no more successfully, they sought to find a way to pay for both military and social expenditures by means of tax reform.[31]

If all of this is true, then how do we explain the offers by Giolitti to Turati in 1903 and to Bissolati in 1911 to join his government? The two cases need to be separated. In 1903, despite Giolitti's protestations that he made no commitments before offering a place in the cabinet to Turati, there is evidence that the prime minister did not expect a successful negotiation.[32] He understood Turati's position in the party and Turati himself doubted Giolitti's seriousness in making the offer. If the Socialist leader had accepted and split the PSI, it would have satisfied Giolitti's desire to domesticate the socialist parliamentary group. When this did not happen, he moved ahead with a different agenda. In forming his 1903 government Giolitti had ambitions that went beyond merely an opening to the left. He also wanted to undermine any challenge to his government from Sonnino's right by enlarging his majority as much a possible. He did this in part by bringing in new faces. Giolitti recalled that except for Luzzatti, most of the others were first-time ministers: Ronchetti at justice, Angelo Majorana at finance, Pedotti at war, Rava at agriculture, industry and commerce, Stelluti-Scala at posts, and Mirabello at navy. He built bridges to the right by recruiting Francesco Tedesco from the Sonnino camp, by bringing in Luzzatti, an ally of Di Rudinì, very early in the cabinet negotiations, and by offering the foreign ministry to the pro-clerical Tittoni.[33]

But Giolitti accomplished a second aim in 1903 and in 1904 that had the long-term effect of creating the Giolittian system. Francesco Barbagallo in his study of southern electoral politics noted that in March 1902, when Zanardelli and Giolitti won a confidence vote on their confrontation with the railway workers, the majority of southern deputies (55 to 43) voted against the government. By June 1903 the split on a confidence vote was even. Even though when Giolitti formed his government, the two southerners, Paternò and Rosano, turned out to be troubled nominations, this proved far from fatal. By opening to the right Giolitti won 82 of 98 members of the southern delegation in the vote of confidence on his government in December 1903. Barbagallo sees this as the moment when the Giolittian majority began to coalesce. Then Giolitti followed up Zanardelli's special legislation for the south with several measures of his own to reward his southern supporters. The final step came in the elections of 1904. Forty percent of the southern delegation was replaced and the southern opposition was gutted.[34] If Turati had joined the government in 1903, the Giolittian era might have taken on a quite different character, but there is a strong probability that it would not have taken place at all. In any case, Giolitti was perfectly at home with the new center-right majority that emerged from the 1904 elections. In fact, Giolitti used the formation of his 1906 government to further weaken the right opposition in the Chamber.[35]

Part of the crisis of reformism was the awareness that the Socialists could make no substantial gains as long as the Giolittian system remained unbroken. The difficulty for both Kuliscioff and Turati was that they had no idea how to undermine it. Although the right reformists like Bissolati and Bonomi were far more flexible in dealing with the obstacles blocking an understanding with Giolitti, they were no more successful in breaking the majority. It was this intellectual impasse that led Kuliscioff, as early as 1909, to consider a clear split within the Estrema that might have eventually put Bissolati in the bourgeois democratic camp.[36] The left reformists seemed to alternate between hope and despair in 1909 and 1911 with despair clearly gaining the upper hand.[37]

The final stage in the prewar relationship between Giolitti and the Italian Socialists came with Giolitti's sudden shift leftward and his adoption of the cause of universal suffrage. The suffrage bill, proposed by Giolitti in 1911, accompanied by the offer to Bissolati to join the government, was again designed to split the PSI. As many contemporary commentators have pointed out, Giolitti's sudden conversion to the suffrage cause was somewhat difficult to explain. The Socialists had been divided on the franchise and had not been able to use the issue to mobilize a mass movement to pressure Parliament. Moreover Giolitti was on record against both universal suffrage and pay for deputies. In March 1911 key Giolittians put themselves to the right of Luzzatti in working to kill a less drastic suffrage law that combined a literacy test with obligatory voting.[38] Even Giolitti's close relationship with prominent Radicals cannot entirely explain it because the Radicals had accepted the substance of Luzzatti's reform as a first step.

While Bissolati and the right reformists and many of Turati's own allies reacted favorably to Giolitti's offer to bring the Socialists in the government, Turati remained suspicious and reserved.[39] Giolitti was undoubtedly far more serious in 1911 than he was in 1903. He had convinced himself that the time was right to divide the reformists from the revolutionaries in the PSI. Giolitti's only personal contacts with the revolutionary faction of the PSI came in Parliament and they were not close. His dealings with the rest of the socialist revolutionary base were matters of police control and surveillance. There is no doubt that Giolitti's remarks about relegating Marx to the attic reveal both an optimistic misreading of the mood at the base of the PSI and a failure to understand the depth of the division within the reformist faction itself.[40] But the statement and the enthusiastic reception to it in the liberal parliamentary camp clearly indicate Giolitti's feelings that the time had come to bring "reasonable socialists" into the constitutional framework. Curiously, Giolitti's position coincided with the ideas that had been germinating in the mind of Anna Kuliscioff. In June, well before the outbreak of the Libyan War, she returned to her idea of 1909 about the formation of a new social democratic party that would be free to move toward Giolitti, while leaving the left reformists within the old party.[41] In light of this, Turati's frantic effort to persuade Bissolati to reject Giolitti's offer in March is all the more incomprehensible.[42]

Certainly the Libyan War would have marked a split in the party and the end of official Socialist cooperation with Giolitti, even if Bissolati had joined the government.[43] The war made it impossible to heal the breach between right and left reformists, although the long-term causes for the break are not easy to understand without taking into account the influence of Kuliscioff's bleak pessimism on Turati. Once the war began, Socialist unity in parliament unraveled.[44] Giolitti's reaction to the split further indicated how his understanding of the socialist movement was restricted to the parliamentary group. On September 25, 1911, Giolitti telegraphed the king: "Movimento socialisti [*sic*] non credo abbia importanza. Parecchi socialisti sono favorevoli all'impresa."[45]

Giolitti used the outbreak of the war to broaden the liberal majority. He had no qualms about cutting off the PSI. The opposition Socialists were rapidly marginalized as they had been between 1906 and 1909.[46] Against the mass base of the party Giolitti resorted to the most severe police actions. He used the full powers of the law to ban meetings and impose rigid censorship on the Socialist party and press.[47]

In conclusion, I would argue that the Socialist party as such was not essential to Giolitti's plans. Much more important in 1903 and in subsequent years was the consolidation of the liberal majority, which might be extended to the right and to the left as circumstances dictated. Instability within the PSI and Giolitti's constant preoccupation with maintaining an alternative majority in case of difficulties also limited the usefulness of the PSI.

On the part of the Socialists, Giolittian tactics hastened the split within the party by separating the right and left reformists. The disappointments of these years were never overcome and the climate of faith that had existed at the turn of the century was never reestablished. Moreover, new leaders who had never been part of Giolitti's system were pushing an agenda that would put the PSI out of the framework of bourgeois politics for many, many years.

Notes

1. Ullrich's argument is summed up in the following: "Fu dunque nella profonda logica della meta più alta della sua politica che Giolitti respinse nel maggio '909, nell'apogeo cioè del 'lungo ministero' e del suo corso di centro-destra, il concetto del 'grande partito liberale.' " See Hartmut Ullrich, *La classe politica nella crisi di partecipazione dell'Italia giolittiana, 1909–1913*, 3 vols. (Rome: Camera dei Deputati-Segretariato Generale Archivio Storico, 1979), 2:635–36; citation from 636. If Giolitti seemed after 1909 to move to the right, as with the appointment of Bertolini to the cabinet in 1912, it was because the Socialist party forced him to do so. A similar position was taken by James Miller who also argued the centrality of the PSI to Giolittian politics until 1912. See James Edward Miller, *From Elite to Mass Politics: Italian Socialism in the Giolittian Era, 1900–1914* (Kent: Kent State University Press, 1990), 26.

2. See *Atti parlamentari, Camera dei Deputati*, legislatura 21, 1 sessione, discussioni, 4 February 1901, p. 2149. Henceforth cited as *AP, Camera*.

3. Alberto Aquarone correctly pointed out: "l'obiettivo primario della politica giolittiana: governare dal centro con oscillazioni tutto sommato lievi e sempre ben controllate ora in senso conservatore, ora in senso progressista, nella preoccupazione costante di allargare quanto possibile, sia in parlamento che nel paese, a destra come a sinistra, la base di consenso a sostegno delle istituzioni e dell'ordine sociale costituito." Alberto Aquarone, *L'Italia giolittiana (1896–1915)*, vol. 1, *Le premesse politiche ed economiche* (Bologna: Il Mulino, 1981), 300.

4. Mola noted that by governing from the center Giolitti "gathered [political] forces, but never succeeded in giving birth to a force." Aldo A. Mola, *Storia dell'amministrazione provinciale di Cuneo dall'Unità al fascismo (1859–1925)* (Turin: AEDA, 1971), 536.

5. Roberto Vivarelli, *Storia delle origini del fascismo*, vol. 2, *L'Italia dalla grande guerra alla marcia su Roma* (Bolgona: Il Mulino, 1991), 205.

6. On the failure of the reforms to break up the basis of Giolitti's system, see Brunello Vigezzi, *Giolitti e Turati: Un incontro mancato*, 2 vols. (Milan:

Riccardo Ricciardi, 1976), 1:50–51. The idea of dividing Giolitti and giolittismo was a constant theme in the Turati-Kuliscioff letters. Commenting on
"il dovere dei successori," *L'Avanti!* 3 December 1909, Turati asked if Kuliscioff saw the article, which was "una specie di inno a Giolitti uccisiore del
giolittismo." See Turati to Kuliscioff, 4 December 1909, in Filippo Turati and
Anna Kuliscioff, *Carteggio,* vol. 2, *1900–1909,* ed. Alessandro Schiavi and
Franco Pedone (Turin: Einaudi, 1971), 1174. He felt that it was a bit exaggerated in form but that 'Il concetto non mi pare falso." The article defined
Giolitti's sudden adoption of a progressive income tax at the end of his 1906–
9 ministry as "un attentato di Giolitti contro il giolittismo" by forcing a clear
choice on his followers. For a later view of the same idea see *L'Avanti!* of 12
April 1911, entitled "Giolitti contro il giolittismo."

7. James Miller's idea that the PSI was a cadre and not a mass party allowed
Giolitti to do this. Reformist indifference to grassroots party organizing and
the structure of the party along the lines of semiautonomous power centers
made it easier to deal individually with each of the constituent elements. See
Miller, *From Elite to Mass,* 39–40.

8. For concrete examples of how Giolitti worked with individual socialist deputies, see Maurizio Degl'Innocenti, *Cittadini e rurali nell'Emilia Romagna rossa
tra '800 e '900* (Milan: Franco Angeli, 1990), esp. chap. 2.

9. See Vigezzi, *Giolitti e Turati,* xv.

10. See Turati, "Sempre in difesa della libertà," 11 June 1902, in Filippo Turati,
Socialismo e riformismo nella storia d'Italia: Scritti politici, 1878–1932, ed. Franco
Livorsi (Milan: Feltrinelli, 1979), 129–30, 144.

11. See *AP, Camera,* legisl. 21, 1 sess. disc., 2 tornata of 21 June 1901, pp. 5505.

12. See Aquarone, *Italia giolittiana,* 303.

13. *AP, Camera,* legisl. 22, 1 sess., disc., 13 December 1904, p. 241.

14. See Turati's remarks in *AP, Camera,* legisl. 22, 1 sess. disc., 2 tornata of May
22, 1907, p. 14539. Giolitti's response to Turati in the debate stressed the
need to educate the working classes by introducing the notions of the labor
contract and arbitration. See the session of 23 May 1907, 14581.

15. See Turati's speech of 11 June 1902, in Turati, *Socialismo e riformismo,* 143.
During the summer of 1901 Talamo, the undersecretary of Grazia e Giustizia
asked Turati if he thought that it would be possible to get through the summer
without disorders. See Turati to Kuliscioff, 18 May 1901, in *Carteggio,* 2:31.
Here and in the encouragement of Bissolati's mediation in the Molinella
strike, Giolitti used the socialists for information as well as a moderating force
on violence. See the letters from Bissolati to Giolitti in Giovanni Giolitti,
Quarant'anni di vita politica, vol. 2. See also the conversations between Giolitti
and Turati over the best way to impose some form of arbitration on the
Molinella strike. Turati to Kuliscioff, 25 and 26 May 1901, *Carteggio,* 2:43, 47.

16. *AP, Camera,* legisl. 22, 1 sess. disc., 13 December 1906, pp. 10995, 10998.

17. The second volume of Giovanni Giolitti, *Quarant'anni di vita politica,* vol. 2,
Dieci anni al potere, 1901–1909, ed. Giampiero Carocci (Milan: Feltrinelli,
1962) has numerous exchanges between Giolitti and the prefects on the disorders of 1901 and 1902. See also the remarks of Fiorenza Fiorentino, *Ordine*

pubblico nell'Italia giolittiana (Rome: Edizioni Carecas, 1978), 18. She stresses that Giolitti could not tolerate general strikes for any reason. See also Giolitti's comments in the Chamber, *AP, Camera,* legisl. 22, 1 sess., disc., 4 March 1908, p. 19870.

18. Giolitti moved harshly to deal with the 1907 Torremaggiore strike in the province of Bari calling the peasant league "a dangerous association of criminals" and even refusing efforts by Bissolati to mediate. See Francesco Barbagallo, *Stato, parlamento e lotte politico-sociali nel Mezzogiorno, 1900–1914* (Naples: Guida, 1980), 233–39. See also his handling of strikes in the Salento in Fabio Grassi, *Il tramonto dell'età giolittiana nel Salento* (Bari: Laterza, 1973), 181, 193–97. An example of the same treatment in the north came when Giolitti insisted that government action during the strike wave in the Ferrara region was really only to deal with violations of common law. *AP, Camera,* legisl. 22, 1 sess., disc., 2 tornata of 3 July 1907, p. 17581.

    Giolitti also took the same position during the crisis of 1898–1900 when he argued against special repressive legislation, saying that existing criminal statues were enough to deal with the excesses of labor unrest. See Sergio Romano, *Giolitti lo stile del potere* (Milan: Bompiani, 1989), 108–9.

19. Alberto Aquarone argued that Giolitti treated unionization in the private and public sectors differently because he wanted total control over the state apparatus, which he used to regulate the process of change. Alberto Aquarone, *Tre capitoli sull'Italia giolittiana* (Bologna: Il Mulino, 1987), 109.

20. On Giolitti and the railway workers, see Adolfo Pepe, *Storia della CGdl dalla fondazione alla guerra di Libia, 1905–1911* (Bari: Laterza, 1972), 174–75. On Giolitti's position on the efforts to combat unionization and the reformist commitment to it, see Guido Melis, *Burocrazia e socialismo nell'Italia liberale: Alle origini dell'organizzazione sindacale del pubblico impiego (1900–1922)* (Bologna: Il Mulino, 1980), chaps 1 and 2. For Turati's personal disappointment, see the letters to Kuliscioff, 1 and 10 December 1907 in *Carteggio,* 2:672, 684–85.

21. See Turati to Kuliscioff, May 16, 1909, in *Carteggio,* 2:1080; also on the same theme of isolation in Giolitti's dictatorship, see Kuliscioff to Turati, 28 February 1908, and his response of 29 February 1908, 2:762 and 770; and Kuliscioff to Turati, 4 April 1090, 2:1052. See also Melis, *Burocrazia e socialismo,* 87.

22. See Turati to Kuliscioff, 22 March 1911 in Vigezzi, *Giolitti e Turati,* 1:233. on the 1911 offer.

23. *AP Camera,* legisl. 22, 1 sess., disc., 13 December 1906, p. 10931.

24. On Giolitti's comments on his 1906–9 government, see Giovanni Giolitti, *Memorie della mia vita,* 9th ed. (Milan: Garzanti, 1967), 178–79. Giolitti pointed out that the budget for education increased from 49 to 85 million lire, that for agriculture from 13 to 27 million, for public works from 79 to 117 million, and for postal and telegraph from 68 to 123 million (pp. 167–68). Aquarone noted that Giolitti did reduce direct taxes but really did little to ease the burden of indirect taxation. He did, however, spend more on education than any government until the republican era. See Aquarone, *Italia giolit-*

tiana, 351, 354–58, 360. On the nature of Giolittian reforms, see *Tre capitoli,* 177–80; for the increases in spending on education, 175–76.

25. This letter was cited by Leo Valiani in "Il problema delle 'Grandi Riforme' fra socialisti italiani dal 1900 al 1914," in Valiani, *Questioni di storia del socialismo* (Turin: Einaudi, 1958), 405.

26. The 1902 Ufficio del Lavoro was put under the reformist socialist Giovanni Montemartini. The 1902 law on municipalization of public services allowed much room for deals among Giolitti, local governments, and the Socialist parlimentary delegation. A similar phenomenon took place with the cooperative movement. Giolitti recalled with pride that he allowed cooperatives to bid on state contracts during his service in the Crispi ministry. On the Ufficio del Lavoro see Aquarone, *Italia giolittiana,* 214–15; for the process of municipalization, see Aquarone, *Tre capitoli,* 124–27; Arturo Labriola commented on the contracts between Giolitti and the cooperatives in *Storia di dieci anni 1899–1909* (Milan: Il Viandante, 1910), 302–3.

27. Pepe notes this fear in Turati and cites articles in *Critica sociale* at the beginning of 1907 that gave this impression. See Pepe, *Storia della CGdl,* 1:67–68, and "La nostra azione parlamentare," *Critica sociale,* 1 January 1907, and "L'inazione parlamentare socialista," *Critica sociale,* 16 January 1907.

28. Kuliscioff to Turati, 16 May 1910, *Carteggio,* 3:160. Also Valiani, "Grandi riforme," 406.

29. Aquarone, *Italia giolittiana,* 106–7.

30. See the letters of Turati to Kuliscioff and her response, 14 June 1907 in which they discussed the efforts of the socialists to direct the inquiry into the war ministry. Turati's fear was that the government would slowly involve the socialists in the process. See *Carteggio,* 2:587, 616. On the involvement in the military budget, see Turati to Kuliscioff, 20 May 1908, 2:868.

31. See Valiani, "Grandi riforme," 408.

32. Giolitti to Romussi, 8 November 1903, ACS, Fondo Giolitti, b. 9, f. 121. In the same letter Giolitti protested against Romussi's obvious desire that Giolitti should renounce the effort to form a government once the Estrema refused to take part. Giolitti argued that the Radicals only constituted 40 of 508 seats and that there was little alternative to Giolitti or the right.

33. "Le trattative dell'on. Giolitti per comporre il Ministero," *La Stampa,* 25 October 1903, which indicated negotiations between Giolitti and Luzzatti. Both Miller and Mammarella indicated that Giolitti was well aware of the problems within PSI. Both feel that Giolitti sought to force a split in the PSI. See Giuseppe Mammarella, *Riformisti e rivoluzionari nel Partito socialista italiano, 1900–1912* (Padova: Marsilio, 1969), 155; Miller, *From Elite to Mass,* 63. Spencer Di Scala in *Dilemmas of Italian Socialism: The Politics of Filippo Turati* (Amherst: University of Massachusetts Press, 1980), 77–78, argued for Giolitti's sincerity in making the offer and sees the move to the right as a reaction to the refusal of the Estrema. See Turati's comments in "L'adunanza dell' Estrema sinistra," on a meeting held on 30 November 1903, in *Il Secolo,* 1–2 December 1903.

    La Tribuna noted that the right pressed Giolitti to include some of its members. See "I partiti di governo," *La Tribuna*, 26 October 1903. See also Giolitti, *Memorie*, 134; Natale, *Giolitti e gli italiani*, 560. Ullrich noted that negotiations between Sonnino and Giolitti for an alliance in 1903 failed when Sonnino blocked the effort, but it does indicate that Giolitti was not exclusively interested in moving left. He was certainly interested in undermining the potential opposition. Tedesco and Del Balzo were brought over in 1903 as was the clerical Suardi. Ullrich, *La classe politica* 116–17. The demands of the radicals for more positions than Giolitti wanted to give him led to the failure of their inclusion and would have limited Giolitti's maneuvers. See "Cose e persone." *La Tribuna*, 2 November 1903.

34. See Francesco Barbagallo, *Stato, parlamento e lotte politico-sociali nel Mezzogiorno, 1900–1914* (Naples: Guida, 1980), 138–43, 293. Not only did Tedesco and Del Balzo reach into the center-south, but he added Codacci-Pisanelli and Giovanni Camera (Finance) as undersecretaries in 1904. This completed Giolitti's raid on southern conservatives. In the passage of the special legislation for Naples, Francesco Girardi, the former clerical mayor, was the *relatore* and Torraca, a former supporter of Pelloux, filled the same role for the law on Basilicata.

35. Ullrich, *Classe politica*, 1:85–86, 118, 121. Ullrich does note that the moderates who joined at this time were not very dependable. Only Bergamasco, Bertolini, and Raineri became firm Giolittians. The 1906 government more or less balanced the center-right and center-left of the government majority with Bertolini, Gianturco, Tittoni, and Fusinato (former undersecretary with Pelloux and Saracco) constituting the right wing and a number of ex-Zanardellians like Cocco-Ortu and Massimini on the left. See Lombroso, "Il nuovo ministero," *Scanciopancia*, 30 May 1906. For the socialists who were not strongly opposed in the elections, see "I pericoli," *La Tribuna*, 22 October 1904. Strangely, Ferri's name is on the list along with those of Costa, Bissolati, and Turati.

36. For a clear explanation of the divisions among the reformists, see Di Scala, *Dilemmas*, 105–9. In a letter to Turati on 31 May 1909 she noted that Bissolati "non può nascondere completamente il suo amore per Giolitti." She wondered about the wisdom of simply breaking off the Estrema and "la costituzione del gruppo democratico autonomo e libero di patteggiare con Giolitti, forse non è un concetto sbagliato." *Carteggio*, 2:1110.

37. Turati's letter to Kuliscioff of 29 May 1909 reveals the problem of finding an adequate response to Giolitti: "La verità non consiste nell'essere ministeriali, ma la vera linea di opposizione non l'abbiamo trovata. Forse sorgerà dalle cose; ma non è un po'ridicolo sequitare ad accusare Giolitti che non crea i partiti, ossia che non crea l'opposizione? Forse il guaio e fuori di noi e fuori della Camera. Se avessimo un proletariato, una democrazia vivi e vibranti e non comiziaioli e ciarlataneschi, le cose sarebbero diverse: ma forse allora sarebbe diverso tutto, sarebbe diverso anche Giolitti." Turati to Kuliscioff, 29 May 1901, *Carteggio* 2:1103.

38. Rastignac's (V. Morello) comments in *La Tribuna* reflected some of the confused reaction when he noted that normally great reforms were taken under

pressure from public opinion, but this major reform seemed to have come entirely out of parliamentary maneuvering. See "Medice, cura te ipsum," *La Tribuna*, 7 January 1911. For the lack of enthusiasm for the reform, see Ullrich, *Classe politica*, 2:712. Prominent Giolittians like Falcioni and Bertolini did their best to sidetrack Luzzatti's reform. Vigezzi, *Giolitti e Turati*, 1:207 n. 2.

Turati noted in his speech to the Congress of Modena in 1911 the failure of the socialists to prepare the issue. See "contro due estremi, per l'azione socialista," 17 October 1911, in Turati, *Socialismo e riformismo*, 233.

39. See Vigezzi, *Giolitti e Turati*, 1:13.
40. See Di Scala, *Dilemmas*, 121–21, 129.
41. Kuliscioff to Turati, 2 June 1911, *Carteggio, 1911–1915*, 3:612. Turati's letter of the same date spoke of a rupture within the parliamentary party (3:613).
42. As late as the Congress of Modena in October 1911 Turati noted how he used his influence to keep Bissolati from accepting the offer. See Turati's speech at Modena, "Contro due estremi, per l'azione socialista," 17 October 1911, in Turati, *Socialismo e riformismo*, 240.
43. Franco Livorsi's argument that with the PSI in the government or even Bissolati "come elemento decisivo per la stessa politica estera, la guerra di Libia non ci sarebbe stata" seems far too extreme; see Livorsi's introduction to Turati, *Socialismo e riformismo*, xlix.
44. See Maurizio Degl'Innocenti, *Il socialismo italiano e la guerra di Libia* (Rome: Riuniti, 1976), 47. Degl'Innocenti also noted that the pressure for a strike did not come from the parliamentary group but from the base of the party.
45. Cited in Ullrich, *Classe politica*, 2:1048.
46. Degl'Innocenti, *Il socialismo italiano*, 62 and 74. Degl'Innocenti indicates that Turati still hoped for renewed cooperation with Giolitti (63). Franco Livorsi has argued in a similar vein; see his remarks in Turati, *Socialismo e riformismo*, 248. While this may be so, there was absolutely no resumption of cooperation during the remainder of Giolitti's ministry.
47. Degl'Innocenti, *Il socialismo italiano*, 65–73. Giolitti simply ignored the protests of Claudio Treves against the censorship of *L'Avanti!* in December 1911; Degl'Innocenti, *Il socialismo italiano*, 66.

4

SOPHISTICATED LIBERALS

John Alcorn

Alexander De Grand has given us a rich taste of his work in progress on Giovanni Giolitti: a reinterpretation of the relations between Giolitti and the Socialists in the period 1903–13. I shall focus here upon the matter of Giolitti's "political faith," as this was put to the test by the claims of the socialist movement during his rule. The core of De Grand's argument on this matter may be summarized as follows: Giolitti, wishing to stay in power, chose a political strategy of "flexible centrism" in coalition formation, a strategy consonant with his "constitutionalist" political culture. Corollary to Giolitti's strategy was a tactic of shifting the coalition's boundaries to the left or to the right as political circumstances changed. The strategy placed constraints on the nature and pace of reforms, and thus contributed to channeling the development of the Socialist party "out of the framework of bourgeois politics for many, many years."

   The argument is not without historical irony; it amounts to a claim that Giolitti was implementing Sidney Sonnino's ideal of government by the center against the extremes, rather than the "English model" of alternation in power of progressive and conservative parties, which had been given forceful expression by Silvio Spaventa in the period of *trasformismo*.[1] The irony, of course, lies in the political rivalry between Giolitti and Sonnino in the period 1903–13. And the argument is not without contemporary resonance, as Italians are grappling with the ill effects of a long period of centrist coalitional rule based upon clientelism; one such ill effect being an "unsatisfied longing for political clarity," as De Grand describes the mood induced by Giolitti's political strategy.

Let us consider in turn the two constraints De Grand identifies in Giolitti's political strategy: the subordination of policy to the desire to stay in power, and a narrow political culture that prevented Giolitti from understanding the Socialists. De Grand cites Roberto Vivarelli's judgment that Giolitti was lacking in "the very quality of his political faith, which was never profound enough to direct his actions and, within certain limits, bind them." If we are to engage in the ambiguous art of bestowing praise and blame upon historical actors, then my position, for what it is worth, is that this judgment of Giolitti's political character is uncharitable. Since I have already noted the contemporary resonance of De Grand's interpretation, perhaps you will not consider it too out of place to liken this characterization of Giolitti's "political faith" to the doubts that have been cast on President Clinton's political integrity. Such judgments do not do justice to two facts of modern political life: namely, that reforms require majority support in legislative assemblies, and that the political representatives whose support the executive branch requires often approach political interaction as a form of bargaining. It is difficult for the executive power to reconcile the plural satisfaction of vested interests with the coherent pursuit of a more abstract, long-term conception of the public good. This tension is especially pronounced where there is a conflict between constitutionalism and democracy, as in Italy before 1911, where political representation was based upon restricted suffrage. To put it another way, again with an eye to the present, we cannot rationally expect statesmen to succeed in the art of high politics if the motives at work in low politics are myopic and selfish. It is perhaps also the case (though this is merely conjecture) that constitutions, such as Italy's then and now, which make the executive power responsible to Parliament rather than to the electorate promote "flexibility" in those who govern, to use De Grand's term, at the expense of resoluteness. I am therefore struck by Giolitti's ability to carry out bank reform without solid support in 1893 and to introduce universal male suffrage, again without solid support, toward the close of the period 1903–13—two major reforms by any measure.

To round out the discussion of the quality of Giolitti's "political faith," consider the related issue of his political culture, as revealed in his attitude toward the Socialists. De Grand argues that cooperation between Giolitti and the Socialists rested upon "a belief in the fragility of Italian political and social development, faith in gradualism, a preference for negotiation over direct action, agnosticism on free trade, and confidence in the expansion of the state sector." He goes on to explain that this common ground was "eventually outweighed by other, more fundamental issues that sepa-rated Giolitti from the vast majority of socialists: tax reform, the military budget, limits on unionization in the public sector, a growing belief in the corruption of the Giolittian majority, and, finally, the Libyan War." With sureness of touch, De Grand relates these disagreements to "four funda-mental distinctions [that Giolitti made] when dealing with labor unrest: first, between economic and political, especially general strikes; second, between private-and public-sector strikes; third, between strikes in the north and those in the agrarian south; and fourth, between strikes led by reformists and those sparked by revolutionaries." This is a clear, accurate, and useful framework.

Let me select for discussion three elements of the framework: strikes in the agrarian south, tax reform, and unionization of the public sector. (Similar remarks could be made about the other elements.) De Grand states that in the period 1903–13, "Giolitti was especially harsh in putting down agricultural leagues in the southern strongholds of his supporters. In doing this he rarely admitted their political or economic content but rather relegated them to violations of criminal laws." It might be instruc-tive to compare Giolitti's early and late policies toward agrarian unrest in the south. Giolitti's first government (1892–93) coincided with the foundation of the Socialist party, and with Italy's first great peasant strike, which took place on the *latifondi* of western Sicily. The strike was led by the *Fasci siciliani*, organizations that were developing in symbiosis with the Socialist party. When, in the summer of 1893, the police discovered that the Central Committee of Sicily's Socialists had decided to make a turn to the peasantry and undertake a strike for better sharecropping contracts on the *latifondi*, Giolitti instructed the prefects in Sicily to conduct a survey of the membership of the *Fasci*, with special attention to persons with criminal records. A high proportion of members with criminal re-cords might justify repression of the *Fasci* as "criminal associations." While the survey was conducted, the peasant strike assumed crisis proportions in the district of Corleone, but the prefect of Palermo reported to Giolitti as follows: "Close scrutiny of each *Fascio* reveals that those with criminal records compared to the rather large number of members are in a signifi-cant minority. Hence I do not think we can dissolve the *Fasci* on this basis." The prefect proceeded to press for repression of the *Fasci* on di-rectly political grounds: "the *Fasci* are but branches of the Central Com-mittee of Palermo . . . led by the fearsome Socialist Garibaldi Bosco, who tirelessly works . . . to keep the *Fasci* ready to seize the first opportunity to rise up against the landowning class and the government. I therefore believe that all the *Fasci* should be forcibly dissolved."² Giolitti did not accept the prefect's recommendation, and made a firm point of pursuing a policy of "constructive mediation and strict enforcement of the rule of law." For reasons that I cannot consider here, a general settlement to the strike remained elusive despite government mediation. The bank scandal brought down Giolitti, who was succeeded by Crispi as the peasant movement spilled over into chaotic agitations against a regressive excise tax, the *dazio di consumo*. After some hesitation, Crispi dissolved the *Fasci* in a state of siege on 3 January 1894. When the state of siege was put before Parliament *post factum*, Giolitti voted to support a policy he had resisted while in power.³ Keeping in mind De Grand's remark that "Giolitti . . . drew an important lesson from his first government in 1892–93, [namely] that it was difficult to maintain power in a stable way with a ministry drawn exclusively from one part of the Chamber [of Deputies]," we are left with the question: Did Giolitti draw a second lesson from his first government; namely, that a policy of constructive mediation could not work in agrarian conflicts in the south, and had to be replaced with a policy of construing such conflicts as matters for criminal law irrespective of the facts? The argument that Giolitti's policy toward peasant unrest in the south became hostage to the makeup of his parliamentary coalition is disturbing, and difficult to refute.

Consider next the issue of tax reform. De Grand writes, with characteristic straightforwardness: "No politician spoke of tax reform so much and over so long a time as Giolitti, but did so little about it once in power." He explains that Giolitti's "failure to live up to the promise of fiscal reform" was a reason for Socialist disillusionment with Giolitti, especially in light of Anna Kuliscioff's belief that tax reform was a *conditio sine qua non* of modernization and progress. The regressive elements in fiscal policy that Giolitti failed to address in his partial reforms were the set of excise taxes on items of basic necessity and the incidence of local taxes. It should be noted that when, in 1882, Giolitti first spoke out for tax reform, in what Giosué Carducci famously termed the "speech for salt in the bread of the poor," he made it clear that he wished to center his efforts at tax reform on making "direct taxes" and national taxes on land and salt less regressive. He actually proposed to compensate for lost revenues by *increasing* the incidence of excise taxes: "I believe that not only the duty of justice, but the promotion of sound finances, require us to ease the burden that weighs on taxpayers in the form of direct taxes, and raise consumption taxes as needed."[4] We are thus left with the question: Did Giolitti in fact fail to deliver on specific promises for specific kinds of tax reform? Or did Giolitti and the Socialists espouse different programs for tax reform, and the Socialists misunderstand Giolitti's program? The latter possibility is consonant with De Grand's general view that leading Socialists were prone to "serious misreading of Giolitti's intentions."

And what about the contrast between the Socialists and Giolitti over unionization in the public sector? De Grand summarizes Alberto Aquarone's view: "Giolitti treated unionization in the private and public sectors differently because he wanted total control over the state apparatus, which he used to regulate the process of change." This goes to the heart of the contrast between Giolitti and the Socialists. Giolitti's aim (I am tempted to say, his "political faith") was to *modernize* Italy. Modernity was understood in reference to the great powers of Continental and Western Europe. It comprised political democracy, economic development, military security, the gradual separation of civil society from political tutelage, sound finance, and cautious establishment of elements of both "social insurance" and "social transfer payments" as part of government. To pursue modernization is not the same thing as to pursue a fully unionized economy. Indeed, there is reason to think the two incompatible in a range of social contexts. To speak with De Grand's straightforwardness, Giolitti was no fool in wishing to discourage unionization of the public sector. Unlike firms, bureaucracies tend to operate with soft budget constraints. To combine union bargaining power and a soft budget constraint with a political culture of patronage is not a program for efficient modernization of the economy or the polity. Italy today stands witness.

If this sounds unfair to workers in the public sector in the period 1903–13, consider another argument. De Grand notes that Giolitti took harsh disciplinary measures against strikers on the railways. Were the railroad workers not an "aristocracy of labor?" Other things being equal, workers in communications, transport, health, and necessary service sectors have more bargaining power than do other workers of comparable skill, because their "strategic" location in the economy enables them credibly to threaten harm to the public if their demands are not met. In the Giolittian period, workers in the private sector stood much more in need of unionization in order to achieve "fair" wages and working conditions than did workers in the public sector. There is something to be said for the fact that Giolitti preferred to restrict the bargaining power of strategically placed workers, while extending government assistance, in the form of pensions, to those without bargaining power: the old and the infirm. In the end, much of high politics is the art of making hard choices about the principles, mechanisms, and criteria for allocating scarce resources with some notion of justice in mind. Giolitti practiced this art within the horizons of his political culture, which, as De Grand shows, was different from and partly at odds with the Socialists' political culture. But I am inclined to think that Giolitti's attitude toward the Socialists was colored less by lack of understanding than by a clearheaded commitment to his "political faith."

In sum, De Grand makes a powerful case for interpreting Giolitti's strategy of coalition formation as flexible centrism, tacking between the Socialist left and the Catholic right. He also argues convincingly that Giolitti's strategy caused a split in the socialist movement, ultimately "pushing" the Socialist party outside the framework of "bourgeois politics." And he offers a clear, accurate, and comprehensive classification of Giolitti's policies and, relatedly, the Socialists' programmatic demands. On the other hand, his judgment of the adequacy and integrity of Giolitti's policies is less persuasive. Giolitti's policy on agrarian strikes in the south appears to have been unprincipled, but his policies on tax reform and unionization in the public sector were more robust. Despite a measure of disagreement, I find De Grand's interpretation stimulating, insightful, thorough, resonant in the present, and forthright. I very much look forward to his larger work on Giolitti.

Notes

1. Sonnino expressed his ideal in the Chamber of Deputies when Giolitti first came to power with a cabinet drawn from the left: "[The Center] should constitute the pivot of a great party of Government, tempered and progressive and abhorrent of extremes. . . . Do you believe that the country, worried over the great financial and economic issues which afflict it will be content to waste time with the flags of the Left and the Right? . . . The historic flags of the Left and the Right have no solutions to offer for the many, many issues before us, about which the country is anxious to know your views: the budget, currency, social pacification, military organization, municipal finance, and many others. And to resolve the greater part of these issues would require uniting elements from all parties, binding as many forces as possible, instead of looking for new arguments for division." *Atti parlamentari. Camera,* 17, session of 10 June 1892.

   Here is how Spaventa justified the English model: "The political parties in a Chamber usually ought not to be more than two, corresponding to the two fundamental tendencies of every human society, conservation and innovation.

In this way, while one governs because it has a majority, the other, that is in the minority, practices opposition and prepares to succeed when it in turn shall have a majority. If the disorganization of parties reaches a point where no cabinet has a solid majority in the assembly; or if only one party can ever hope to have a majority; then the country's government cannot but be highly pernicious and contemptible. For, either the government shrinks to ruling without the consent of the majority in order to fulfill its most elementary duties; or the government's majority is so entrenched and compact that the government cannot lose its support, and becomes incorrigible for the lack of another party that might succeed it, right its wrongs, and correct its mistakes." S. Spaventa, *La politica della Destra. Scritti e discorsi raccolti da Benedetto Croce* (Bari, 1910), 467.

2. Secret report from prefect of Palermo to minister of interior, 17 September 1893, Archivio di Stato di Palermo, Gab. Pref. 1861–1905, b. 137, cat. 16, N. 4677. This document, together with twenty-eight other documents bearing on the strike and related events summarized in this paragraph, is to be published in J. Alcorn, "I Fasci siciliani ed il primo grande sciopero contadino dell'Italia liberale (1893)," *Nuove Prospettive Meridionali* 3, no. 5 (April 1993).

3. *Atti Parlamentari. Camera*, session of 3 March 1894.

4. G. Giolitti, program presented 15 October 1882 in Rome, *Discorsi extraparlamentari* (Turin, 1952), 91–92.

5

THE PSI AND THE POSTWAR CRISIS

Giovanni Sabbatucci

In an extraordinarily short space of time—between the end of World War I and the middle of the 1920s—the Italian Socialist party (PSI) went through a concentrated dose of dramatic experiences, a succession of victories and defeats that had no precedents even in the eventful history of this party. On one side it was involved with the crisis of the Italian liberal state; on the other, it was caught up in the schism of the international workers' movement—and more than anything in the "European civil war" (to use Nolte's debatable expression) that began in October 1917. Let us very briefly consider its basic stages.

At the end of the great war, the PSI was a weakened party, its nucleus and members decimated, politically marginalized on the national scene, but with a great prestige because of its intransigent rejection of the war. In this situation, the "maximalist" party leaders made an extremely radical choice: instead of trying to overcome the fractures inherited from the war and to reinsert themselves in the parliamentary-political game, they decided to play on their diversity and put all their cards on a revolutionary line closely linked to the example of Red October and to the Soviet model. On the basis of this project—more announced than consistently pursued —the PSI obtained a great number of votes: it increased its membership (but without ever reaching the dimensions of a real mass party, not even at the time of its greatest expansion). It won the first political elections after the war by tripling the seats it had in 1913 and became the strongest Italian party. It consolidated its position in local government, even beyond its traditional areas. And it reaped the political benefits of the great wave of trade-union struggles of the "two Red years."

When the cycle of struggles ceased between the end of 1920 and the beginning of 1921 and the political trend was reversed in Italy—as in all of Europe—the PSI still had no coherent strategy of frontal opposition to the bourgeois state and liberal institutions. And its strategy did not change even after the "anomalous" schism of Leghorn (when the more revolutionary and pro-Bolshevik wing broke away from the party) and when the first rumblings of the Fascist action squads' offensives were heard. The maximalist PSI, blocked as it was by its rigid ideological prejudices, was not able to offer any political response to these attacks, which struck at the real base of socialist power with systematic violence and cleverly exploited its contradictions and internal weaknesses. The reformist element, the only one that realized, albeit after some time, the need to get out of the straitjacket of its class-based intransigence, remained as a minority, like a prisoner inside the party. It only decided to leave the party a few days before the March on Rome, when it was too late to influence the outcome of the political crisis.

At the end of 1922, with Mussolini in power, the situation of the Italian workers' movement was completely the reverse of its position only two years before. Instead of a great party at the height of its powers, there were now three more or less equal groups, divided among themselves and on the sidelines of the political game: the maximalist PSI, the reformist PSU (United Socialist party) and the Communist party of Italy. The least vital of the three parties was the PSI, defender of an empty ideological heritage and divided up between preservers of tradition and advocates of confluence with the Italian Communist party.

After the elections of 1924 (where the total electoral force of the two Socialist parties was more than halved with respect to that of the PSI in 1921) and after the Matteotti crisis, the PSI and PSU had to fight to protect even the elementary conditions of their existence and maintain areas of political and trade-union freedom, which were gradually reduced until they finally disappeared. Uprooted from the Italian political situation, separated from its social base, forced to move its leadership abroad and to place its hope for rebirth in events it could not bring about, Italian socialism found itself in the condition of someone who has lost everything and is forced to start from scratch.

The reasons for this defeat, which left an indelible mark on the PSI's history, were numerous and complex. Obviously, the Italian Socialists can not bear all the responsibility for this, but anybody studying the history of socialism—as Angelo Tasca, in his conclusion to *Nascita e avvento del fascismo*, had already realized half a century before—has to concentrate his or her attention on the PSI's faults and errors, even at the cost of being "guilty of injustice toward the Italian workers' movement" and toward the figures of its leaders. In particular, we must ask ourselves what the basic reasons were and what contingent motives forced the PSI along a road so different from the one taken, albeit with many uncertainties, by most of European socialism; a road that prevented it from solving some fundamental problems, and principally the one concerning its relations with democracy.

The schism of the international workers' movement, which opened with the October revolution and was implemented with the foundation of the Third International and of the national Communist parties had, alongside many tragic consequences, at least one positive effect: it separated the advocates of a violent seizure of power and proletarian dictatorship from the supporters of reformist gradualism; it also forced democratic socialism to recognize itself as such, to rediscover the value of representative institutions, to continue (albeit among a thousand contradictions) that process of integration in the states and national systems which had begun with the Great War. In Italy this development did not take place. The hope tardily expressed by Treves to the Rome congress of 1922 ("the Socialists with the Socialists, the Communists with the Communists") was not realized, or was realized too late. At that time, the PSI represented, and continued to represent, an entirely anomalous case in the framework of European socialism.

This anomaly was based on a phenomenon that has deep roots in the history of the Italian workers' movement (and in general in the history of Italy): maximalism. Maximalism understood in a general sense, as a refusal of gradualism and intermediate solutions in the name of purity based on the class concept and the revolutionary ideal, is certainly not just an Italian phenomenon. But in no other country did it have the ability to rule the workers' movement as it did in Italy. The historic roots and permanent features of Italian maximalism have been acutely reviewed by Roberto Vivarelli. Vivarelli has justly emphasized the link between maximalism and an intransigent and millenarian tradition of a Risorgimento-Mazzini origin (in fact most of the first leaders of the Italian workers' movement were influenced by Mazzini or Garibaldi), fueled by the refusal of the monarchical state; he notes also that a strong maximalist tendency (mainly involving rural workers) was also present in individuals and factions usually classified under the reformist label.

Understood in this broad sense, maximalism is thus a structural component of the Italian Socialist movement, a component that remained strong even in periods of reformist hegemony over the party and that finally divided in 1911–12. This intransigent and antistate characteristic of Italian socialism was mainly due to its refusal to support Italian participation in World War I. This refusal was also prompted by contingent reasons (Italy's position as regards the conflict was different from that of France and Germany) and which, in the given situation, was probably inevitable. But it certainly had the effect of stressing its sense of extraneousness, its separateness from the Italian workers' movement with respect to the national community and of emphasizing the PSI's diversity with regard to the major European Socialist parties.

By insisting too much on maximalism as a historical constant and permanent feature of Italian socialism, we risk however underestimating the fracture represented by the Bolshevik revolution and not fully grasping the novelty of maximalism as such (which took shape in 1917–18) with respect to old-style intransigentism, personified above all by Costantino Lazzari and which, not by chance, maintained its own physiognomy and its own autonomous organization between 1918 and 1920, distinct from the new maximalism of Serrati. The old intransigentism had given the PSI a strong class-based and antisystem connotation, but had not stopped it from remaining a party of the Second International, of playing its own role in the political life of the nation, thanks also to the relative autonomy of the parliamentary group, and of maintaining at least a relationship of cohabitation with liberal institutions. The myth of the socialist revolution, planned in an indefinite future, had the function of blocking any integration in the "bourgeois" state, to which reformism fatally led, and of keeping the party's purity as regards class concepts. In November 1917, the socialist revolution stopped being an essentially ideological formula and became a concrete and topical reality with which to contend, a model to which it could immediately adapt. The term "maximalism" itself (now officially adopted by the majority faction of the party in place of the old "revolutionary-intransent" denomination) acquired a different significance, also because, thanks to a linguistic distortion, it was used both for the revolutionaries of the PSI and the Russian "majority party," that is, the Bolsheviks.

If you read the official documents of the party from 1918 to 1920—

starting with the famous resolution of December 1918, in which for the first time the dictatorship of the proletariat is indicated as an immediate goal—you cannot help being struck by the extremist nature of the pronouncements, by the continual reference to the violence of the final battle, the almost disdainful rejection of any representative institution (national and local) based on the hated "bourgeois democracy" and the almost disarming frankness with which it is affirmed that those institutions are nothing else but enemy strongholds to be conquered and then destroyed.

This extremism, as has been observed more than once, was more of words than deeds. But this only partly relieves the responsibilities of the maximalists. The inflammatory formulas and slogans of the two Red years, albeit never translated into a coherent program of revolutionary action, set the tone of the political and social battles of those years, introduced further elements of radicalization into Italian society, hurt widespread interests and sensitivities, and produced fear and the desire for revenge. The proof of all this lies not so much in the Fascist reaction, but in the isolation in which the Socialists found themselves in supporting it, in the badly concealed complacency with which numerous observers not suspected of being Fascist sympathizers (one only has to recall the case of Salvemini) watched the PSI's defeats.

The passivity and fatalism that the maximalists showed, first by announcing the revolution without seriously preparing for it, then by not effectively addressing the reaction, were not, however, the result of incapacity or a lack of moral fiber. They were the logical result of a culture and a mentality. Despite the fact that they sincerely admired the Soviet experience and were really convinced that the problem of the revolution was on the agenda, Serrati and the maximalists remained the positivist-determinists they had always been. They had none of the steely voluntarism that characterized a Lenin, or in a different manner, a Gramsci (and in general all the real revolutionary leaders). For them, the revolution was a natural event that as such, had to occur. Red October had only brought the fatal deadline nearer. So the revolutionaries should not force the situation with impulsive initiatives and sudden attacks. They must gird themselves, be ready for the task awaiting them, and strengthen their control over the party and the party's control over the entire workers' movement, with the aim of protecting it from reformist temptations. And this was the sense of the attempt, mainly by Bombacci, to reorganize the party in a more centralized manner and above all to reduce the autonomy of the parliamentary group.

For Serrati and the majority of the maximalists, this did not necessarily mean breaking up the unity of the workers' movement—nor compromising the link between the party and the mass bodies that represented its real membership and electoral reservoir—to embrace the Bolshevik model of the elitist party, the "steel nucleus" of the proletariat, proposed by the "pure" Communists. On the contrary, Serrati's plan consisted of keeping the main part of the workers' movement united (with its organizations and traditions) on an intransigent and revolutionary platform, without paying the price requested by the Communists. This was even more the case when Serrati realized (between the summer and autumn of 1920) that the revolutionary wave was flowing back and that it was necessary to give the party a more "defensive" tendency, to realign it on the position of the old intransigentism.

In this key it is easier to understand Serrati's behavior and that of the maximalist leadership in the long confrontation with the Comintern that led to the "anomalous" schism of Leghorn. This behavior is explained not only by personal pride, party patriotism, or dissent on tactics, but also and above all by the fear (confessed by Serrati himself) of losing the "technical" nucleus of reformism and, with it, contact with the members organized in the trade unions, cooperatives, and local government.

The line of the maximalists, albeit lacking a true strategic breadth, did have its own coherence. I think the behavior of the reformists is more difficult to explain. Reduced to a small minority among the party members, the reformists in fact kept their strong positions in the economic organizations and the parliamentary group. Using this solid situation— only partly compromised by the maximalist wave of the two Red years— as a base, they would have been able to rebuild a strong and potentially majority party among the electorate (as the Socialists of the SFIO [Section française de l'internationale óuvière, i.e., the French Socialist party] did in France, after their defeat in the Tours congress), leaving Serrati to deal with the "pure" Communists, a party with few members but many deputies, capable of having a positive influence on the Italian political crisis.

Why didn't the reformists take this road? First of all, we must remember that, in the immediate postwar period, even the reformists (with the exception of Turati and a few others) were attracted by the Russian Revolution and had a kind of inferiority complex with respect to the maximalists, which led them to tone down their positions and lower themselves to those of the intransigents (at the Bologna congress they did not even present a motion). At the end of 1920, after maximalism had demonstrated all its inconsistency with the occupation of the factories and with the events of Bologna, their inferiority complex lessened. But it was precisely because of this that the reformists, led by Turati, deluded themselves that they could regain control of the party as they had done between 1906 and 1908, counting on the Communists leaving and the maximalist phenomenon ending. In other words, Turati made a calculation very similar to that of Serrati: he tried to bring the entire workers' movement on his side and not just a fraction of it.

In the long term, Turati's plan was sounder than Serrati's. This was because the reformists had a wider and more solid membership than their adversaries, and also because—with regard to balance within the party—after the Leghorn congress the maximalists rapidly began to lose power. What neither Turati nor Serrati had calculated was the time factor: between the end of 1920 and the beginning of 1921, with the Fascist action squads invading agrarian areas, and with the sudden growth of the Fascist movement, the Italian crisis rapidly accelerated, thus thwarting long-term strategies and forcing the socialist movement to deal with problems of defense and survival for which it was entirely unprepared.

We now come to another fundamental aspect of the socialist tragedy of the post-World War I period: the lack of or, at best, tardy understanding of the Fascist phenomenon. While the Fascists were familiar with Italian Socialism, if only for the fact that many of them (starting with Mussolini) had been active in it in the past, the Socialists did not understand Fascism and underestimated its strength for a long time.

For the maximalists, the problem of Fascism was more or less irrelevant from a theoretical angle. If the bourgeois state, as an expression of the dominion of class, were an intrinsically oppressive organization with which the workers' movement must avoid dealing, then the way in which that oppression operated did not constitute an important problem. The Fascist reaction, since it was a class reaction, was immediately identified with the reaction of the state; the violence of its demonstrations was even a symptom of the crisis in which the bourgeois state found itself. Faced with the fury of the reaction, a prelude to the inevitable proletarian victory, there was nothing else to do but hold fast to one's principles and keep a firm grip on intransigence while waiting for the storm to pass.

Naturally, the reformists could not share the maximalist diagnosis. Their culture and their historical experience were founded on the idea that the liberal state was not an instrument of oppression (on the contrary, the representative institutions could be used for the emancipation of the proletariat), and above all that the bourgeoisie was not a single reactionary block, but had a progressive component with which the workers' movement must walk a part of the way. But also behind this vision there was a determinist philosophy based on economics; the bourgeoisie was pushed toward progress and democracy by the laws of capitalism, which made any form of oppression and repression incompatible with modernity. The reformists, unable to declare that Fascism was a product of the capitalist bourgeoisie (with which, strictly speaking, it was incompatible) but also incapable, with their cultural background, of recognizing that it had the autonomous dimension of a political phenomenon, were forced to fall back on an explanation in a psychological key: Fascism was a kind of war neurosis, one of the many bitter results of the conflict, a passing state of mind, like maximalism. And, like maximalism, it would soon disappear. Although based on an opposite premise, the reformists arrived at a conclusion not very different from that of the maximalists: you had to hold fast to your principles, not return violence for violence, wait for the phenomenon to pass before proceeding as you had before.

In fact, the reformists—precisely because they considered democracy to be a positive value and did not share the catastrophic opinion about the future of the capitalist system—were willing, at least in theory, to intervene in the political crisis by making their parliamentary weight felt to form a democratic majority. It was the real membership of the movement that pushed them in this direction, and in particular the Red organizations of the Po valley area, already protagonists in the peasants' struggles of 1919–20 and now directly under fire from the Fascist action squads. But this willingness remained theoretical as long as the deputies were bound to a party discipline that imposed the strictest intransigence. The rebellion of the parliamentary group against the leadership, which led to the schism of Rome, only occurred in the summer of 1922, when almost all bets were off.

The freedom gained with the split, on the eve of the March of Rome, was not enough for the reformists to change a political situation by now stabilized around Mussolini's "national government," nor to create in 1923, a parliamentary majority capable of blocking the Acerbo law, a decisive step toward the authoritarian regime. Even the antifascist battle fought by Matteotti before and after the elections of 1924 was not always followed and adequately supported by the political and trade-union leaders of reformist Socialism, often inclined (not unlike the maximalists, albeit for different reasons) to underestimate the subversive nature of the Fascist phenomenon, and its ability to endure and take over the state.

The underestimation and the more or less radical incomprehension of Fascism were certainly not prerogatives of the Socialists. All the Italian political forces—from the conservatives to the Communists—committed serious errors in assessing a phenomenon that had no precedents or terms of reference in the political history of Europe. All were trying to fit it into normal categories. All deluded themselves either that they could use it or that it would shortly disappear. All paid a high price for their error of judgment. But it was the Socialists who paid the highest price: not only immediately, as the main target of Fascist violence and victims of state repression, but also in a long-term perspective. The sense of defeat weighed on the party for a long time, weakening its action in the years of exile and during the Resistance, and making its return to the national scene more difficult (especially with such a dynamic and unscrupulous competitor as the PCI). After the Liberation, the PSI again became one of the protagonists of Italian politics. But it never fully recovered those roots in society that had constituted its special characteristic and greatest strength during the first thirty years of its history.

6

INTERNATIONAL AND DOMESTIC REALITIES AFTER WORLD WAR I

Thomas Row

The postwar crisis is one of those periods in Italian history that can rightly be called a turning point. Between the end of the First World War and the Fascist seizure of power, decisions were either made or not made, and actions were either taken or not taken, that set the country on a fateful course and that have had repercussions lasting up to the present time. As historians, we return again and again to the basic questions raised by this period: What was the real nature of the breakdown of the Liberal regime? Why was it that the Fascists were able to succeed in taking control of the state? How do we evaluate the strategy and tactics of those who aided and abetted it? To be sure, these are familiar questions, but I believe that with the end of the cold war and the collapse of communism we will look at them in an new light and reassess many traditional interpretations.

Of central importance to any understanding of these questions is the subject treated by Giovanni Sabbatucci in his paper: the role of the Italian Socialist party (which, in my view, he quite rightly considers in its broad political-cultural sense rather than in a narrow institutional way), and the postwar crisis.

Here was a moment in which, despite the great difficulties faced during the war years, the Socialists had much going for them: as Sabbatucci reminds us, between the end of the war and 1920 the party acquired large popular support; in the 1919 elections it tripled its seats in Parliament, becoming the strongest Italian political party; at the same time, the socialists consolidated their positions in the cooperatives, in the unions, and in local administration. Yet, just two years later Mussolini came to power and the socialist movement was profoundly divided into three marginalized groupings. After the 1924 elections and the Matteotti affair the game was more or less up. As Sabbatucci so well puts it, at this point, "Italian socialism finds itself in the condition of a person who has lost everything and who is compelled to start again from zero."

One might well have asked then a question that has often been posed in recent days: "What's left of the Left?" Why did the Italian Left find itself so weak and divided? Why was the Left unable to mount an effective opposition to Fascism? What, in other words, went wrong? In attempting to answer these questions, it is all too easy to play—again to use a recent expression—the "Blame Game." Goodness knows there is plenty of blame to go around. For a long time, depending upon one's political inclinations, it has been open season against one and all: the maximalists can be condemned for stubbornly pursuing a revolutionary dream that flew in the face of reality; the reformists can be criticized for their passivity, for catering to the fantasies of the Left and for failing to assert their autonomy until it was too late; the communists can be criticized for practically everything, for dividing the movement and upsetting the apple cart. And so forth and so on.

It is not the least of the virtues of Giovanni Sabbatucci's paper that his aim is to understand the socialists of this time rather than to sit in judgment upon the them. Even so, and taking his cue from Angelo Tasca, he is afraid to focus his attention on the very real mistakes and errors made by the PSI in these years of crisis.

I think that it is essential, in evaluating the actions of the socialists in this period, to keep in mind the international dimension: the broader European context within which the postwar crisis unfolded in Italy. As a result of the war, the old order was everywhere challenged. Revolution spread through east and central Europe and threatened the West. Grand new ideologies: Leninism and Wilsonianism offered to recast bourgeois Europe as a whole, from the Atlantic to the Urals.

Then, as well as now, the Italian political system showed a very great sensibility to systemic changes on an international level. I cannot but think of the enormous impact the end of the cold war had on the post-World War II political system in Italy. There is always a temptation in talking about Italian politics to keep within the echo chamber of the domestic scene. In great moments of crisis and transition, though—after the First

World War, after the Second World War, and now after the cold war—the broader dimension is crucial.

As Sabbatucci points out, the history of the PSI in this period has to be placed in the broader context of the general crisis and eventual schism of the international workers' movement. The great catalytic event, of course, is the Russian Revolution. Here, Sabbatucci makes some important distinctions. For the maximalists, the Russian Revolution marked a fracture, a real development from the prewar past. Sabbatucci modifies or refines Roberto Vivarelli's emphasis on maximalism as a historical constant. After 1917, "maximalism" took on a new meaning: revolution has become a real and concrete possibility (at least in Russia).

The reformists, too, succumbed to the allure of the great October revolution. They came, in Sabbatucci's words, to suffer from a kind of "inferiority complex" with respect to the maximalists. He sees a reformist "delusion," paralleled ironically by the maximalists who sought "to bring the entire workers' movement on [their] side and not just a fraction of it." This goes a long way, in his view (and I agree) toward explaining the strategic thinking of the reformists at least up to 1920 and even later.

In looking at postwar Italian socialism in European perspective, I would pose two questions in need of further development. First, why was Italian socialism so idiosyncratic in this period? How exactly can the differences between the Italian case and those of other countries be best explained? Some kind of comparative dimension would be helpful to account for the relative strength of the maximalists and the relative weakness of the reformists in Italy. Second, an intriguing mention is made of Nolte's notion of a "European civil war." I would be curious to know in detail where the author might place Italian socialism in this framework.

If we then turn to the domestic political context faced by the socialist movement in the postwar years, a different series of questions emerges. The great drama experienced by the socialists is played out against the backdrop of the collapse of the liberal regime. Some of the basic elements of this crisis have a very familiar ring today.

First, there is the bankruptcy of the political class. The Liberal political class was not prepared to deal with the new realities of the country created by the war. Here, it is useful to keep in mind a distinction made by Alexander De Grand in his book on the Italian Left between the problems of the state and those of the political class. As a result of the war, the state emerges in many respects strengthened, but the Parliament, at least, and the political class have been considerably weakened. Second, there is a virtual explosion of what today we would call protest movements, as well as the emergence or reorganization of new political forces: ex-combatants, d'annunziani, popolari, nationalists, etc.—not to mention fascists. There is a widespread, diffuse, and contradictory popular opposition to the old regime. Third, the moment seemed to have arrived for "a great reform," for a radical change that would bring the political system in line with the new social realities. In the face of this, though, there is on the one hand a political class reluctant to give up its hold on power; on the other, a bitterly divided series of opposition forces that do not seem capable of offering any viable alternative.

Giovanni Sabbatucci's explication of the socialist positions, of the attitudes of the reformists and maximalists toward the state, is exemplary. I would suggest, though, that here again some sort of comparative dimension—a "comparative domestic dimension"—would be useful. How do interactions with other political forces, and with the political class in particular, shape socialist strategies in this period? How do the other political movements pose limits as well as offer opportunities to socialist action?

Toward the end of the paper, Sabbatucci raises what strikes me as a very crucial point: that is, the failure of the Italian Socialist party to understand the real nature of Fascism (or at any rate the failure to understand Fascism until it was too late). As he points out: "While the Fascists understood Italian Socialism perfectly well (many of them, beginning with Mussolini, having been Socialists), the Socialists did not understand Fascism and underestimated its force." Why was this so?

The question demands, I think, a fuller consideration of socialist "culture and mentality," of socialist "interpretative categories"—these are all terms used in the paper, and I found them highly suggestive. If I understand correctly, there is a distinction meant between formal socialist theory and this notion of a socialist mentality/culture, or rather mentalities and cultures. Spencer Di Scala referred this morning to "the mystical nature of the general strike." Perhaps mysticism rather than Marx is more relevant to understanding socialist mentalities and behavior in this period. As Sabbatucci shows, the maximalists and the reformists had rather different analyses of Fascism. Even so, they both come to the same conclusions about how to respond: hold fast to your principles and wait for the phenomenon to pass before proceeding as before.

What was it about socialist political culture that blinded the movement to the realities of the situation in the postwar crisis? To the realities of

Fascism? Why was it that, "They just didn't get it?." Conversely, what was it about the Fascists that enabled them "to get it" (or get to power, anyway)? I found the hint of an answer in a phrase of Sabbatucci's where he talks about the "reinsertion" of the PSI into the *realtà nazionale* after the fall of Fascism. This raised for me the important question of the ties between political movement and Italian society, between the PSI and the *realtà nazionale*.

I would like to push the matter further and suggest that a key to the problem lies with the question of nationalism; nationalism not so much in the narrow sense of the nationalist movement, but in the broad, diffuse cultural sense in which nationalism had permeated Italian "mentalities," in differing ways and in differing degrees, since the end of the nineteenth century. The intervention crisis and the great upheaval and sacrifices of the war alter and intensify this cultural strain. While the Fascists were able to connect to nationalism, the Socialists were not.

I end by asking what conclusions we might draw from the experiences of the Italian Socialist movement during the postwar crisis. Giovanni Sabbatucci's answer strikes me as somewhat harsh and melancholy, yet ultimately very convincing. The postwar crisis does indeed mark a turning point in the fortunes of Italian socialism. Nothing would ever be the same again. The Socialists, as he argues, "paid the highest price of all the Italian political forces, not only in the short, but in the long run." He writes: "even after the Liberation, when the PSI once again becomes a protagonist of Italian politics, the party never recovers that rootedness [*quel radicamento*] in society that had constituted its peculiarity and its force during the first thirty years of its history."

It is precisely this question of the loss of "rootedness," of the weakening connection between the Socialist party and Italian society that most intrigues me in this account of the postwar crisis and that resonates most when I think about the present crisis of the country.

7

SURVIVAL IN DEFEAT: PIETRO NENNI

Giuseppe Tamburrano

Pietro Nenni arrived as an exile in Paris on 21 November 1926, after Mussolini had eliminated every trace of freedom and democracy in Italy. Once in Paris, Nenni had two basic issues to face: his own personal survival and how to continue the battle for democracy and socialist unity. The first problem was easily solved. He had a lot of friends in the French capital, having spent some time there in the past, and he received a warm welcome from the French Left. He had no trouble finding work especially with French and foreign French-language papers, such as the Belgian *Le Soir*. The second issue was more complex: there was a profound division and even open conflict between the Socialists and other democratic forces that had taken refuge in Paris.

A brief look at the history of this period may be useful for understanding the complexity of the issues faced by Pietro Nenni. Nenni had abandoned the Republican party just after the split between the Socialists and the Communists. Coinciding as it did with the peak of the fascist threat, the split had greatly weakened the party. It is even difficult to understand why the two factions—the Maximalist, led by Giacinto Menotti Serrati, and the Communist, led by Amadeo Bordiga—decided to split, given that, at least verbally, they seemed to agree on almost everything. They certainly agreed on what was considered the main issue: the proletarian revolution that Lenin was anxious should take place in Italy as soon as possible.

Lenin was convinced that the time was ripe for such a revolution and that Turati's Reformists (who opposed any form of violence and who were under the illusion that socialism could be achieved through existing institutions) were the only obstacle. Although Lenin had urged Serrati to expel the "social traitors," Serrati had refused to do so. The reformists were not particularly strong within the party (14,000 versus Bordiga's 58,000) but they represented the working-class bodies, the cooperatives, and especially the trade unions. Serrati thought that there could be no revolution without the support of the working classes through the trade unions. What still remains a mystery is why Serrati, and his majority faction, should have been so in favor of a revolution not supported by the working classes.

Of course the answer is that while the maximalists were very good at proclaiming the revolution at the drop of a hat, they were absolutely incapable of organizing one. They were good honest people, loyal to the workers' cause, but light-years away from the idea of taking up arms and using violence. They believed that the revolution was an "ineluctable historical process," and were confident that the proletariat, an abstract entity, would rise up and fulfill Marx's prophesy once the time was ripe.

The contrasts persisted within the Italian Socialist party (PSI) even after the Leghorn split. The profound rift between the maximalists and reformists led to another division a little more than a year and a half later, in October 1922. The Communist party concentrated all its efforts on fighting the two other parties, in the effort to win over the masses and proletarian bodies it needed for the revolution. The maximalists and the reformists were in conflict with the Communists and with each other. To sum up, the Left had split into three different parties that spent all their time and energy fighting their own bitter internal battles despite the inexorable advance of Fascism.

Although Italy had won the war, the mood in the country was one of profound disappointment. The allies were accused of failing to keep their promise and granting a so-called mutilated victory. Discontent was especially strong among the civil population, which had already put up with so much hardship during the war, among those who had supported the war from the beginning and, especially, among those who had actually fought in trenches.

Indeed Italy had paid a high price, in terms of deaths and territory, with the invasion of northwest Italy. The weaker, more vulnerable sectors of society had been especially affected by the impact of the severe postwar depression. The workers belonging to the Socialist party and the CGL had been against the war from the start and now had ample grounds for resenting the middle classes who had insisted on the war in the first place.

How dare they now complain that the war had not achieved its purposes, that it had been a useless massacre condemned even by the pope? The soldiers and veterans resented the political leadership for not keeping its promises—especially to distribute land—and the Socialists who criticized them for having participated in the war.

In January 1919, Don Sturzo, a Catholic priest, founded what was called the Catholic party. This new party opposed the "atheist" Socialists, the Liberals for having deprived the pope of his temporal possessions, and the bourgeois state. Before dissolving, Parliament voted in favor of an electoral reform, introducing a proportional voting system, which was to be the downfall of the Liberals, the dominant governing party.

In the November 1919 elections, the Socialists and the "Popolari" triumphed, just gaining an absolute majority. Although Don Sturzo was as anti-Giolitti as he was anti-Socialist, the Catholics and Socialists joined forces to promote the renewal and reform of the former leading classes. The country was in the throes of social unrest: land and factories were occupied, there were popular uprisings against inflation, continual strikes and demonstrations—a profound economic crisis. Public opinion soon tired of endemic rebellion with no revolutionary outlet. Rightist solutions became increasingly attractive. First the landowners, and then the entrepreneurs, handed themselves over to the truncheons of the Fascists.

The antifascist groups that did manage to get themselves organized and fight the Fascists in the streets by their own methods were disowned by their parties. In Parma and Sarzana, the Arditi movement had fostered the resistance of the workers and forced the Fascists to retreat, yet it was disowned by the Communists (who disapproved of the use of violence for democracy instead of for the proletarian revolution) by the Reformists (against violence on principle), and the maximalists (foolishly ambitious by definition).

Having just expelled the reformists from the party, the maximalists were convinced that the Comintern would consider them fully qualified to participate with the Communists in reconstructing unity, and embarked on the journey to the revolutionary Mecca. Nenni has described the reaction of the leaders of the maximalist faction (including Serrati) when Mussolini was getting ready to march on Rome with his squads, in the following terms:

> There was a meeting of the directorate of the party and I remember going into the room with "Stefani" (a well-known press agency of the time) who told us about the Fascist conference in Milan and

Mussolini's speech in Naples announcing his imminent "arrival" in Rome. Nobody took the threat seriously. The next day, the whole delegation, including Serrati, got on the train for Moscow, absolutely convinced that nothing would happen in Rome.

Nenni and Mussolini had been friends, and Nenni knew that Mussolini always meant what he said.

By this time the young Nenni had become a major figure in the Socialist party. He was chief of *Avanti!* and had been placed in charge of the campaign against the amalgamation of the Italian Socialist and Communist delegations (the latter led by Gramsci) with the participation of Zinoviev. In Nenni's opinion, this would have simply resulted in the Socialist party's being swallowed up by the Communist party. Nenni organized an extraordinary conference and successfully thwarted the designs of the Comintern and the greed of the Communists. The conference also enabled the Italian Socialist party to get rid of Serrati and his faction: after being overruled at the conference, the maximalists left the party and persisted in pursuing what might be called their "theoretical" extremism.

Nenni then embarked on another battle to persuade PSI leaders to work toward the recomposition of the Socialist movement. Nenni referred to this as "Socialist unity," meaning unification with the Reformists. After their expulsion from the PSI, the reformists had formed another party, the PSU, led by Turati, Treves, and Matteotti. "One morning," writes Nenni, "I heard a knock on the door. When I opened the door, there was a young man, with a smile on his face. He introduced himself as Professor Carlo Rosselli."

Although Rosselli was a member of the PSU, he agreed with Nenni's theory of Socialist unity. The meeting between Nenni and Rosselli eventually led to the publication of the *Fourth Estate*, a journal entirely devoted to a discussion of the theoretical and political issues involved in the rebirth of Italian socialism, over and beyond the limits represented by maximalism and reformism.

Nenni accused the reformists of lack of courage and shortsighted vision in the postwar crisis. In his view the parliamentary-type proposals put forward by the Reformists were incapable of solving the crisis. Nenni believed that Turati had underestimated the severity of the situation after the war, and wrongly considered that an agreement with Giolitti would be sufficient to foster recovery. According to Nenni, Giolitti was a shadow of his former self and the only possible solution lay in a democratic revolution. The country needed to become a republic with the foundation of a constituent assembly and a new constitution. Moreover, major reforms, including agrarian reform, could no longer be delayed. Conversely, the maximalists and Communists believed in only one form of revolution, proletarian revolution; and the reformists in only one possible democracy, parliamentary democracy.

The reaction of the antifascist forces to Matteotti's assassination is evidence of their failure (indeed, everyone's failure) to perceive the gravity of the situation and take action. The reformists still had confidence in the monarchy, the Communists in direct action to establish the Soviet, and the maximalists were somewhere between the two. Everyone, including Turati, Amendola, and Gramsci was convinced, though, that fascism had been defeated. No action was taken to resist or prepare a counteroffensive to combat Mussolini and save democracy.

The preface to the first edition of the *History of Four Years*, edited by Carlo Rosselli (never distributed because of the "exceptional" fascist laws) shows how much Nenni had learned from the above events.

> Whoever looks at the history of the Socialist party since 1910 must be struck by the following: by opposing the war in Libya, the party had become the natural vehicle of opposition to the whole enterprise, yet it made almost no use of these powers. The same applied, to a larger extent, to the World War. The party, showing a dignity to which I would like to pay homage (remember I was on the other side), had fearlessly resisted succumbing to the appeal and illusion of the war. Yet, when the time came to reap the reward, it became the accuser rather than the accused, and gathered under its wing those who were disappointed, discontented, and rebellious, started to play with words, got drunk on words and theories, raved on about the Russian myth, and showed not even an iota of the political intuition and action needed to find a socialist-oriented solution to the crisis of the Italian state and society.
>
> And, if only we had learned something from all this! Despite the heroic battle waged by the Socialists against fascism, a fight that sooner or later will successfully lead to a change in the situation, there is every reason to believe that unfortunately the proletariat will gain nothing. The socialist movement is still anchored to ideological positions that belong to the past, is still worrying about the orthodoxy of doctrine, carefully avoiding formulating any concrete programs that respond to the need of the moment or acting as a banner for the opposition, polarizing the working classes, the economically

exploited, and politically oppressed. In short, it is acting as if social-ism were the result of a process that has to evolve over centuries and not a reality of the immediate future. Yet, it is obvious—one need only look at the Aventino—that the solution to the present crisis of the Italian state and society (and therefore of liberty) can only be a socialist solution and that the political aim can only be the establish-ment of a democratic, workers' republic of Italy.

In Paris, Nenni continued to fight the same battles that had been waged and lost (along with democracy) in Italy. His aim was to reunite all the antifascist forces and Socialists. The antifascist *Concentration* was founded at a symposium in Nerac in April 1927; it included the PSI socialists, the reformists, the Republicans, the General Confederation of Labor (CGL), the League of Rights of Man, but not the Catholics or the Communists. The latter were critical of the Concentration for remaining loyal to the illusion of "bourgeois democracy" and were particularly hostile to Nenni, whom they had not yet forgiven for his role in preventing the amalgam-ation advocated by Moscow.

Nenni had been particularly anxious for the Communists to join, in part because of their role in the Italian underground resistance movement and also because the Soviet Union was still the only truly antifascist power, if only because fascism was anti-Soviet. However, in those years Moscow was even more antisocialist than it was antifascist. This was the period of "socialfascism," the theory—which Stalin used also as a pretext to snatch power from his former ally Bukharin—according to which the Socialists were considered to obstruct the proletarian revolution (which they did not believe in) more than the Fascists, who were at least openly counter-revolutionary. The Socialists, especially those more to the left than the Reformists, were cheating the proletariat and therefore had to be opposed by every possible means and forced to reveal their real identity. The masses who continued to support them had to be drawn away from them. Not only was Nenni responsible for the nonamalgamation of Communists and Socialists, he was a left-wing Socialist and therefore a major enemy.

The situation in Italy left little hope for antifascists. Mussolini was increasingly ensconced. The only possible justification for the continued Communist belief that the proletarian revolution and the establishment of a Soviet republic could be achieved by the simultaneous elimination of fascism and capitalism lies in ideological blindness and subservience to Stalin. Another possible, albeit extremely superficial justification, might be the economic depression in the late 1930s, which fueled the ideological mystifications of Marxism, according to which the economic crisis represented the final and definitive crisis of capitalism.

Mussolini was becoming increasingly powerful in Italy and fascism was spreading all over Europe: in Hungary, Poland, Austria, Finland, Portugal, and Spain, with ramifications even in England and France. The situation in Germany was particularly worrying: the open battle between the "opportunism" of the Social Democrats and the "sectarism" of the Communists paved the way for the Brownshirts.

Nenni used every possible opportunity (press, meetings, etc.) to underline that Fascism was not a purely Italian phenomenon; it was a potential danger also for other countries less backward than Italy. He traveled all over Europe, especially in Germany, tirelessly putting people on their guard. Not one German city was left out of his itinerary of meetings and conferences. His words went unheeded. The Italian and German experience had demonstrated the grave repercussions of the divisions within the proletariat and within the Left in general. Nenni devoted all his energy to reconstructing unity, first and foremost among the Socialists. With the help of Turati and the young Saragat, who was extremely active (especially culturally) from his refuge in Austria, Nenni finally managed to bring the Socialists and the reformists together at a major conference held in Paris in July 1930.

However, Nenni was striving for something more than Socialist unity. His second objective was a rapprochement with the Communists, who continued to be firm supporters of the "social fascist" policy. In late 1932 there were the first, hesitant, signs of dialogue between Socialists and Communists and, in particular, between the two Internationals. After Hitler's victory, even the blind were forced to admit that the division between the two parties was contributing to the success of fascism. In August of that year, Austrian Socialist Friedrich Adler made the first reference to a possible understanding between the two Internationals in the effort to combat fascism. Nenni did not miss the opportunity and went even further. In his presentation to the 22d Conference (originally to have been held that same year but subsequently postponed to April 1933) he referred to "proletarian unity," provoking the negative reaction of both Modigliani and Treves. The reaction of the Communists was also negative.

Nenni continued the battle, regardless of the mounting opposition within his own party. He was convinced that Hitler's victory had made an alliance of the Left not only possible but indeed imperative and inevitable.

It was only a matter of time. In February 1933, the Socialist International proposed united action against fascism and the war. This time the response from the Comintern was not negative, merely evasive.

In March 1933, Hitler won the elections and gained full powers. At that point, the Soviet Union sought a nonaggression agreement with the Fascists and, in September 1933 signed a nonaggression pact with Mussolini. Nenni was unrestrainable, envisaging at last a possible "organic unity of the working classes." He tried to bridge the gap separating the Socialists and the Communists and at the same time accentuated the differences with the non-Marxist factions of the antifascist forces.

The main dispute was with Rosselli who had managed to escape from Lipari, where he had been in political confinement with antifascist leaders Lussu and Nitti. On his arrival in Paris, he concentrated all his efforts on "Justice and Liberty," which had already achieved considerable success against fascism in Italy, but not a political formation as such, with a definite program and ideology. Rosselli was responsible for the policies and doctrine expressed in "Justice and Liberty," as is clearly stated in his book *Socialisme liberal*, published in Paris in the autumn of 1930.

Although Carlo Rosselli was in favor of establishing a new non-Marxist socialism, and agreed with Nenni on the need to eliminate both reformism and maximalism, they could not agree on the characteristics of the new socialism. Rosselli believed that Marxism, by advocating determinism and collectivism, denied individual liberty, placing all the emphasis on class. Nenni believed that the new socialism ought to be loyal to true Marxism, which did not deny liberty but strove for the liberation of all men.

Nenni was not alone in rejecting Rosselli's liberal socialism. Treves and Saragat were even more against it than he was. Like Nenni, Saragat was in favor of a profound renewal of Italian socialism, but within the framework of the rigorous interpretation of Marxism to be found in Bauer and Adler's texts. The ideological dispute became a political one. The first issue of the *Quaderni di Giustizia e Libertà* published 1 January 1932, contained an article outlining the program of the "New Socialism," based on Rosselli's ideas. The February 1934 issue (no. 10) contained a proposal for the constitution of a "New Socialist" party. The author of the article, Emilio Lussu, stated that the old socialism was finished and would never be resurrected; that a new "socialist movement, then party, would have to be created on its ashes."

The division was inevitable. In May 1934, Nenni referred to the "anti-Socialist twitching of the small-bourgeois world. . . . These tendencies are crystallized around Justice and Liberty. . . . With the 'Socialism' of Justice and Liberty, the Party could share neither ends nor means. . . . Socialism is Marxist, classist, materialistic, proletarian. . . . Its indestructible foundations are in the war of class." The General Council of *Concentration* declared itself dissolved and just over three months later, the Socialists and Communists signed their first pact of unity of action.

Of the Socialist leaders, Giuseppe Saragat came closest to sharing Nenni's claims on the Marxist, classist, and internationalistic nature of socialism and unity with the Communist party in the effort to achieve organic unity. The correspondence between the two Socialists (copies of which have been preserved at the Nenni Foundation) show that Saragat was more Marxist than Nenni and even more determined to achieve organic unity (although he firmly defended the role of the Socialist party in striving to reach it). However, there was no general consensus within the Socialist party on this issue. Modigliani and Tasca, for example, were in favor of unity of action with the Communist Party but only in the framework of the resistance to fascism. They excluded any prospect of organic unity.

In fact the Communists, the International, and especially the Italian Communist party made no mystery of the fact that for them unity only served the purpose of combating fascism. Their goal was still to absorb and eliminate the socialist movement. In an article that appeared in the *Internationale Communiste*, the Socialists are explicitly castigated as an antipopular front and as "those who seek . . . organic unity, in order to eliminate the difference between Communism and Social Democracy." We are also informed by this same paper that the International's new policy is to "assist the Social democratic masses in the passage to Communism with a view to arriving at the victory of Soviet power." The day after the signature of the pact with the Socialists, Ruggero Grieco reassured the Communists in political confinement on the island of Ponza, stressing that nothing had changed in Communist policy and that the ideological battle "must even be intensified."

Hence the change in Communist policy was tactical, quite simply due to the advance to the Nazi-fascists in Europe and to their declared anticommunism. The Soviet Union sought allies to face this threat wherever it could, among all antifascist forces. At the Seventh Conference of the Communist International in July 1935, the Popular Front announced its new policy. The Communist parties were surprisingly quick to respond to the new directives, overtaking even the left-wing Socialists and Nenni himself in their overtures toward "democratic-bourgeois" countries and parties. Nenni realized that Soviet policy only responded to cynical opportunism and that there was no question of the Communists giving up their objective of absolute hegemony. They would have been prepared to establish an alliance with God himself or even the devil to achieve their immediate and long-term goals.

Basically this singlemindedness also justifies Nenni's persistent belief in organic unity. A single party could not be so subservient to Moscow and would have to develop new characteristics, those very characteristics described and defended by Nenni and Saragat in their polemic with liberal socialism. In these terms, Nenni's "organic unity" was more or less an illusion.

The situation was, however, precipitating and programs and illusions were fast overtaken by the urgency of events. Fascism was becoming increasingly threatening and unity was linked to the immediate requirement of defense. The unity of Socialists and Communists was not only a question of tactics on the part of the International. In France especially it was in response to strong pressure from below to react against a dangerous extreme-right movement that was developing. On 12 February 1934, during a march to protest against the fascist threat, the Socialist and Communist groups joined forces, enthusiastically overcoming all their earlier clashes and conflicts to proclaim "unity."

Meantime Austria was in the throes of a civil war that eventually led to the clerical-fascist Dollfuss coup d'état, which paved the way for the Nazi putsch. Fascism spread all over Europe: "Today the restoration triumphed in Rome, Berlin, Budapest, Vienna, Warsaw, and Madrid," wrote Nenni. A united Left was the only barrier against fascism. On 16 February 1936, the elections in Spain were won by the Spanish People's Front, which included Socialists, Communists, Republicans, the General Labor Union, and the trade union and workers' party. Less than three months later, the Popular Front also won the elections in France. Socialists were increasing in France and Spain. Nenni's theory was proving itself to be true. Wherever the Left had been divided, as in Italy and Germany, fascism had succeeded. Wherever the Left had joined forces, the right had been forced to retreat. The Socialists were undoubtedly in the lead in terms of the overall success of the forces of the Left.

But the victory was short-lived. Only five months after the victory of the Popular Front in Spain, General Franco ("el Caudillo") declared civil war on the Spanish republic. It took three years of bloody fighting for

Franco's Fascist forces—and the help of Mussolini and Hitler—to defeat the Spanish Popular Front, abandoned by democratic countries, especially the government of the French Popular Front led by Léon Blum.

The success of the French Left government was also short-lived and tormented. Opposed by the other anticommunist European countries, and tormented by its own internal contrasts, it seemed incapable of acting and going to the aid of the Spanish republic. Nenni threw himself into its defense. He knew that the fight both to beat fascism and to achieve a united Left was at stake in Spain. Despite the advance of fascism, the Left was still united and even gaining in strength. It had managed to survive the difficult test posed by the cynical, violent authoritarian attitude of the Communists and forget for a moment its theoretical disputes and conflicts. Nenni, Pacciardi, Longo, and Rosselli all knew (as Rosselli had written) that Spain was a general rehearsal of the war between fascist and antifascist nations, and of the battle that had to be fought in Italy with absolute unity if it was to have any hope of success.

The contacts between the Socialists (especially Nenni) and the Soviet Union increased during the Spanish civil war. Solidarity with the country of "real socialism" increased for the simple, but extraordinarily eloquent, reason that the Soviet Union had been the only country that had helped the Spanish republic (as best it could and receiving payment for it in gold), whereas the French Social Democrats and the French government had merely washed their hands of the Spanish issue.

However, Nenni and the Socialists were not blinded by this solidarity; it had simply induced them to put up with Stalin's methods, which included the extermination of anarchists in Barcelona and the moral and physical destruction of dissidents. Although Nenni was more than critical of the Moscow trials, he did not allow that macabre farce to induce him to break with Moscow or with the Italian Communists, who supported Stalin and believed, or pretended they did, that Trotzky and Zinoviev, Kamenev and Radek, Tukhacevski and Bukharin really were spies and traitors: "Unity of action must continue," he wrote, "the trials divide us but the fight against fascism unites us." However, discord within the party was increasing.

The united policy was to receive its final coup de grâce on 22 August 1939 when newspapers revealed that Stalin and Hitler had decided to agree on a nonaggression pact. It was signed only a few days later by von Ribbentrop and Molotov in Moscow: "It is a crime," commented Nenni, "against which our conscience reacts with absolute vehemence."

Nenni still did not change his mind. In the first place he was convinced that the pact was unnatural and would be short-lived because (1) fascism and communism were absolutely incompatible; and (2) the need for a union between Socialists and Communists stemmed from the need to combat fascism.

This time Nenni had the majority of the party against him, including Saragat, who had been a firm supporter of the unity with the Communist party right up until the end. Nenni resigned from the secretariat and as editor of the *New Avanti!*

The Communists—with the exception of Terracini who criticized the Russian-German pact (and was later expelled from the party) and other prestigious militants such as Leo Valiani and Altiero Spinelli who abandoned the party—accepted Stalin's betrayal submissively and proceed to adapt the opinions and slogans expressed only a few days earlier to the new circumstances. What particularly upset Terracini was the theory of his comrades claiming capitalism was no different, whether "democratic" or fascist. Nenni proved right: Hitler broke the Russian-German pact and invaded Russia. The Communists revived the idea of antifascist unity: "The events of the last ten days," writes Nenni, "give me the satisfaction of knowing that I was right."

And he was to prove to his own comrades and especially the Communists that he had been right. At last things started to move in the right direction. Only four months after Germany's invasion of Russia, the third pact of unity of action was signed by the Socialists, Communists, and Justice and Liberty in Toulouse. Nenni's isolation had come to an end. He took up the fight with renewed energy and vigor.

We all know the rest of the story. The democratic nations and the Soviet Union became allies, defeated the Nazi-fascist powers and won the war. The parties of the Left and all democratic forces joined forces in the Resistance movement and freed northern Italy from German occupation.

Undoubtedly, despite the many difficulties, Nenni's policy had been successful. Surprisingly, the various splits and internal divisions did not prevent the Socialist party from being the second strongest party in the first political elections held in Italy on 2 June 1946 (two points ahead of the Communist party: 21% against 19%). Most people had expected the Communists, who had undoubtedly contributed the most to the fight against fascism and to the liberation, and were well-organized throughout the country, to do better than the Socialists and even be part of a relative majority.

A tripolar system emerged from the 1946 elections: the Christian Democrat party, the Italian Socialist party (the Italian Socialist party of Proletarian Unity) and the Italian Communist party. Of the other parties, the Right (Monarchists and Every man) and the Liberals could be more or less grouped with the Christian Democrats, and the Republicans and "Azionisti" with the Socialist party. If the Socialists had implemented a truly democratic, independent policy, not hostile to the Communists, they would have had a distinct advantage over the Christian Democrats. Immediately after the war and the victory of the republic over the monarchy in the referendum of 2 June 1946, the Christian Democrats could not afford to break away from the Republican, antifascist Left and make a government with the Right (which included the monarchists and the reactionary elements of the Right). It was doubtful whether such a government would have had a sufficient majority, and, even if it had managed to obtain a very narrow one, it would have caused a split among the Christian Democrats themselves.

But Nenni decided to pursue a different route. He was afraid that, despite the destruction of fascism, the moderate clerical forces still represented a potential danger. He wanted to be sure that the values of the Resistance, the hopes of the workers, the ideal for a "democratic revolution" would not be disappointed by the "Restoration." Nenni believed that a united Left was the only defense against the danger. He also believed that after the tragedy of the fascist war, Europe could only move more to the Left; that the Soviet Union and Labour-ruled England would find the basis for an understanding in the framework of the antifascist alliance; that Roosevelt's democratic America could not oppose such an alliance, which would also be a reference point for an Italian republic with a government of the Left.

In the beginning Saragat had also believed in the Moscow-London axis and defended the united action pact between the Socialists and Communists, in accordance with the general trends of European policy. However, as ambassador to Paris, Saragat realized before Nenni did that things were going in a different direction and heading toward a split between the West and Soviet Union. He anticipated the decision to opt for the West with the January 1947 split.

Nenni remained firmly convinced that the unity of the Left was the only way to defend democracy, the values of the Resistance, and the advantages that the workers had managed to gain. He believed that all this had been endangered by the breakdown in the cooperation between the forces who had won the war, and the Christian Democrat leader Alcide De Gasperi's expulsion of the Left from the government.

The events of the 1920s and 1930s clearly had some influence on Nenni's attitude. He knew that the division of the Left had allowed fascism to gain ground, while the unity of the Left had paved the way for the victory of the parties representing the workers. Nenni also believed (wrongly) that the Left carried more clout than the Christian Democrats and moderates. Nenni's main mistake was that he failed to perceive that the situation in Europe in the 1920s through the 1930s and the 1940s was quite different. Prior to the war, fascism had represented a threat to democracy; after the war, communism.

This does not mean that Saragat was right. Nenni had been correct to oppose any restoration, moderatism, clericalism, anticommunism, persecution of political militants, and trade unions of the Left. However, this should not have involved getting mixed up with the Communists and marrying Soviet foreign policy. Saragat was in part responsible for driving Nenni into the arms of the Communists by deciding in favor of the split in 1947. The division produced a centrifugal effect with some forces within the ranks of socialism opting for the PCI (Nenni) and others for the Christian Democrats (Saragat).

Had the Italian Socialist party been united, this would not have happened and the party would have continued to weigh significantly on public life. With the division of the PSI and its consequent loss of power—from which it never recovered—the Italian political system ceased to be tripolar and became a bipolar one: the Christian Democrats, the "irreplaceable barrier against Communism in the government," became "State," and the Communist opposition lost any chance of government participation. Thus the fifty-year-old institutional crisis of Italian democracy, which remained firmly anchored to one system, without alternation, stems from those long-past events of 1947.

8

HISTORICIZING NENNI

Borden W. Painter Jr.

Giuseppe Tamburrano's paper provides fresh historical testimony to Pietro Nenni as a survivor. Of course, he demonstrates that Nenni was not merely a survivor, but rather a man whose long political career contributed to the struggle against fascism and for a socialist and democratic society. Nenni, in fact, consistently worked to unify the left and to defend democracy. That consistent pattern also included a dilemma: the dilemma that not all the Left had the same commitment to democracy as he did. Thus, Nenni had to fail politically insofar as he had set himself an impossible task. Yet, in retrospect, we may recognize that in a certain sense he won, for Italy is democratic and the nondemocratic Left has collapsed; only time will tell if a unified and democratic left will take shape in post-cold war Italy.

Tamburrano's paper touches on many important points, but I shall focus on only those points of particular interest to me as one outside of Italian politics and academic life. They are points that I think are now of interest given the chronological distance from the events that shaped Nenni's life. In fact, his long career as a great survivor offers us a lens through which to view some of the important events and forces of twentieth-century Europe.

Nenni labored in the midst of those great themes and forces that determined so much of twentieth-century political life: nationalism, liberalism, socialism, communism and anticommunism, fascism and antifascism, and democracy. His firm adherence to two of those forces, socialism and democracy, led him to antifascism *and* an uncertain, ever-changing and difficult relationship with a third: communism.

In looking at Nenni as a socialist, democrat, and antifascist facing communism I shall remain largely within the chronological framework of Tamburrano's paper from World War I to 1947, except to consider Nenni's reaction to the revelations of Stalin's brutalities in the 1950s. In addition, I have very much in mind the current reconsidering, rethinking, and reshuffling of historians' views on those twentieth-century forces in the wake of the collapse of communism. Indeed it is the combination of chronological distance—nearly half a century from the end of World War II, seventy years since the March on Rome, seventy-five years since the Russian Revolution—and the collapse of communism that calls for historical reexamination of the period from 1918 to 1947. The historigraphical and interpretive changes now emerging are making and will make differences in viewing Nenni's career in its relationship to socialism, democracy, fascism, and communism.

Also, I believe that it is time to "historicize" the study of these shaping forces of the twentieth century, their interaction, and their influence on one another. I believe, for example, that it is imperative to examine very closely the interactions among fascism, communism, socialism, and democracy in the first half of this century. Furthermore, we need to study these interactions as historians, clearly separated from our own political allegiances. This may sound strange, perhaps heretical, at a meeting commemorating the founding of the Partitio Socialista Italiano! Let me simply say that I want to approach Nenni's career during the fascist period as a historian who is not Italian, not a socialist, and obviously not a member of the PSI. In fact, I shall refer to the opinions of several American historians and political scientists on Nenni. American assessments of Nenni are obviously appropriate at this conference.

Let me begin by enlisting the help of Alex De Grand. De Grand defined the purpose of his book, *In Stalin's Shadow: Angelo Tasca and the Crisis of the Left in Italy and France, 1910–1945*, in words that apply to Nenni's career about as well as they do to Tasca's:

> [This book] centers on the troubled relationship between the Socialist and Communist movements from the origins of the split in the Bolshevik Revolution to the crises leading up to World War II. Once the proletarian movement broke into two distinct parties, there were only three options: continued civil war on the Left, absorption of one party by the other, or cooperation and alliance. Each of these strategies was attempted along the way. Tasca's career is an ideal medium for viewing the problems created by the split on the Left because he

was involved in both parties and took clear positions on each of the three positions. But Tasca's life [and for our purposes here, Nenni's also] is important in a larger perspective; it revolved around the essential issues that confronted the European Left during the first fifty years of the century: the integration of the Bolshevik legacy into socialist practice, the challenge of fascism, and the polarization caused by the cold war.[1]

Nenni's historical and political reputation is one of pragmatism, and a man who "responded primarily to tactical situations."[2] Thus, following World War I, he attempted to respond to the circumstances created by the war, the postwar crisis, and the emergence of Bolshevism. Nenni adhered to socialism and joined the PSI in 1921, but he rejected the ideological pretensions of the maximalists and refused to support a union of socialists if it meant domination by the communists (see Chapter 7). Nenni believed that Bordiga, Gramsci, and the communist leadership mistook the situation as ripe for a Leninist-type revolution.[3]

The victory of fascism again forced Nenni to rethink his position and that of his brand of socialism. Thus began his career as a firm and consistent antifascist, attempting to adhere to his socialism and democracy. Here we begin to get at the heart of the matter concerning Nenni's relationship to those great shaping forces of the twentieth century. He seemed prepared, at times, to make any sacrifice or concession in order to bring about a coalition of parties and movements against fascism, but, to his credit, he never went so far as to sacrifice his commitment to democracy for the sake of that much-desired coalition.

Nenni saw fascism as a European, not just an Italian problem, and thus was more than ready to join the Popular Front efforts following the rise of Hitler and the beginning of the Spanish civil war.[4] When Nenni signed the Unity of Action pact with the Communists in 1934 it began that subordination of reformism to a dominant communist presence that, according to De Grand, would last until 1956 (*The Italian Left*, 165). Unlike Tasca, he did not consider the Stalinist menace comparable to the fascist one (De Grand, *In Stalin's Shadow*, 140).

The Spanish civil war became, of course, the defining moment for antifascism. We may note a certain irony in this fact, as most historians consider Franco's coalition of conservative and reactionary forces to have only a small fascist component and Franco to be no fascist at all. War demands and requires a basic definition of who is the enemy and who are the allies against the common enemy. For many Europeans of either the

Left or the Right, the struggle in Spain offered the moment of choice to be either Red or Black.

Nenni, the committed antifascist, could hardly stand aside from this decisive moment. Thus he played his role in forging the antifascist coalition of the Popular Front days of the 1930s. De Grand notes that "Nenni understood better than Tasca the need to focus on the antifascist struggle" (*In Stalin's Shadow*, 180). Tasca and Nenni differed in the appraisal of Stalin and whether the necessity of antifascism overrode any doubts about Stalin's regime. For participants such as Nenni and Tasca, and for historians ever since, there emerged in the 1930s the dilemma of how to forge the alliance against fascism without compromising one's commitment to democracy or, if worried about Stalin, increasing the power and influence of Stalin's Soviet Union. De Grand's conclusion is that Tasca "came dangerously close to lumping the Fascist powers and the Soviet Union as symbols of evil against which the democracies had to struggle" (*In Stalin's Shadow*, 190). Today we are, in fact, closer to such a "lumping." The privileged position of Stalin the antifascist, the Stalin who led his country to victory in the Great Patriotic War, is itself being "historicized."[5]

At the risk of oversimplifying, I would submit that this historical reconsideration may enhance our view of Nenni. But here I go beyond stating these issues in only personal terms and again look through the lens of Nenni's career to the larger historical issues. Specifically we need to examine carefully the dilemma of democratic socialism in the 1930s, which had to face several difficult and insuperable problems: (1) the division between democratic and nondemocratic socialism; (2) the division between reformist and revolutionary socialism; and (3) the role of Bolshevik-Leninist-Stalinist communism through the Comintern and the Soviet state.

Commenting on this dilemma takes us onto controversial ground where it is admittedly difficult to separate historical from political points of view. My main point here is that the Soviet Union in the 1930s was, in fact and perception, a socialist state. It represented one kind of socialism, obviously neither democratic socialism nor reformist socialism. Therefore, it is incorrect from a historical point of view to say that, in retrospect, Stalin's state was not *truly* socialist. Here is a recent example of such a disavowal that I believe leads to a historical muddle:

> [During the Cold War] it was near-impossible to gain a hearing for either a critical reading of Soviet history or the argument that such states were not really socialist, given the absence of democratic free-

doms and the suppression of struggles for human rights (not to mention the fact that liberties and freedoms supposedly associated with capitalism historically had been nowhere to be found as recently as the *capitalist* states of Nazi Germany and Fascist Italy!).[6]

The point I make is simply this: that westerners, including socialists, assumed that the Soviet state was socialist, although some doubted or denied its democratic nature. Any doubts in the 1930s about the nature of Stalin's rule were set aside for those determined to oppose fascism. The Nazi-Soviet Pact of August 1939 obviously caused anxiety and confusion, but with Hitler's invasion of Russia on 22 June 1941 all doubts were cast aside. As Tamburrano notes, "the necessity of the union of socialists and communists was born from the imperatives of the struggle against fascism." After 22 June 1941 that union would include a wider spectrum of political parties than socialist and communist or even the left. No middle position was possible.

At the end of the war the great contribution of the Soviet Union in Germany's defeat and the role of the Italian communists in the armed resistance transformed the political scene in Italy. Norman Kogan points out that Nenni "believed that divisions among the left had been responsible for the past victories of Fascism and Nazism and that the workers could not afford to be divided in the future if the triumph of reaction were to be prevented. This outlook, however, sincere, would make the Socialists vulnerable to Communist strategy."[7] Let us remember, however, that Nenni's outlook was shared by many on the Left immediately after the war, and it is easily understood within the historical context of the time.

The outbreak of the cold war then complicated matters and made political choices even more difficult. Nenni adhered to what he understood was a traditional socialist opposition to alliances (Kogan, *A Political History*, 20). His opposition to NATO seemed plausible, as did his favorable attitude toward the Soviet bloc. His postwar years, culminating in the award of the Stalin Peace Prize in 1951 marked the high-water mark of his adherence to a policy of unity and solidarity of the left.

Nenni changed his mind when it became clear to him that the Soviet state's practices could not be reconciled with democracy. The revelations at the Twentieth Congress of the Soviet Party led Nenni to the conclusion that "the defects revealed by Khrushchev were not the results of the errors of one man, but were due to the degeneration of the Soviet political and legal system. It was the method of dictatorship that had to be abandoned:

the mere replacement of one man by some others was not enough" (Kogan, *A Political History*, 89).

Richard Drake has compared the reaction of Raniero Panzieri and Nenni.[8] to the revelations of Stalinism. Panzieri had rejected any thought of compromise with social democrats like Giuseppe Saragat immediately after the war. Once Saragat had departed from the PSI, Panzieri saw a new opportunity for unity on the Left and therefore cooperation between the PSI and the PCI. Not surprisingly he became Rodolfo Morandi's protégé. Panzieri's reaction to the Twentieth Congress was similar to Nenni's, but he drew a very different conclusion:

> Panzieri began with the same premise that Nenni did: Stalinism had put Marxism in a bad odor. But how should destalinization be accomplished? What should be its results? The two colleagues offered radically different answers to these questions. Whereas Nenni called for more democracy as an antidote to Stalinism and the regrettably existent legacy of Stalin in Russia, Panzieri called for more Marxism-Leninism, emphatically rejecting the ideas, as Morandi had before him, that Marxism could ever be reduced to social democracy. Reformism had always been and always would be an irredeemable error because it contradicted what Marx himself had said about the dialectic of history. Only revolution could bring about a socialist state; this, for Panzieri, was the inviolable core of Marxism. (Drake, *Revolutionary Mystique*, 39)

Spencer Di Scala has commented on the two sides of Nenni's attitudes and policy shifts in the late 1940s and 1950s. On the one hand Nenni "retained his integrity" by not falling prey to a rigid ideological position. His position rested on "nostalgia and analogy" with the earlier antifascist coalition. Unlike Morandi, Nenni's flexibility and pragmatism allowed him "to disengage from the Communists when he understood the front's detrimental effect on the PSI and the country." On the other hand, Di Scala concludes, "Nenni's politics during the Popular Front period . . . had devastating and permanent effects on the socialist movement and cannot be condoned by heightening cold war tensions. . . . By subordinating the Socialist party to the Communist, Nenni and Morandi not only disregarded one of Europe's most glorious socialist traditions, but also justified thirty-five years of Christian democratic hegemony by depriving Italy of a viable political alternative to Catholics or Communists."[9]

I have strayed beyond the chronological boundaries of Tamburrano's essay and perhaps raised some questions that call for comment and discussion. Let me conclude therefore with a few comments. First, Tamburrano succeeds admirably in highlighting Nenni's ability to survive, but reminds us also that Nenni was more than a survivor. What earlier critics might have seen as a weakness, namely, his changes of policy, his pragmatism, may now appear more accurately as his way of trying to remain faithful to both socialism and democracy throughout the long and torturous history of the struggle against fascism and then Soviet communism. Second, Nenni's career, with all its twists and turns, does give us a very important case study of the interaction of the great shaping forces of twentieth-century Europe. John Lukacs suggests in his new book, *The End of the Twentieth Century and the End of the Modern Age*,[10] that the twentieth century for Europe is 1914 to 1989, from World War I to the collapse of communism. He emphasizes the role of nationalism as a greater and more significant force than socialism, communism, democracy, or liberalism. He sees fascism as primarily an exaggerated form of nationalism. I have read only excerpts of his book; his points await debate and discussion. My point is only this: historigraphically we are entering a time of reassessment that will change at least some of the ways we have treated those seventy-five years. Nenni survives as an important figure in that period, and this conference offers us an opportunity at some reassessment of his role.

Notes

1. Alexander J. De Grand, *In Stalin's Shadow, Angelo Tasca and the Crisis of the Left in Italy and France, 1910–1945*, (Dekalb, Ill., 1986), 7.
2. Alexander J. De Grand, *The Italian Left in the Twentieth Century, A History of the Socialist and Communist Parties* (Bloomington, 1989), 56.
3. Pietro Nenni, *Intervista sul socialismo italiano*, ed. Giuseppe Tamburrano (Rome, 1977), 30.
4. See Nenni, *Intervista*, 49f.; see also Chapter 7.
5. For a recent example, see Alan Bullock, *Hitler and Stalin, Parallel Lives* (New York, 1992).
6. Harvey J. Kaye, *The Powers of the Past: Reflections on the Crisis and the Promise of History* (Minneapolis, 1991), 136.
7. Norman Kogan, *A Political History of Italy: The Postwar Years*, (New York, 1983), 89.
8. Richard Drake, *The Revolutionary Mystique and Terrorism in Contemporary Italy* (Bloomington, 1989), 33–58.
9. Spencer M. Di Scala, *Renewing Italian Socialism, Nenni to Craxi* (New York, 1988), 79.
10. I have read only an excerpt in *Harper's* (January 1993).

9

CARLO ROSSELLI'S SOCIALISM

Joel Blatt

Arthur Schlesinger Jr. began his memoir of the John F. Kennedy presidency with these words from Ernest Hemingway: "If people bring so much courage to this world the world has to kill them to break them, so of course it kills them. The world breaks every one and afterward many are strong at the broken places. But those that will not break it kills. It kills the very good and very gentle and the very brave impartially."[1] Two of those who "would not break" were killed near Bagnoles de l'Orne in Normandy in western France on 9 June 1937, an event that created one of the "broken places" of twentieth-century Italian history. Six men and a woman, all French, ambushed Carlo Rosselli and his brother Nello in a plot carried out by the Organisation Secret d'Action Révolutionnaire Nationale (OSAR), nicknamed the Cagoule, a French extreme-right group.[2] Perceiving Carlo Rosselli as perhaps their most dangerous antifascist opponent, the upper echelons of Italian Fascism had set the conspiracy in motion as part of a no-holds-barred battle between Italian Fascism on one side, and Carlo Rosselli and Giustizia e Libertà on the other.[3]

This paper will concentrate on Carlo Rosselli's socialism, comparing and contrasting him with other Socialists, focusing on the components of his socialism that led to Bagnoles de l'Orne, and placing him within a century of Italian Socialism. Fine historians, some in attendance, one the chair for this panel, have preceded me down these paths.[4] There may be some Giellisti in the audience. I offer this paper in a nonpolemical spirit, but Carlo Rosselli was controversial and I have included personal value judgments in my conclusion. I look forward to the discussion. I would like to thank Spencer Di Scala for bringing us together. Finally, my excursion into these areas owes much to the wisdom and encouragement of my mentor in Italian history, a great historian of Italian and European history, A. William Salomone.

Carlo Rosselli's socialism originated in his heritage and personal formation, Italy's tumultuous history in which he participated, and in his mentors. He was born into a prominent Jewish-Italian family as Italian Jews strode with gratitude into the new world of equal opportunity brought by the Risorgimento.[5] As we shall see, Rosselli ascribed his fundamental morality to the Judeo-Christian-humanistic tradition.[6] He learned patriotism, liberty, and duty at home, in large part from his remarkable mother, Amelia Pincherle Rosselli, a well-known writer. Parenthetically, let me note here that one can call neither Italy nor France democracies until after World War II when Amelia Pincherle Rosselli and half their populations could finally vote. Rosselli's family had fought for unification and liberty; Mazzini had died in the home of Rosselli's great-aunt and -uncle.[7] It was a family for whom love of country meant love of freedom. Although Amelia Pincherle Rosselli was intensely patriotic and had personal contact with leading Italian nationalists,[8] the family spirit of inquiry differed from the conservative, patriotic, patriarchal Jewish-Italian family of the Ovazzas described in Alexander Stille's recent book, *Benevolence and Betrayal.*[9] During World War I, the camaraderie across class lines forged between Lieutenant Carlo Rosselli and his men provided a formative influence on his socialism.[10] Rosselli emerged from the war as a twenty-year-old searching for a meaningful personal path, and perhaps with a heightened critical spirit looking toward a postwar Italy that would be commensurate with the sacrifices of his oldest brother, Aldo, who died a war hero in 1916, and so many others.[11]

As he turned to the intensive study of economics and political economy, Rosselli watched the rise of Fascism from 1920 to 1922 and its first consolidation of power from 1922 to 1924. The assassination of Giacomo Matteotti on 10 June 1924, catapulted Rosselli into intransigent opposition to the intensifying Fascist dictatorship as he joined the Partito Socialista Unitario and played major roles in the publication of significant antifascist journals, *Non Mollare* in 1925 and *Il Quarto Stato* (with Pietro Nenni) the next year. By mid-1926, he chose militant antifascism rather than a promising career as a professor of economics. Arrested for his roles in aiding the evasions from Italy of Mussolini's opponents, particularly the leading Reformist Socialist, Filippo Turati, Rosselli spent two and a half years in Fascist prisons and *confino*. In July 1929 he escaped from the island of Lipari off the coast of Sicily to France, where he and others established his political movement, Giustizia e Libertà.[12]

The rise of Fascism, the murder of Matteotti and extensive Fascist brutality, the snuffing out of liberty by an increasingly sophisticated police state, and what Rosselli perceived as an inadequate response by Italy's Liberals and Socialists all contributed to the making of the Liberal-Socialist-Antifascist. Rosselli, himself, said in 1931: "I had a home; they devastated it. I had a journal; they suppressed it. I had a professorship; they forced me to abandon it. I had, as I have today, ideas, dignity, and ideal; to defend them, I had to go to prison. I had teachers, friends— Amendola, Matteotti, Gobetti—they killed them."[13] The battle against Fascism became for Rosselli an ethical imperative, a battle to which he devoted his thought and action. Rosselli also threw his wealth into the fray, perhaps resolving a sense of guilt about his prosperous origins.[14] I am reminded of my interview with Sandro Pertini, another prosperous Social-ist (if not so well-to-do as Rosselli). The president described with relish his manual labor in France from 1927 to 1929 as a taxicab washer, brick-layer, and housepainter, and then how, with money inherited from his father, he had set up a clandestine radio transmitter beaming into Italy. After Pertini's arrest, a "simpaticissimo" French police inspector thanked him for causing his temporary assignment to Nice with its beautiful women before asking, "But why didn't you stay quiet?"[15] Pertini and Rosselli both followed their consciences and willingly backed their Social-ist beliefs with their personal financial means. What were the components of Rosselli's socialism?

Carlo Rosselli constructed his liberal socialism on a moral foundation. In his seminal *Socialismo liberale*, written from confino on Lipari, he traced his beliefs to "Greek rationalism and the messianism of Israel," learning liberty from the former and justice and equality from the latter.[16] Rosselli's book and much of his early postwar intellectual and political development began as a sharp critique of Marxism, which he condemned as a pseudosci-ence that ignored human will and assumed too rigid class conflict. He contested the primacy of economic factors and the existence of any law of history.

Under the Marxist rubric, Rosselli attacked Italian maximalist socialists, Soviet Communists, and Italian reformist socialists. He blamed the Fascist victory in part on maximalists, who, in 1919–1920, had threatened revolu-tion and dictatorship even though they were a minority, thereby providing reactionaries with a rationale for illegality. Rosselli urged Socialist acceptance of "democratic method" and liberty on principle.[17] There was no "Marxist ethic," he declared, "only one ethic, . . . of Socrates, Christ and Kant."[18] He contested Communist dictatorship and bureaucracy in the Soviet Union, at one time conceived of socialism cultivating a position between "two bestial extremes" (presumably communism and fascism), and ridiculed "the grotesque phantom of 'socialfascism.' "[19] Having studied revolutionary syndicalism for his *tesi di Laurea*, Rosselli favored decentralization, autonomy, and federalism over Leninism. Yet he noted the conditions that had given rise to the Russian Revolution, during the 1930s moved toward practical cooperation with Communists against Fascism, and was not an anti-Communist. Rosselli launched some of his sharpest, and perhaps least fair, barbs toward reformists, the Socialists with whom he was in closest proximity. He seems to have included them in a general criticism of Giolittian Italy and the parliamentary practices of *trasformismo*, resembling in this regard the contemporary views of Gaetano Salvemini. Rosselli castigated the reformists' positivism for losing the younger generation: "The new generation, all idealistic, voluntaristic, pragmatic, did not understand the materialist, postivist, scientific language of the old."[20] Reformist passivity stemming from Marxist determinism, he alleged, contributed to the rise and consolidation of Fascist power and to the failure of the Aventine opposition.[21] He posed a question to the reformists: "Transformation of things or of consciousness?"[22] and his answer carries us toward the core of his beliefs.

Carlo Rosselli's socialism had its roots in liberty, but his "Socialismo liberale" would extend nineteenth-century liberalism from a "privileged minority" to everyone. He stated, "Socialism is only the logical development, up to its extreme consequences, of the principle of liberty. Socialism, . . . concrete emancipation of the proletariat, is liberalism in action, liberty for the poor."[23] To attain "effective liberty," Rosselli called for "a more equal distribution of riches and the assurance in any event and for every person of a life worthy of the name."[24] For him, socialism was "above all . . . active adhesion to the cause of the poor and the oppressed."[25] Socialism was also "faith."

The future remained open, to be shaped by human initiative. He did not offer an "ultimate truth" or a "transcendent law." In fact, "the forces of privilege, injustice, oppression . . . can continue to prevail," he asserted.[26] His "motto" was, "The socialist regime will be, but even might not be."[27] Human will would decide.

Rosselli added that socialism required changes within individuals before it could be implemented. A fundamental "transformation of conditions" required as an "indispensible premise" the cultivation of certain "essential values" through "education and the efforts of a long series of generations." "If men have rooted neither the sense of dignity nor responsibility, if they don't feel pride in their autonomy, if they don't emancipate themselves in their interior world, Socialism cannot be built." Instead the "barracks state" would emerge.[28] Distinctly revealed here was Rosselli's reformism and the influence on him during the 1920s of British Fabianism. His emphasis on values and his critique of Marxism led Rosselli into a more complex interpretation of Italian Fascism than many others on the Left.

Although a significant factor, Rosselli argued that those who looked only at class would never understand the full dimensions of the Fascist threat. Nationalistic sentiments, "factiousness," the romantic lure of action, postwar "restlessness," "latent weaknesses" from the deeper Italian past, a "cult of unanimity," a waiting for "pope, king, or Mussolini" to act, and poverty all had an impact. Mussolini knew how to appeal to certain "feelings" *(tasti)*, and his opponents had to struggle against "a certain type of mentality" as well as "a fierce and blind class reaction."[29] Rosselli's breadth of vision contributed to a keen realism toward the historical evolution in Italy in spite of his exile vantage point. Given its synthesis of old and new, Rosselli regarded Italian Fascism as a formidable enemy whose strength would even burden the remaking of Italian democracy after Mussolini's defeat. As his analysis of Italian Fascism emerged, his emotional reaction to the establishment of the Fascist dictatorship created an implacable revolutionary antifascist resistance.

Fascism threatened with extinction Carlo Rosselli's deepest beliefs, and he threw his own life in front of the juggernaut. In a liberal and democratic regime, Rosselli advocated peaceful means, but no compromise was possible across the divide between "two mutually exclusive principles and moral worlds." Fascism, "first and foremost antiliberalism," had destroyed all the middle ground, necessitating for anyone who wished to push it from power the adoption of the "revolutionary method" and "violence."[30] In prison, he rejected a proffered deal, explaining to his mother that for an example to be effective, it had to be "pure, perfect, uncontaminated," and "follow . . . a line of morality, of absolute intransigence."[31]

He looked for "heroes," ready for self-sacrifice, finding his own inspiration in Giacomo Matteotti and Ferruccio Parri, a prison cellmate in 1927. Resembling Martin Luther King, Rosselli wrote: "All our life is concentrated on this effort to arrive, for one hour at the highest point. Whoever has pulled himself up a rocky mountain will understand me. Even we are a group of climbers tied together. Parri helps me, I help others. We will arrive at the summit." [32] The battle would be long, "not . . . years but . . . generations," he thought in 1930, and in 1934 he stated, "We work for eternity." [33]

Soon after his arrival in France in August 1929, Rosselli and others established Guistizia e Libertà, which attracted Liberals, democrats, Republicans, and Socialists, and from 1931 to 1934 joined another exile coalition of the non-Communist Left, the Concentrazione Antifascista. The movement's own internal politics and its frequently strained interactions with the Concentration provide chapters in the perennial saga of the relations of Socialists with each other and with their closest allies-potential rivals. [34] Since Italian Fascism appealed across class lines as well as to class interest, Rosselli favored a coalition of the proletariat and other groups.

Rosselli and his chief collaborators, particularly Alberto Tarchiani, had an eye for daring action, symbolic gesture, and propaganda in Italy that rivaled Mussolini's, as shown by the evasion of Turati, the escape from Lipari (organized by Tarchiani), and the propaganda flight of Giovanni Bassanesi and Gioacchino Dolci from a Swiss meadow to Milan's central piazza (July 1930). The latter was a perfect Rosselli-Tarchiani-Giellisti venture: Audacious, innovative, using a symbol of modernity, the airplane, [35] reaching the minds of Italians living in the "consensus factory." Throughout the rest of their lives, Rosselli and Tarchiani attempted repeatedly to launch flights toward the peninsula, without success.

In 1932, Giustizia e Libertà published a program for a post-Fascist Italy based on "liberty," "justice," "essentially on the working classes," and "a profound economic-political transformation" instead of "a return to the past." The framework offered a republic, a constituent assembly elected by universal suffrage, substantial agrarian reform, significant industrial "reorganization" combining central planning, some "socialization" but not of industries that were competitive and with "autonomous management," "workers' control" in major workplaces, a state based on "the widest autonomy," and other changes. [36]

A year later, with one of his bursts of insight, Rosselli understood almost at once the significance of Hitler's "spiritual 'blitzkrieg.' " [37] In 1932, even before Hitler reached power, Rosselli saw the momentum shifting to the Fascists leaving antifascists with "a desperate defense of our reasons for living." [38] In a notable essay of November 1933, "La Guerra che torna"

(The war that returns), Rosselli asserted that fascism in power in Germany and Italy meant war. As bluntly, he prescribed preventive revolutions to topple Hitler and Mussolini. He criticized sharply the pacifism and support for disarmament of many Socialists, in contrast with his own vivid "interventionism."[39] For Rosselli, Hitler's rise and the inadequate reponses to Nazism's threat raised the danger posed by Italian Fascism to a European and international level and underscored an enormous crisis of democracy.

From 1933 to 1936, various developments drove Giustizia e Libertà toward greater isolation and independence. In 1933, Rosselli's thirst for revitalization through innovation led to a flirtation with the French Neosocialists. In 1934, a multifaceted competition for turf between Giustizia e Libertà and Pietro Nenni's Socialists and other issues contributed to the demise of the *Concentrazione Antifascista.*[40] Soon thereafter, in his new weekly newspaper, *Giustizia e Libertà,* Rosselli downplayed temporarily the "inert" Italian masses in contrast to the revolutionary elite when "50–100–200" people remained politically active in any Italian city.[41] In another essay, he inveighed against the modern "dictatorial state" for "devouring society." "Man is the end. Not the state," he concluded.[42] At the same time, as the Western democracies responded feebly to Hitler and Italian Fascism strengthened its grip, Rosselli lost faith in the middle classes and emphasized more the proletariat in future antifascist battles, and looked more to the Soviet Union as a potential opponent of Germany. His iconoclasm alienated the Italian Socialist party while his socialism worried some liberal Giellisti. Thus, two of Giustizia e Libertà's major leaders, Emilio Lussu, leaning Left, and Alberto Tarchiani, leaning toward the center, retreated to different degrees from the movement, although Tarchiani continued his collaboration in clandestine operations.[43] At first, but not for long, Rosselli hoped that the Ethiopian War might open a revolutionary window for the antifascists. In March 1936 with his stark realism, he immediately drew the full consequences of the French failure to roll back the German remilitarization of the Rhineland: "A France that has not gone to war over the Rhineland will not do it for Austria, perhaps not even for Czechoslovakia."[44] Four months later, events in Spain ended his decade-long wait for a revolutionary opportunity.

The Spanish civil war climaxed Carlo Rosselli's intense activity against Italian Fascism and led to his death. Giustizia e Libertà plotted unsuccessfully for many years to assassinate Mussolini using planes and other means. When I asked the former Giellista Max Salvadori if his organization had tried to assassinate the dictator, he replied, "We viewed Mussolini and the men around him as common criminals." Mussolini killed to reach power and killed to keep it.[45] Aldo Garosci discussed Giustizia e Libertà's always fruitless efforts to organize flights to bomb the Palazzo Venezia, Mussolini's workplace in Rome, which he thought "foolish"; the United States failed in an attempt against Colonel Kaddafi with many planes, he said.[46] The Giellisti moved closer to the Anarchists. When I asked Garosci whether Tarchiani played a role (in accord with Anarchists) in helping to arm Angelo Sbardellotto, an Italian Anarchist subsequently arrested and executed in Rome in 1932, he responded, "Sì, certo."[47] With humor, Garosci described a commemoration in Rome after World War II, with the then distinguished ambassador to the United States Alberto Tarchiani in attendance, at which half the toasts recalled the evanescent "bombing of Rome and the Palazzo Venezia."[48] In spite of Tarchiani's distinctly more centrist political orientation, my sense is that he matched Rosselli as a conspirator.

Responding apocalyptically, Rosselli leaped into the Spanish civil war, stating, "The battle in Spain will be decisive for the fate of Fascism and antifascism in Europe."[49] After meeting with André Malraux in Paris,[50] Rosselli personally led the first group of Italian antifascists, mainly Anarchists, into early battles of the Spanish civil war. He suffered a light wound, subsequently developing the phlebitis that led him to the health spa of Bagnoles de l'Orne. In November 1936, Rosselli beamed his striking radio address from Barcelona toward Italy, "Oggi in Spagna, domani in Italia" (Today in Spain, tomorrow in Italy), in which he predicted the spread of revolutionary antifascism from Spain to Italy.[51] After the Italian Fascist defeat at Guadalajara in March 1937, he appealed "for a Guadalajara on Italian soil" and *Giustizia e Libertá* published photographs of Italian Fascist prisoners.[52] Finally, in what became his last battle, Rosselli sent Garosci (Magrini) to Spain to attempt to borrow planes from the Spanish government for an assault on Rome and the Giellisti also discussed a ground incursion into Italy. These imprecise schemes faded into a frustrating campaign to launch one plane from France on a propaganda flight to break the Fascist "silence" concealing Guadalajara.[53]

Italian Fascism feared three things most: (1) communism in Italy; (2) assassination attempts against Mussolini; (3) someone who might unite the Italian antifascist opposition.[54] Carlo Rosselli posed the latter two threats, and in the last months of his life, on practical grounds, sought better relations with Italy's Communists.[55]

Rosselli became an Italian Fascist obsession. From 1931 onward, Arturo Bocchini, chief of police, and Michelangelo Di Stefano, director of the Division Polizia Politica and of OVRA, became convinced that Giustizia e Libertà threatened Italian Fascism and the Duce.[56] Di Stefano's greatest triumph became René Odin, code-named Togo, a French engineer portrayed as acting out of Fascist idealism,[57] who infiltrated Giustizia e Libertà in 1933 and worked against Rosselli and the organization with devastating impact throughout the remainder of Rosselli's life. As OVRA arrested Giellisti on the peninsula, Rosselli relied ever more on Togo, who passed himself off as a businessman traveling at times to Italy.[58] Information from Togo played a role in the first wave of arrests of the Turin section of Giustizia e Libertà in 1934. Bocchini handled the investigation with extreme care and the sentences were surprisingly light at first, apparently at least in part because Fascist authorities wanted to preserve Togo's cover.[59]

Following the breakup of the Concentrazione Antifascista, Di Stefano demanded from his agents a thorough assessment of its components.[60] One report described Giustizia e Libertà as "more dangerous than the . . . pure Anarchists."[61] Another report assessed Giustizia e Libertà's "possibilities" as "increased" and portrayed Rosselli as "the most terrible . . . ambitious to excess, cold, calculating, ready to risk when it appeared to him that there was even a lone probability of success." The agent concluded, "The major danger comes from Rosselli, and . . . it is absolutely necessary to assassinate him ("sopprimerlo")."[62]

Thus, a blunt appeal to kill the antifascist leader circulated as early as June 1934 in the upper reaches of OVRA. A first assassination attempt may have been made in March 1936 (the Zanatta episode),[63] perhaps reacting against Rosselli's militancy during the Ethiopian War. The same month, Togo wrote, "I have needed to convince myself that Rosselli is without doubt the most dangerous of all the exiles."[64]

The Spanish civil war intensified Italian Fascism's hatred and paranoia toward Rosselli. From Spain, a Fascist agent positioned Rosselli "on the road to becoming the duce of Italian antifascism."[65] In November 1936, shortly after the "Oggi in Spagna, domani in Italia" address, Di Stefano alleged that Rosselli toughened Italian antifascists in Spain for subsequent "action" in Italy.[66] OVRA's chief warned of Giustizia e Libertà's "fixed idea" of bombing the Palazzo Venezia and the Palazzo Torlonia in Rome, where Mussolini worked and lived respectively.[67] On 4 May 1937, while one police official wrote, "Almost all the activity of 'Giustizia e Libertà' in the kingdom is now in our hands through the network of informers," high-ranking representatives of the army, navy, air force, finance ministry and militia met under Bocchini's auspices to prepare the air defenses of Rome and Italy against what had become a single Giellista plane under Togo's constant gaze.[68] Finally, leaving nothing to chance, Fascist authorities approached and successfully requested the French to stop the flight.[69] Months earlier, though, Italian Fascist leaders had ordered Rosselli's assassination.

As the Spanish civil war lengthened, as the Italian Fascist commitment to Franco deepened, and as Mussolini's relationship with Hitler's Germany became stronger and more complex,[70] Italian Fascism developed an extensive sabotage plot, one aspect of which entailed Rosselli's assassination. On 29 January and 3 February 1937, Santo Emanuele, head of the counterintelligence section of the Servizio Informazione Militare (SIM, Italian military intelligence), and Roberto Navale, chief of the Turin branch of the same organization responsible for France, developed a wide-ranging plan for destruction in southern France and elsewhere of material being sent to the Spanish government.[71] Within a month, explosions began to rock southern France.[72] They also targeted two men for assassination: Ernesto Bonomini and Carlo Rosselli. Bonomini, an Anarchist who in 1924 had assassinated the leading Italian Fascist in France, Nicola Bonservizi, and who the Fascists thought was plotting to kill Mussolini and Hitler, survived the Spanish civil war and escaped to the United States.[73]

To assassinate Rosselli, Italian Fascism struck an accord with the OSAR (The Cagoule) as the extreme-right group prepared a coup d'état against the French Popular Front government and the Third French Republic. The Cagoule committed the crime for "one hundred semi-automatic Beretta rifles" and hopes of future aid, even an alliance, with Italian Fascism. Filippo Anfuso, Foreign Minister Count Galeazzo Ciano's chief troubleshooter, served as a link between the highest Fascist leadership and the Cagoule. I have no doubt that Mussolini and Ciano made the decision to kill Carlo Rosselli. On 22 March 1937, in Monte Carlo, just after the conclusion of the battle of Guadalajara, representatives of Italian Fascism and the OSAR reached the accord that had its tragic denouement on that desolate patch of sacred earth in France two and one half months later.[74]

Italian Fascism had Carlo Rosselli eliminated at the point where the Italian civil war merged with a European civil war that Rosselli was utilizing as a fulcrum to turn revolution toward Italy. His faith in justice and liberty, his quest for innovation,[75] his strongminded realism in assessing historical currents, his charisma and force of personality,[76] his implacable antifascist resistance, and the persistent attempts by Giustizia e Libertà to assassinate the Duce put Rosselli atop the antifascist ramparts. Di Stefano and Bocchini deceived him as he made mistakes of judgment that contributed to the loss of Giellista cadres in Italy. Fascist leaders defeated him most of the time. Even with all the weapons of the police state, though, they feared him, could not control him, and killed him.

Let me add some concluding remarks. I have qualms about Rosselli's and Tarchiani's *attentati*, but Rosselli sharply distinguished between a free society in which he condemned such violence, and the repressive Fascist dictatorship that justified resistance by every means. I would add, following Thomas Jefferson, what should one do when a dictator violates natural rights to "life and liberty?" In Rosselli's plotting against Mussolini, he approached the Anarchist conception of power. Moreover, in explaining Giellista policy, Garosci traced a tradition of tyrannicide back to the Renaissance, while Max Salvadori bluntly said, "We admired Brutus," not Caesar.[77] Although he recognized that Italian Fascism embodied far more than the dictator; still, both Rosselli (and Police Chief Bocchini) thought Mussolini's demise would lead to the unravelling of the regime.[78] Rosselli clearly believed in the historical significance of the individual. Has not the twentieth century proved him correct?

Carlo Rosselli's *Socialismo liberale* represents one of the significant chapters in the history of Italian Socialism, even though Rosselli only belonged to the Socialist party for a relatively brief time. He was a socialist heretic. Similar to the Hebrew prophets and Christian heretics, he contrasted a bleak present with a heroic past. Gaetano Arfé placed Rosselli's and Nenni's *Quarto Stato* as a vigorous transition linking pre-Fascist and antifascist socialism.[79] Rosselli asserted that in an age of mass politics only a revitalized socialism could defeat Mussolini's dictatorship. A socialist maverick, his liberty-centered, voluntaristic, decentralized, in one respect elitist, and non-Marxist socialism alienated many contemporary Socialists and Communists, while his vigorous commitment to equality and social justice pushed away many Liberals. Giustizia e Libertà's path was lonely. Carlo Rosselli's open-ended vision of history contrasts profoundly with the "terrible simplifications" of this century. How much greater strength was shown by Rosselli's tragic and heroic embrace of spontaneity than by the so-called strongmen of his era, Hitler, Stalin—and yes, Mussolini— who crushed liberty.

A liberal-socialist prophet, Rosselli comprehended almost at once the Fascist challenge to the highest Judeo-Christian-humanist moral tradition of the West, that each individual's life is sacred, deserving of dignity. He understood early one of the most brutal realities of the 1930s: that if one wished to restore or preserve liberty, one needed to be willing to risk death. Winston Churchill's supreme moment in 1940, one of the greatest in the history of the West, lay not only in his choice to resist Hitler but in couching his intransigent resistance in terms of the Western heritage of freedom. Carlo Rosselli made a similar choice fifteen years earlier, during a period in which Churchill was "being charmed . . . by . . . Mussolini's gentle and simple bearing."[80]

With startling bursts of insight and courage, during the swift approach of one of the darkest moments in the long history of the West, Carlo Rosselli remained a protagonist in the field to the end. He deserves to be recognized as perhaps the greatest Third Force figure in twentieth-century Italian history,[81] as one of the greatest Italian Socialists, as one of the greatest twentieth-century Italians, and as one of the greatest European antifascists.

Historians usually are little better than anyone else at predicting the future. No one can know with certainty what Carlo Rosselli might have accomplished if he had survived the ambush at Bagnoles. In his home country, soon he would have been proscribed as a Jew as well as an antifascist. With the men and women whom he inspired, he certainly would have participated in the Italian civil war in the north from 1943 to 1945. If he had survived the Holocaust and civil war, one might speculate about his postwar role. Max Salvadori stated that Rosselli "would undoubtedly have been the major political figure at the end of the war, combining in his own personality what was represented by Parri, De Gasperi, and Pertini."[82] Aldo Garosci wondered what a political leader with Rosselli's exuberant energy and extensive knowledge of economics, who was already teaching Keynes to college students in the mid-1920s, might have contributed to an era of reconstruction.[83] With reference to our own time, traditional wisdom in the twentieth century has been that historical fortune never knocks and stops at Third Force doors, but recent years have been unkind to traditional wisdom. Rosselli grappled with one of the most nettlesome questions for the twentieth-century Left: How can one utilize central authority to create greater equality without fostering fearsome totalitarian dictatorships.[84] Rosselli's answer of a large measure of autonomy with some degree of planning always affirmed the duality of justice (equality) and liberty. As the century nears its end, might a moment for Carlo Rosselli's and the Giellisti's *Socialismo liberale* come round at last?

The costs of the twenty-five-year Italian civil war were enormous for

Italy.[85] Among them, Italian Fascism selectively killed or truncated and circumscribed the lives of a number of the most extraordinary twentieth-century Italian political leaders: Matteotti, Giovanni Amendola, Gobetti, Gramsci, Rosselli, and others.

Nevertheless, I insist that Carlo and Nello Rosselli were not solely victims. Listen to these defiant words of Nello writing to his brother in 1931: "I am proud of you and of your activity. . . . If at some time you feel alone or *unheeded*, chase away the thought: There is much fire under the ashes in Italy, even if the layer is heavy and hides it entirely. You will finish, we will finish with victory, if you never give up, not even for one moment, not even one inch."[86]

Listen to Nello Rosselli's stunning epitaph for an earlier maverick Italian Socialist, Carlo Pisacane, and unintentionally for himself and his brother: "The wayfarer anxious to cross the torrent throws stones one on top of the other, into the depths of the water then steps on the last ones that surface, securely, because he knows that those which have disappeared into the whirlpool will support his weight.

Pisacane, even he, seemed to disappear into nothingness. But on his life, on his death, one was able to put down, one puts down, one of the granite pillars of the Italian edifice."[87]

Listen to Piero Calamandrei, representing the Rosselli family, as he speaks in 1945 in a courtroom in Rome during the Processo Roatta, the trial of some of the assassins of the Rosselli brothers: "*Disgraziati*, you more than we, because you wanted to kill them and you made them immortal: and in the mud of this trial they bring a light of sunrise. Are the Rossellis dead? No. You are dead, you on that bench and the sad ghosts who are behind you, but Carlo and Nello, sweet friends, youthful and smiling are here, (profoundly moved) beside us. They watch all this immense ruin, this emptiness, but their brows are clear, and their eyes serene, and they say: "Non Mollare" (Don't give in)."[88]

Notes

ABBREVIATIONS

ACS	Archivio Centrale Dello Stato, Rome
AGR	Pubblica Sicurezza, Divisione Affari Generali e Riservati
ASMAE	Archivio Storico Ministero degli Affari Esteri, Rome
B	Busta

CPC   Caselario Politico Centrale
F   Fascicolo
ISRT   Istituto Storico della Resistenza in Toscana, Florence
PP   Pubblica Sicurezza, Divisione Polizia Politica
PS   Pubblica Sicurezza
SPD, CR   Segretaria Particolare del Duce, Carteggio Riservato
US   Ufficio Spagna

1. Arthur Schlesinger Jr., *A Thousand Days: John F. Kennedy in The White House* (Boston: Houghton Mifflin and The Riverside Press, 1965).

2. For the OSAR, see Philippe Bourdrel, *La Cagoule* (Paris: Albin Michel, 1970 new ed. 1992), and Dagore (pseudonym of Aristide Corre), *Les carnets secrets de la Cagoule*, ed. and intro. Christian Bernadac (Paris: Editions France-Empire, 1977).

3. For the assassination itself, see the confession by Fernand Jakubiez in J. R. Tournoux, *L' Histoire secrète: La Cagoule, Le Front Populaire, Vichy, Londres, Deuxième Bureau, L' Algérie Francaise, L'O.A.S.*, (Paris: Plon, 1962), 310–14. For the Italian side, see *Il Processo Roatta: I documenti* (Rome: Universale De Luigi, 1945). Franco Bandini, *Il cono d' ombra: Chi armò la mano degli assassini dei fratelli Rosselli* (Milan: SugarCo, 1990), includes much detail on the crime, but adopts a different interpretation than my own.

4. Charles Delzell, "The Assassination of Carlo and Nello Rosselli June 9, 1937: Closing a Chapter of Italian Anti-Fascism," *Italian Quarterly* 28, no. 107 (winter 1987): 47–64; Charles Delzell, *Mussolini's Enemies: The Italian Anti-Fascist Resistance* (Princeton: Princeton University Press, 1961); Aldo Garosci, *La vita di Carlo Rosselli*, 2 vols. (Florence: Edizioni U, 1945); Nicola Tranfaglia, *Carlo Rosselli dall'interventismo a "Giustizia e Libertà"* (Bari: Laternza, 1968); Gaetano Salvemini, *Carlo and Nello Rosselli: A Memoir* (London: For Intellectual Liberty, 1937); Salvemini, "L'assassinio dei Rosselli," *Opere di Gaetano Salvemini*, vol. 6, *Scritti sul fascismo*, Part 2, ed. Nino Valeri and Alberto Merola (Milan: Feltrinelli, 1966), 295–340; the excellent collection of essays in *Giustizia e Libertà nella lotta antifascista e nella storia d'Italia: Attualità dei fratelli Rosselli a quaranta anni dal loro sacrificio*, intro. Carlo Francovich (Florence: La Nuova Italia, 1978); G. Arfé et al., *L' Emigrazione socialista nella lotta contro il fascismo (1926–1939)* (Florence: Sansoni, 1982).

5. For the meaning of their Jewishness to Nello Rosselli and Carlo Rosselli, see Bruno di Porto, "Il problema ebraico in Nello Rosselli," in the collection cited above, *Giustizia e Libertà nella lotta antifascista* 491–499. Also see Leo Valiani's introduction to *Epistolario familiare Carlo, Nello Rosselli e la madre (1914–1937)* (Milan: SugarCo, 1979), 12; Tranfaglia, *Carlo Rosselli*, 13.

6. Carlo Rosselli, *Socialismo liberale*, in *Opere scelte di Carlo Rosselli*, vol. 1. *Socialismo liberale*, ed. John Rosselli (Turin: Giulio Einaudi, 1973), 352 and 425. Giorgio Spini recently observed that Carlo Rosselli's Jewish heritage influenced him more than is commonly recognized, even though he was completely secular and less interested in Jewish questions than his brother Nello (Giorgio Spini et al., "Role and Destiny of Minorities in a Changing Europe,"

13 May 1992, Italian Cultural Institute, New York City, and a conversation with Professor Spini the same day). Also see Tranfaglia, *Carlo Rosselli*, 63.

7. Salvemini, *Carlo and Nello Rosselli: A Memoir*, 7.

8. Tranfaglia, *Carlo Rosselli*, 12, 13, and 33 (note 7); Valiani, introduction to *Epistolario familiare*, 10.

9. Alexander Stille, *Benevolence and Betrayal: Five Italian Jewish Families under Fascism* (New York: Summit, 1991), 17–89.

10. Salvemini, *Carlo and Nello Rosselli: A Memoir*, 8; Valiani, introduction to *Epistolario familiare*, 13; Tranfaglia, *Carlo Rosselli*, chapter 1.

11. Tranfaglia, *Carlo Rosselli*, chapter 2.

12. There is much literature on these various episodes. For a detailed overview, see Garosci, *Vita*, vol. 1, and Tranfaglia, *Carlo Rosselli*.

13. Carlo Rosselli, *Scritti dell' esilio I. 'Giustizia e Libertà' e la Concentrazione Antifascista (1929–1934)*, ed. and intro. Costanzo Casucci (Turin: Einaudi, 1988), 21. ("Avevo una casa: me l'hanno devastata. Avevo un giornale: me l'hanno soppresso. Avevo una cattedra: l'ho dovuta abbandonare. Avevo, come ho oggi, delle idee, una dignità, un ideale: per difenderli ho dovuto andare in galera. Avevo dei maestri, degli amici-Amendola, Matteotti, Gobetti-me li hanno uccisi.")

14. Tranfaglia, *Carlo Rosselli*, 20, 121.

15. Interview, Joel Blatt and President Sandro Pertini, 8 February 1984, Quirinale Palace, Rome. ("Ma come, perchè lei non se ne è rimasto tranquillo?")

16. Carlo Rosselli, *Socialismo liberale*, 352. ("Il razionalismo greco e il messianismo d' Israele.") The book has recently been translated into English as *Liberal Socialism* (Princeton: Princeton University Press, 1994), ed. Nadio Urbinati and trans. by William McCuaig.

17. Ibid., 449–450: Garosci, *Vita*, 1:145.

18. Carlo Rosselli, *Socialismo liberale*, 425. ("L'etica marxista—in realtà inesistente, che di etica ve n'è una sola, senza aggettivi: l'etica di Socrate, di Cristo e di Kant.)"

19. Tranfaglia, *Carlo Rosselli*, 353. ("due bestiali estremi"); Carlo Rosselli, "Risposta a Giorgio Amendola," in *Scritti politici*, ed. Zeffiro Ciuffoletti and Paolo Bagnoli (Naples: Guida, 1988), 211. ("fantasma grottesco del 'socialfascismo' ").

20. Carlo Rosselli, *Socialismo liberale*, 395. ("La nuova generazione tutta idealista, volontarista, pragmatista, non capiva il linguaggio materialistico, positivistico, scientificistico dei vecchi.")

21. In general, see Rosselli, *Socialismo liberale;* Tranfaglia, *Carlo Rosselli,*; Garosci, *Vita*, vol. 1.

22. Rosselli, *Socialismo liberale*, 429. ("trasformazione delle cose o delle coscienze?")

23. Ibid., 436. ("Il socialismo non è che lo sviluppo logico, sino alle sue estreme conseguenze, del principio di libertà. Il socialismo ... concreta l'emancipazione del proletariato—è liberalismo in azione, è libertà che si fa per la povera gente.")

24. Ibid., 437. ("una effettiva libertà")("una più equa distribuzione delle ricchezze

e l'assicurazione in ogni caso ad ogni uomo di una vita degna di questo nome").

25. Ibid., 455. ("soprattutto . . . adesione attiva . . . alla causa dei poveri e degli opressi").

26. Ibid., 454–55. ("verità ultima")("legge trascendente")("le forze del privilegio, della ingiustizia, della oppressione dei molti nell'interesse dei pochi, possano contiuare a prevalere").

27. Ibid., 455. ("il regime socialista sarà, ma potrebbe anche non essere").

28. Ibid., 461. ("trasformazione ambientale")("presupposto indispensabile")("valori essenziali")("educazione e gli sforzi di una lunga serie di generazioni")("Se gli uomini non hanno radicato né il senso della dignità né quello della responsabilità, se non sentono la fierezza della loro autonomia, se non si sono emancipati nel loro mondo interiore, non si fa il socialismo.")("lo Stato caserma").

29. Ibid., 456–62. ("faziosità")("inquieta")("debolezze latenti")("il culto dell' unanimità")("un certo tipo di mentalità")("una feroce e cieco reazione di classe").

30. Ibid., 467–68; Tranfaglia, *Carlo Rosselli*, 289–90. ("due principi e . . . due mondi morali reciprocamente escludentisi")("prima e soprattutto antiliberalismo")("il metodo rivoluzionario").

31. Tranfaglia, *Carlo Rosselli*, 351; Letter, Carlo Rosselli to Amelia Pincherle Rosselli, Como, 2 May 1927, in *Epistolario familiare*, 340. ("puro, perfetto, incontaminato")("seguire . . . una linea di moralità, di intransigenza assoluta").

32. Garosci, *Vita*, 1:109–10; Carlo Rosselli, "Fuga in quattro tempi," in *Opere scelte di Carlo Rosselli*, vol. 1, *Socialismo liberale*, ed. John Rosselli, 514, and for Rosselli's deep admiration of Parri, 511–14. ("Tutta la nostra vita è tesa in questo sforzo di arrivare, per un' ora, altissimi. Che importa sapere che si dovrà poi ridiscendere? Chi si è sollevato su per un 'camino' nella montagna rocciosa, mi capisce. Anche noi siamo in cordata. Parri aiuta me, io aiuto altri. Arriveremo alla cima.")

33. Valiani, introduction to *Epistolario familiare*, 17, 19; Letters, Carlo Rosselli to Amelia Pincherle Rosselli, *Epistorario familiare*, Paris, 31 December 1930 (p. 482) and 14 May 1934 (p. 562). ("non . . . anni, ma . . . generazioni") ("Lavoriamo per l'eternità").

34. Delzell, *Mussolini's Enemies*, chap. 2; Santi Fedele, *Storia della Concentrazione Antifascista 1927/1934* (Milan: Feltrinelli, 1976); Alexander De Grand, *The Italian Left in the Twentieth Century: A History of the Socialist and Communist Parties* (Bloomington: Indiana University Press, 1989), 67–68; De Grand, *In Stalin's Shadow: Angeo Tasca and The Crisis of the Left in Italy and France, 1910–1945* (DeKalb: Northern Illinois University Press, 1986), 85–90; Spencer Di Scala, *Renewing Italian Socialism: Nenni to Craxi* (New York: Oxford University Press, 1988), 6.

35. For the Bassanesi-Dolci flight, see Garosci, *Vita*, 1:213–14; Egidio Reale, "Il volo su Milano," in *No al fascismo*, ed. Ernesto Rossi, 2d ed. (Turin: Einaudi, 1963), 203–16; Franco Fuci, *Ali contro Mussolini: I raid aerei antifascisti degli anni trenta* (Milan: Mursia, 1978), 9–87.

36. *Quaderni di "Gustizia e Libertà,"* no. 1 (January 1932): 1–20; Leo Valiani, "Carlo e Nello Rosselli: Il pensiero e l' azione," in *Giustizia e Libertà nella lotta,*

16–17; Garosci, *Vita*, 1:246–53. ("essenzialmente sulle classi lavoratrici")("una profonda trasformazione economico-politica")("un ritorno al passato")("gestione autonoma")("controllo operaio")("sulle più ampie autonomie").

37. The phrase is from Garosci, *Vita*, 2:8.

38. Garosci, *Vita*, 1:268. ("Una disperata difesa delle nostre ragioni di vita").

39. Carlo Rosselli, "La guerra che torna," in *Scritti politici*, ed. Ciuffoletti and Bagnoli, 274–82; Garosci, *Vita*, 2:22–27.

40. See note 34.

41. "G.L. e le masse inerte," in *Scritti politici*, 291–94. For Giellisti publications and more, see Frank Rosengarten, *The Italian Anti-Fascist Press (1919–1945)* (Cleveland: Case Western Reserve University Press, 1968), 62–42.

42. "Contro lo Stato," 295–98, "Lo Stato dittatoriale" [77])("divorando la Società")("L' uomo è il fine, Non lo stato.")

43. Garosci, *Vita*, 2:65–102.

44. Ibid., 88. ("Una Francia che non ha fatto la guerra per il Reno non la farà per l'Austria, forse neppure per la Cecoslovacchia").

45. Conversation, Joel Blatt and Max Salvadori, New York City, October 1989, and telephone conversation, 21 June 1992.

46. Interview, Joel Blatt and Max Salvadori, Rome, 28 June 1990.

47. Ibid. Tarchiani's role in the Sbardellotto Affair is debated. When shown photos of Tarchiani by his captors, Sbardellotto said that Tarchiani was the man he met in a railroad station in Paris (ACS, CPC, 4639, Sbardellotto). The Fascist police accused Tarchiani. On the other hand, Tarchiani denied it (ISRT, Giustizia e Libertà, Fondo Alberto Tarchiani). The Fascists executed Sbardellotto even though he did not actually carry out an assassination attempt.

48. Interview with Garosci, *Vita*.

49. No number, no author cited, 2 August 1936, ACS, SPD, CR, B 77, F Carlo Rosselli. The Fascist agent, possibly Togo, said "Secondo lui la lotta in Spagna sarà decisiva per le sorti del Fascismo e dell'antifascismo in Europa."

50. No number, no author cited but probably Togo, Paris, 4 August 1936, ACS, SPD, CR, B 77, F Carlo Rosselli.

51. Carlo Rosselli, "La Guerra che torna," *Scritti dell' esilio*, ed. Casucci, 250–58.

52. "Per una Guadalajara in terra italiana," *Giustizia e Libertà*, 23 April 1937, ASMAE, US, B 43: also see *Scritti politici*, 365–68.

53. Interview, Joel Blatt and Aldo Garosci, Rome, 28 June 1990; ACS, Pubblica Sicurezza, H2, B 129.

54. Giacomo Matteotti and Giovanni Amendola are other examples. Paolo Bagnoli emphasized this point in conversation, New York, 28 May 1992.

55. Garosci, *Vita*, 2:237–47; Delzell, "The Assassination of Carlo and Nello Rosselli, June 9, 1937" 57–58. As early as April–May 1936, Rosselli and Giustizia e Libertà had approached the Italian Communist party in pursuit of a "Revolutionary Antifascist Front" or "Revolutionary Antifascist Alliance." The Italian Communist party rejected Rosselli as too prone to "adventure," in part choosing to guard Communist relations with the Italian Socialists rather than Giustizia e Libertà. See correspondence, Istituto Gramsci, APC 1917–1940,

Fascicoli 1457/1 (18–24, 26–27) and 1397 (7–8 and 9). (Elena Dundavich Scalamandre brought this archival source to my attention); *Socialismo e democrazia nella lotta antifascista 1927–1939: Dalle carte Nenni e dagli archivi di "Giustizia e Libertà" e del Partito Communista Italiano*, ed. by Domenico Zucàro (Milan: Feltrinelli, 1988), 292–303.

56. For example, see Appunto 500. 3526, PS, Direttore, PP, to AGR, 18 February 1931, ACS, H2, B 57. For Bocchini, see Paola Carucci, "Arturo Bocchini," in *Uomini e volti del fascismo*, ed. Ferdinando Cordova (Rome: Bulzoni, 1980), 63–103: Franco Fuci, *Le polizie di Mussolini: La repressione dell'antifascismo nel "ventennio"* (Milan: Mursia, 1985).

57. Pro-Memoria, author not given but sounds like Di Stefano, 26 March 1934, ACS, PP, B 122. OVRA infiltrated a number of other agents into Giustizia e Libertà too.

58. See many documents in ACS, PP, Buste 114, 122, 123.

59. See many documents in ACS, PP, B 114, F Giustizia e Libertà, Togo 1 and Togo 4. For the story of the role of another agent, Pitigrilli (Dino Segre), see Stille, *Benevolence and Betrayal*, 91–165.

60. No number, no author cited but probably Di Stefano, 1 June 1934, and Appunto 500/18559, Direttore, PP, to AGR, 28 June 1934, ACS, PP, B 141, F Movimenti di partiti sovversivi italiani all'estero in seguito allo scioglimento della concentrazione, 1932–1934.

61. No number, no author cited, 12 June 1934, ibid. ("più pericoloso del gruppo degli anarchici puri").

62. No number, No author cited, Paris, 11 June 1934, ibid. ("è terribilissimo. Ambizioso all' ecesso, freddo, calcolatore, pronto a rischiare quando gli appaia che vi sia anche una sola probabilità di successo")("In conclusione, il maggiore pericolo viene da Rosselli, e . . . è assolutamente necessario sopprimerlo") idem., 55–56. Also see "Introduzione," Costanzo Casucci, to Carlo Rosselli, *Scritti dall'esilio II: Dallo scioglimento della concentrazione antifascista alla guerra di Spagna (1934–1937)* (Turin: Einaudi, 1992), lxxxi–lxxxii

63. Salvemini, *Carlo and Nello Rosselli: A Memoir*, 55–56.

64. No signature but apparently Togo, 23 March 1936, ACS, CR, B 77, F Rosslli-Carlo. ("Ho dovuto persuadermi che il Rosselli è, senza dubbio, l'uomo più pericoloso di tutto il fuoruscitismo.")

65. No number, no author cited, Barcellona, 30 October 1936, ACS, PP, B 50, F Notizie dirette dalla Spagna. ("È sulla strada di diventare il duce dell'antifascismo italiano.")

66. Appunto 500.34584, Di Stefano, Capo, PP, to AGR, 25 November 1936, ACS, PS, He 129.

67. Appunto 500.10876, Di Stefano to AGR, 2 April 1937, ACS, PS H2, B 129.

68. No author cited, 4 May 1937, ACS, PP, B 127. ("quasi tutta l'attività di 'g.l.' nel Regno è ora nelle nostre mani attraverso i servizi fiduciari"). For the meeting of the officials, see appunto, no number, PS, AGR, May 1937 (no precise date on the document but the meeting had been scheduled for 4 May), ACS, PS, H2, B 129. For Togo's reports, see ACS, PS. H2, B 129.

69. Telegram 629, Ministero degli Affari Esteri to Ministero dell' Interno, 2 May 1937, ACS, PS, H2, B 129, and other documents in the same file.

70. John Coverdale, *Italian Intervention in the Spanish Civil War* (Princeton: Princeton University Press, 1975); Robert Whealey, *Hitler and Spain: The Nazi Role in the Spanish Civil War* (Lexington: University Press of Kentucky, 1989); Ciano, "Colloquio del Ministro Ciano col Fuhrer," Berchtesgaden, 24 October 1936, ASMAE, US 1, allegato 1; Verbale della Riunione a Palazzo Venezia, December 6, 1936, ASMAE, US 1, allegato 2; Verbale della Riunione a Palazzo Venezia, 14 January 1936, ASMAE, US 1, allegato 7.

71. See the documents at the end of J.-R. Tournoux, *L'Histoire secrète*.

72. Document with no number or date, relating to Candella, alias Cantelli, Mission of the Archives Nationales at the Ministère de l'Interiéur, Paris, Fonds Panthéon, MI 25393, Troncoso No. 1, Dossier-Rapports d' Ensemble.

73. For Italian Fascist rumors that Bonomini was contemplating attempts on Hitler and Mussolini, see ACS, PS, H2, B 129; for the Fascist police file on his activity, see ACS, CPC, B 740 (Bonomini, Ernesto). Bonomini served eight years in prison in France, and then returned to Anarchist political activity in 1932.

74. See notes 2 and 3; Delzell, "The Assassination of Carlo and Nello Rosselli June 9, 1937"; Salvemini, "L'assassinio dei Rosselli." I am working on a long article and a book on the subject of this paragraph.

75. I am indebted to a conversation with Paolo Bagnoli, New York City, 28 May 1992. Bagnoli stated that Rosselli was killed because of his potential to build a coalition and because he urged the creation of a new society.

76. Both Aldo Garosci and Max Salvadori discussed with me the force of Carlo Rosselli's personality. Paolo Bagnoli said that Riccardo Bauer had told him that Rosselli had been a strong leader even as a youth.

77. Telephone conversation, Joel Blatt and Max Salvadori, 21 June 1992.

78. Guido Leto, *OVRA, fascismo antifascismo* (Bologna: Cappelli, 1951), 77.

79. Gaetano Arfé, "Carlo Rosselli nella storia del socialismo italiano," in *Giustizia e Libertà, nella lotta antifascista,* 25.

80. Arno J. Mayer, "The Power Politician and Counterrevolutionary," in *Churchill: A Profile* ed. Peter Stansky (New York: Hill and Wang, 1973), 182. Churchill was chancellor of the exchequer and made these comments during the period of strikes in Great Britain. A more extended version of his remarks follows: "I could not help being charmed as so many other people by Signor Mussolini's gentle and simple bearing. . . . If I had been an Italian I am sure that I should have been whole-heartedly with you from start to finish in your triumphant struggle against the bestial appetites and passions of Leninism. . . . Externally, your movement has rendered a service to the whole world. . . . Hereafter, no great nation will be unprovided with an ultimate means of protection against cancerous growths."

81. I am indebted to a conversation with Margherita Repetto Alaia, who also provided help in some instances with translation.

82. Telephone conversation, Joel Blatt and Max Salvadori, 21 June 1992.

83. Garosci, *Vita,* 2:50 n. 2.

84. Franco Venturi, "Carlo Rosselli e la cultura Francese," in *Giustizia e Libertá nella lotta antifascista* 175–77, notes that Rosselli developed a friendship with the French historian Elie Halévy, who had written about this issue. Also see Valiani, introduction to *Epistolario familiare*, 22.

85. I am indebted to a conversation with Margherita Repetto Alaia.

86. Nello Rosselli to Carlo Rosselli, Vienna, 4 December 1931, *Epistolario familiare*, 516, and Valiani, introduction to *Epistolario familiare*, 20. ("Sono fiero di te e della tua attività. . . . Se qualche volta ti parrà d' esser solo o inascoltato, scaccia il pensiero: c'è molto fuoco sotto la cenere in Italia, seppure lo stato di cenere è spesso e lo nasconde affatto. Finirete, finiremo col vincere se non mollerete mai, neppure un momento, neppure un pollice.")

87. Nello Rosselli, *Carlo Pisacane nel risorgimento italiano* (Turin: Einaudi, 1977), 272. ("Il viandante ansioso di varcare il torrente getta pietre una sull'altra, nel profondo dell' acqua, poi posa sicuro il suo piede sulle ultime, che affiorano, perché sa anche lui, pareva sparito nel nulla. Ma sulla sua vita, sulla sua morte poteva posare, e posa, uno dei piloni grantici dell'edificio italiano.")

88. *Il processo Roatta: I documenti*, 114 ("Disgraziati, voi più di noi, perché voi voleste ucciderli e li avete resi immortali: e nel fango di questo processo sono loro che portano una luce di aurora. Morti i Rosselli? No. Siete voi i morti, voi su quel banco e le tristi ombre che sono dietro a voi, ma Carlo e Nello, i dolci amici biondi e sorridenti sono qui, (profondamente commosso) accanto a noi, essi guardano tutta questa immensa rovina, questo vuoto, ma la loro fronte è chiara, i loro occhi sereni, e ci dicono: 'Non mollare.' ")

10

FLORENTINE ANTIFASCISM: THE JEWISH MILIEU

Giorgio Spini

Surely you have admired the masterly essay in which Joel Blatt has outlined the personality and the political thought of Carlo Rosselli. I am sure
that you have considered his penetrating analysis a contribution of the
highest value to our discussions. Now I would like to underline, personally, that the paper has a peculiar value because of the very fact of being
the work of an American student. It seems to me a sort of drastic denial
of certain stereotypes that so often circulate in the history departments of
the United States when modern history is considered. But Joel Blatt has
made absolutely clear that Italy was not always and only the country of
Mussolini or an alternate of Gramsci. Even less was Italy only Don Camillo [a character in Giovanni Guareschi's novels] and his opponents'
country. So if we want to have a realistic vision of Italian events of the last
one hundred years, we must give serious consideration to the democratic
and socialist currents, to their intellectual richness, and to their often
dramatic vicissitudes. Yes, socialist and democratic Italians have been less
colorful than the Blackshirts and the Don Camillos, but they have been
far more important and constructive.

At this point I could keep silent and say nothing else, and perhaps it
would be polite since many of you are probably tired. I could simply add
that Joel Blatt brought me back to the times of my earliest youth. I think
that I was eighteen or nineteen years old when I entered into the Archivio
di Stato of Florence. My goal was to investigate the history of the human-
ists of the sixteenth century and of Antonio Brucioli. I wrote an essay on

this man, and there in the study room of the Archivio di Stato in Florence, I saw a distinguished young gentleman, fair-haired, blue-eyed, with a vaguely British countenance, and I thought that was Nello Rosselli, already famous as a student. But Joel Blatt's paper was so stimulating intellectually that I cannot resist the temptation of proposing a couple of topics upon which further historical analysis could be developed in the future.

First, the relationship between Carlo Rosselli and his brother Nello. Nello was not only the younger but also the less conspicuous for bravery or for brilliant political stands. He was not a man of action but a man of books. Carlo identified himself with the cause of socialism immediately after Matteotti's murder. Nello joined the Unione democratica, Amendola's organization; that is, he chose a position less toward the Left. Nevertheless, one has to ask if this man of study, outwardly harmless, peaceful, if this man in reality did not contribute more than one would think to the building of the *liberalsocialismo*, liberal socialism, of Carlo Rosselli. It is known that Carlo considered seriously suggestions and observations by Nello while he was writing the text of *Socialismo liberale*. But beyond that Nello gave, with his historical investigations, the evidence that *socialismo liberale* existed because it was already present in Italian history. Since the times of the Risorgimento, with men like Pisacane and Montanelli, *socialismo liberale* existed, so it was not a utopia, something fantastic, but rather a concrete political movement, a reality, and a concrete revolutionary project. As you remember, Nello, in his work *Mazzini and Bakunin*, gave a historical picture that is today considered a classic of Italian historiography. In this picture he outlined the beginnings of the socialist workers' movement in Italy, and he underlined clearly its libertarian characteristics and the fact that the early workers' movement in Italy, the early socialist movement, was not Marxist. In other words, Nello showed that Carlo's liberal socialism was not abstract but continued a line of thought and of action, a historical line that was rooted in Italian reality.

One could also ask oneself if Nello would influence Carlo to identify socialism with the ethical religious heritage of Judaism and Christianity (to which Joel Blatt alluded so well in his paper). Of the two brothers, Carlo was the more secularized, and Nello the more thoughtful with regard to religious problems. Nello was also a member of the Jewish youth organization Federazione giovanile ebraica italiana. I would think that without Nello, Carlo's secularism would probably have become so total that it would have become all-encompassing. Nello's influence of the brother was most likely then instrumental, in Carlo's considering the religious factor more deeply. I am thinking of Nello's influence when one reads the beautiful pages of *Socialismo liberale* and the link of socialism with the prophets of the Old Testament.

With this I arrive at my second point. Joel Blatt underlined very well that the liberal socialism of Rosselli derives largely from the Judeo-Christian heritage. It could be important to investigate *which* Judaism and *which* Christianity is involved. Judaism, and let me use this other Italian word *Ebraismo*, because the common people in Italy do not call the Jews "Jews"; they call them "Ebrei" ("Jews" are associated with Judas the traitor). "Ebrei" is more kind and respectful; Italians also call the Jews "Israelites," a term associated with the glory of Israel and the kingdom of Israel. The common people of Italy have made a sort of self-censorship and eliminated a word that seemed offensive. So "Ebraismo," the Rossellis' "Hebraism," was the Italian variant; it stemmed from a family background of Hebraic faith, or at least the family background of the times of liberal Italy.

It is a kind of rare and exquisite flower, a precious flower that bloomed around the middle of the nineteenth century and lived until the tragic 1938, the year of the racial laws in Italy. I call it a rare flower because I don't believe that there are any equivalents outside of Italy. We are here in America where more Jews live than in any other part of the world. Therefore it would be worthwhile that I try to say something about this rare flower, the *ebraismo italiano*. I think it is worthwhile because I am not a Jew and there is no Jewish connection in my family at all. I am a gentile from head to toe; therefore I think I can be historically objective. In many countries of Europe, Jews have felt themselves as guests, sometimes well-accepted, sometimes tolerated, sometimes ill-treated by the owners of the house, and they had to learn the language of the homeowners. But the Jews of Rome are among the very few Romans who can surely trace their ancestry back to the times of Caesar. No Roman is so Roman as the Jew. The other Italians immigrated into Rome. The Roman Jew feels that *he* is the owner of the house. He is not a guest in the house of other people; the other people flocked in later. The Roman Jews always spoke that peculiar Roman vernacular; the Roman Jews taught the other Romans certain dishes as the *carciofi alla Judea*. The Tuscan Jews often have ancestors who once spoke Spanish. Only part of the Tuscan Jews are of Sephardic descent, especially the Leghorn Sephardim. But for generations they have spoken Italian or, better, they speak the local vernacular of Leghorn. Leghorn was built by the will, by the decree of the grand dukes. In order to increase its population, the Jews were offered particular liberties, particular privileges, and so they had a share in the building of the fortune of the city. In the image I used they are the masters of the dwelling; they are the masters of the house, not anybody's guests. So for a long time the commercial law of the port of Leghorn was based upon the Sephardic tradition and even the Christians were ruled by Sephardic rules. Something of the kind could be mentioned for Venice or Trieste, although in these places Jews from different origins arrived, including Askenazis.

Italians of Jewish extraction felt themselves so strong because they had taken part in the building of the common house, Italy; together with other Italians they had contributed with enthusiasm since the beginnings of the Risorgimento. If you go to Rome, on the capital there is a large inscription that commemorates the citizens of Rome who died fighting for the Italian Risorgimento. One is impressed by the number of clearly Jewish names that are on that stone; Jews fought and died together with other Romans. Joel Blatt very well remembers that the Rossellis were a family, a Jewish family of strong Risorgimento traditions. From that derived a very important consequence. In Italy, Jews identify themselves, and were identified by others, exclusively because of their religion, not because of some ethnic or linguistic factor. A Roman Jew is exactly a Roman, the difference being that he goes or does not go to the temple on Saturday, while the rest of the Romans usually don't go to mass on Sunday. That is the difference. In Italy there were only Italians of the Jewish persuasion, not Italian Jews. Under certain aspects their religious heritage made Italian Jews more strongly Italian. The Italy of the Risorgimento fought against the pope to make Rome its own capital. Under this profile, the Jews, Italian Jews, were champions of Risorgimento orthodoxy; reaction was identified with ultraconservative Catholicism, and that was the enemy of both the Jews and the rest of the Risorgimento Italians. Many Italian patriots followed the religious faith of Mazzini. The Rossellis were of "Mazzinian" ancestry. Now, according to Mazzini, Christianity was to be abandoned for a sort of a universalist religion, a humanitarian religion whose god had all the traits of the God of the Old Testament, so a Jew could become a Mazzinian without giving up anything of his or her peculiar Jewish heritage. In the ranks of the Mazzinian party, which was also a religion, in certain ways he could join with total equality with other Italians.

And I come to another point; Italian Jews adopted a generous and open-minded attitude toward the Italian gentiles. In general, when the history of the Jews is discussed in modern times, there is much attention paid to the question of the tolerance by others toward the Jews, never to the reverse: how the Jews saw the gentiles and behaved toward them. From this point of view the case of the Italian Jews is really unique. The very day the Jews were liberated from the exclusion under which they suffered for centuries, that very day, in Italy, they asked, "What can we do for the others?" That is the beginning of the bright and splendid history of Jewish humanitarianism that was the faith of socialists such as Claudio Treves and Emanuele Modigliani, such as the two brothers Rosselli. Their flight to liberty is a sort of symbol in a certain sense.

Three exiles can be compared: Carlo Rosselli, the modernist Jew; Lussu, born Catholic but entirely secularistic; and Nitti, the son of a Methodist pastor. So this generous attitude led to forms of cooperation with men of different experiences and of different confessional backgrounds. Therefore Italian Jews didn't feel their heritage, the Old Testament, as something to be kept closed inside their narrow circle as a minority, but as something that should be enjoyed in common with others, something that could be an impulse for humanitarianism, in the generous brotherly attitude toward the humble and the suffering. One cannot, in my humble opinion, understand the lofty idealism of the two brothers that has been described so well by Joel Blatt, without keeping in mind that at the bottom of their motivations there was this particular heritage (the same heritage of Treves, for instance, with whose family the Rossellis were tied through marriage).

Let me say that there is something more to explore in this case, something that at first appears to be mere curiosity. Rosselli fought in the First World War and later in the Spanish civil war. I am not an expert in either military history or in Jewish history, but as far as I know the first Jews who fought in wars after the destruction of the kingdom of Israel were the Italian Jews who participated in the Risorgimento wars. They found the military life attractive enough that in united Italy it was quite common for young men of the Jewish middle class to enter military life. The career officer was typical of more than one Jewish family.

Italy's Jews thus have had an unique role in Italian and European history and are a fascinating subject for further study.

PART 2

POLITICS

11

THE DIVIDED LEFT:
AFTER FASCISM, WHAT?

Domenico Settembrini

After Fascism, what? We know the reply of history: the Christian Demo-cratic hegemony in the government and that of the Italian Communist Party (PCI) in the opposition, with the consequent Sovietization of a large part of the working class and intelligentsia; these phenomena sustained each other for decades, making any changes in the majority impossible. Hence a blocked democracy, with all the evils—party power, jobs for the boys, corruption, etc.—that find in this lack of change fertile ground for taking on abnormal dimensions.

The topic of my essay is therefore that of analyzing if the elements existed, in the cultural and political background with which the Left—and in particular the Italian Socialist party (PSI)—emerged from its first twenty years, to steer the course of Italian politics in a different direction; and if so, by what tactical "errors" or by what insuperable adversity of "fortune" this alternative remained in the limbo of things that could have been.

Leo Valiani maintained that the Left did possess a plan for this alterna-tive, and that it only abandoned it because of the indolence of its leaders. But one has only to read his description of this plan to realize that it was an entirely unrealistic alternative: "After the insurrection a new state could have been built, in which De Gasperi would probably have been in the opposition. The Socialists and Communists, who would have been its main leaders, did not believe this. The old, pre-Fascist state could also have been restored, on the understanding that the political class would be renewed. De Gasperi believed this."[1] Today no one (not even, one would think, Valiani) can delude himself or herself that, had the De Gasperi plan to graft the rebirth of democracy onto the pre-Fascist liberal and parliamentary traditions been defeated, there would have been any lasting opposition worthy of the name in the "new state" that would have arisen on the ruins of that tradition.

On the other hand, De Gasperi's plan had the merit of meeting the opposition halfway; that opposition in which—instead of militant antifascism, whether Marxist or that of "Justice and Liberty"—"another political element, another ideological and moral force had done much to conserve a certain antifascist conscience: the liberal and parliamentary tradition of pre-Fascist Italy," as the liberal historian Alberto Aquarone has observed. And much of that "mass antifascism produced by the war and the defeat," again according to Aquarone, "was of the same nature, that is looking toward the 'past' rather than the 'future,' " if only because "militant antifascism had trouble in producing [a] coherent and credible political program" for "that future."[2]

This was a typical understatement. Militant antifascism (that is, of the Left, divided and therefore uncertain about many things) had a unanimous and inflexible program on one point: that it was necessary to eradicate entirely that pre-Fascist Italy, on which instead a spontaneous, internal antifascism was to be based. Here, as Pietro Scoppola wrote, we are looking at a "paradox," consisting of the "fact that the idea of the revolution is a common element in a line of pre-Fascist mentality, in Fascist mentality, and in most of antifascist mentality."[3] "Paradox" because it follows that antifascism (at least "militant" and left-wing antifascism) was fueled by the same voluntarist and idealistic humors, by the same religious desire for renewal and thus by the same hostility to the only form of democracy possible: the representative liberal one. A hostility prevailed in most of the thinking of the Giolitti age, from the nationalistic tendencies to those that could generally be defined as "democratic."

In the opinion of its most uncompromising opponents, Fascism had won because it had "betrayed" that original common hostility to "Italietta," turning aside a part of its own revolutionary forces in defense of the constituted order precisely when most of these forces had joined the school of the October revolution (in its congress of 1919, the PSI unanimously voted to support the Comintern) and were thus ready to launch a decisive attack on the system. Hence, in the militant antifascist mentality, Fascism was overhastily identified with capitalism, instead of making it a creature of the system, a kind of "white guard." Although less approximate visions of the phenomenon were not lacking on a more reasoned level of thinking, they had no effect either on the *communis opinio* of the militants or on the Left's strategic orientation.

In his Moscow lessons, Togliatti defined Fascism as "a mass reactionary regime." This was an authentic oxymoron, since the "reaction" came from an attempt to stop and reverse the course of events, put in motion with the French Revolution, for letting the masses enter history. But Pietro Nenni was more penetrating in grasping Fascism's tendency, or at least its aspiration, to go beyond compromise, when he wrote in the *Almanacco socialista* of 1932: "it is certain that Fascism has some points of contact with the Bolshevik state on the issue of democratic and civil liberties and that . . . it aims at forms of direct and controlled economies that can open new possibilities of mass action. . . . Thus it is possible to predict the day in which Fascism will be unable to govern the forces that it has unleashed and in which the revolution could assume the task of dismantling the bourgeois individualist economy once and for all." And in *Avanti* of 9 January 1932, Nenni goes even further: "Fascism is basically a popular and demagogic movement, it is of the masses, and must give satisfaction to these masses. . . . It has destroyed the old political class to make space for its own and it wants above all to destroy the old economic ruling class, to put in its own creatures."[4]

Hence the conviction that once Fascism fell, the Left would have to resume the journey interrupted by the "reaction" of the Fascist action squads in the post–World War I period, finally completing that radical revolution ("totalitarian" as Nenni defined it in 1926)[5] of which Fascism had been both the excavator and the heir or, at least, the hibernator. In the end, it involved digging out the roots of régime-Fascism, of compromise-Fascism, implementing that anticapitalist program of the Marxist left that the Fascist left, movement-Fascism, had made its own, without however managing to impose it.

Agreement in the militant antifascist ranks on this radical negation of the pre-Fascist past, considered the necessary and sufficient cause of regime-Fascism, went well beyond the Marxist forces. The case of Carlo Rosselli is exemplary: "only through a profound revolution can Fascism be overthrown," because only with a radical revolution "can the economic, moral and political causes be eliminated that, after the failed Risorgimento and corrupting Giolittism, led to an easy victory for [Fascism] in Italy."[6]

This is why the Action party's program of April 1943, drafted by Ragghianti with the help of La Malfa, demanded "the nationalization of all the great financial, insurance, and industrial groups" in order "to cut at the roots . . . every reactionary power of great capital."[7] It was evident that they wanted to distinguish themselves from Marxism; that is, to maintain a market economy covering all the large enterprises. But it was just as evident that all the small and medium enterprises could never aspire to become big, under penalty of expropriation, prefiguring a system that in fact had nothing to do with a so-called mixed economy. That is to say, with state intervention alongside private initiative, prohibited from expanding, private business would have been fatally destined to lose impetus, if not actually to perish, until it "spontaneously" left the scene. La Malfa continued for a long time, even after the split with the Action party, to trace the roots of Fascism to the entire post-Risorgimento history: "Italy has never been a real democracy": "the private management of the great industrial, financial, commercial and insurance groups" is "one of the greatest obstacles to democracy, to the prosperity of the working classes." In May 1944, La Malfa legitimized the union of all the parties of the left as the only way to ensure a "complete break with Fascism and pre-Fascism," since "the traditional structure of the Italian state" is "the one that led to Fascism," and will lead it there again if it is not radically dismantled. He reached the conclusion, after logical demonstration, that "a liberal-democratic society of an individualist nature is by now outside history." Hence the "need for a third way," of "a progressive democracy" placed "between the individualist state and the Marxist": "a solution that without being Marxist is not anti-Marxist." After becoming leader of the Italian Republican Party (PRI), La Malfa took a position of neutrality on the international level. Do not link up with either the West or the East, he advised in July 1947, a position he was to reaffirm after his party entered De Gasperi's government. "We are neither with Russia nor the United States of America. . . . Italy must reconstruct its civilization in peace and prosperity."[8]

No socialist could evidently advise less than this. All the critical reflection of the years of exile, albeit taking a certain distance from the radical Communist condemnation of any kind of "formal" and "bourgeois" democracy, was concentrated on the poor revolutionary spirit shown by maximalism during the early postwar period, and ended with the conclusion that, next time, a more programmed and verbal intransigence was needed. "Do as in Russia," which in the two Red years of 1919–1920 had been little more than a slogan, now actually had to be applied. In this framework, the tactical turning point of the Comintern, caused by Hitler coming to power, made unity of action pacts between the two parties possible, but also led to preoccupations within the PSI that the Communists, prompted by the USSR's defense policy, could become overfriendly toward the nonsocialist, generally democratic forces. That is, the Socialists were frightened of the risk that, by placing the USSR's foreign policy interests before the revolution, the Communists would be satisfied by "demolishing Fascism," which would cause "compromise solutions with the forces of reaction," as Morandi wrote in *Nuovo Avanti* of 7 March 1936.

Nenni, in his *Diari*, revealed that the armed battle against Fascism had reawakened the memory of that fiery subversivism of his youthful republican phase, when he had kept his distance from the PSI, and even from the PSI ruled by Mussolini, because he had believed that party would never have had a truly revolutionary strategy. In the meeting of the Socialist leadership, held on 12 October 1944 in a liberated Italy, the problem was raised of some "companions who say they have been told to establish bands"; "the armchair revolutionaries are alarmed." Nenni's comment: "But if they don't want a military organization, at least of the nucleus, then with whom do they want to make the revolution? The *carabinieri?*" [9] On the other hand, Nenni had made no mystery of his real intentions the previous April, when Togliatti, returning from the USSR, wanted the PCI and PSI to stop their frontal attack on the monarchy and the Badoglio government to collaborate in the war against Nazism (this latter goal was given absolute priority by Stalin). Commenting in the underground *Avanti* of 3 April 1944 on what was called the "Salerno turning point," the Socialist leader recognized that Togliatti's move thwarted the agenda of 9 February, where the Socialist party had wanted to "channel the fight for power" along "the road that had been historically illuminated by the French precedents of the revolutionary and Marat terrors when, to conquer the enemy from outside, it was a power game to crush the one inside first." [10] Nenni and the PSI's alignment with Togliatti was based more on a power relationship—since Stalin's approval made the Communist leader the unquestionable interpreter of the revolutionary line—than real conviction. In fact, in the PSI there was the hope that it was a tactical move. More than a year later, with the insurrection in the north approaching, Nenni, believing that the moment had arrived to end the tactical interruption and return to the revolutionary strategy, wrote in *Avanti* of 30 January 1945: "The popular forces are urging an attack on capitalist privileges under the Socialist banner or under the Communist banner. Besides Nazi-fascism, they want to strike out at bourgeois society. Twenty years ago they won in Russia; everything makes us think that they are, that we are, about to win in Europe."[11] However, the incorrigibly subversive Socialist leader was impatient about the slowness (with the Anglo-Americans still there and only leaving at the end of 1947) with which Togliatti's strategy moved. For Togliatti, the destiny of the revolution in Italy now depended very largely on the worldwide triumph of the social model of the USSR, a triumph whose realization was a dogma to add to that of the inevitable collapse of capitalism. Nenni showed very evident signs of this impatience and threatened to upset Togliatti's plans in a meeting in La Spezia on 23 November 1946, when the Socialist leader launched the slogan "from government to power." Togliatti asked Lizzadri if Nenni "had not by chance gone mad" and responded, speaking in Genoa, that, with this formula, the Socialist leader was justifying the suspicion that the left wing wanted to abandon the democratic method, whereas in reality it only wanted to gain a majority in the first legislature of the Republic to continue cooperating with the Christian Democrats (DC).[12] This policy would remain in effect, obviously, until the favorable international and domestic circumstances existed to pass "from government to power," along the lines of the plan successfully implemented in February 1948 in Czechoslovakia, where the Communist party had found itself acting after the war in conditions (albeit much more favorable) most like, or less unlike, those existing in Italy.

It is true that there was a great, albeit confused, aspiration within the PSI to place the relationship between socialism and institutions and the values of the so-called bourgeois democracy not in terms of alternative opposition, but to consider socialism as the universalization, and thus the realization and reinforcement, of those values. Giuseppe Saragat was the most famous supporter of this tendency to reconcile Marxism and democracy, even to see in a correctly interpreted Marxism the logical aspiration of democratic thinking; in the 1930s he devoted a book, L'humanisme marxiste, to this theme, in which he reproached "orthodox Communists" for "holding more or less the same position as Fascism with respect to political democracy." Instead, in his opinion, "in a democracy in which the guiding principle is the suppression of classes, everyone, including the middle classes who have been expropriated, should be ensured their *real* rights."[13] So it can be understood why, when the Ribbentrop-Stalin pact was signed in 1939, Saragat was the first Socialist to separate Marxism and

Stalinism, accusing the latter of totalitarianism. However, for the Marxist Saragat in exile, there was a point that presented a great problem in the reconciliation of Marxism and democracy, and the evolution of Saragat in the post–World War II period confirmed its impossibility. The point was that of how socialism was going to achieve power. Affirming, as it was then affirmed, that it was only possible to achieve power—even in a democratic system—by revolution, prompted serious doubts about the destiny of democracy after the revolution. It was impossible to admit, on the other hand, that power could be achieved by democratic methods without questioning the identification of capitalism with Fascism, on which the entire political thinking of militant antifascism was based. That identification, by placing the entire responsibility for Fascism on the shoulders of capitalism, stopped any efforts toward a radical self-criticism, which the Left would have had to make anyway if it really wanted to play a constructive role in the post-Fascism period; at that time, however, such criticism would have paralyzed the Left. In the early postwar period the conditions for saving the institutions and strengthening the bases of democracy in Italy were not affected by an initiative of capitalism that was seeking in vain cooperation for reform from the workers' and peasants' movements. Turati repeatedly affirmed this in his correspondence with Kulishov. Roberto Vivarelli's recent *Storia delle origini del fascismo*, definitive for its rigor and amplitude of documentation, has categoric judgments: "One cannot speak of a presumed united front of the bourgeoisie to repel the advance of democracy." In fact, with the introduction of the eight-hour working day on 20 February 1919 and various insurance provisions, the ruling class autonomously initiated "profound innovations, the importance of which cannot be overestimated," hoping in vain for the other side's willingness to cooperate. Contrary to what is believed, the behavior of farmers was not much different at the start: "many of the peasants' requests were initially accepted by the landowners."[14] But militant antifascism could not acknowledge this state of things without reaching the disturbing conclusion that the institutions had collapsed because of being attacked by the Marxist Left. Thus, by refusing to admit any failure of its responsibilities, militant antifascism avoided an identity crisis that could have been fatal for its survival (even though the inevitable day of reckoning was to come in the post-Fascism period).

Even Saragat reinforced this refusal when, in 1926, he declared he was so convinced of the "profound iniquity of the capitalist system" that he considered its abolition could not be "ruled by a numerical criterion," but should be included in the "unavoidable issue of the class war."[15] The serious implications of this assertion are obvious: if democratic rule does not apply with regards to capitalism, it follows that when it is abolished, it can—in fact, it must—be done against the conviction of the majority, including that large part of workers without whose support no majority can be formed in an industrialized society. Saragat also returned to this position in *L'humanisme marxiste*, in which he wrote that "the inexpiable error of reformism is that of having lulled the proletariat with the hope of achieving, without shocks and without problems, the prodigious leap from the reign of necessity to the reign of liberty through a gradual, peaceful increase of suffrage".[16] And Saragat once again stressed his fierce anticapitalism, entirely in line with Marxist orthodoxy, just after the courageous schism of Palazzo Barberini, writing in *L'Umanità* of 18 January 1947: "we realize that a capitalist society cannot free people from the slavery of need and cannot remove the tragic threat of new dictatorships and new wars."[17]

It is thus impossible to have any doubts about "what" would have happened in Italy after Fascism, if the forces of the Left had had the capacity and possibility to shape the destiny of the country according to their program. As Franco Gaeta affirmed at the Florence conference devoted to the Left in Europe after World War II: "The socialist and communist left, at least up to 1949, had no prospects of managing the system; they only had the prospect of bringing it down." But the entire proceedings of that conference should be read, because they shed much light on our topic. Just take the problem of economic reconstruction, which De Gasperi entrusted to the free-trader Einaudi. Did the Left have an alternative model? Valerio Castronovo denies it: "immediately after the Liberation, the Italian Left did not possess an economic formation to cope with the situation, and even less was it able to propose a concrete alternative solution. . . . that was not a tactical formula or an ideological exercise without time or place, to that of the free-traders." The Left certainly had a program. As we have seen, the destruction (or anyway, the theoretical correction) of capitalism constituted the only point on which all the militant antifascist forces agreed. But what would have happened had that program been implemented, as it certainly would have been if the Left had not been defeated? In Florence, Luciano Cafagna noted the contradiction between lamenting the failure of the attempt to establish in Europe "a regime similar or sympathetic with that of the USSR" and realizing the "ideal failure" of that same Soviet regime. Nor was it possible to avoid this contradiction by judging that this attempt, carried out "in a context different from that of the USSR model-country would not necessarily have led to the same perverse results." A very implausible hypothesis, both because of the "weight of the great power [of the] model-country," and because of the "intrinsic logic of that model." Hence Di Nolfo's rhetorical question at the end of the conference: "Isn't it right to be pleased about these defeats, after having considered certain situations and certain assumptions?" But why were the militant antifascists unable to "produce" that "coherent and credible program" about which Aquarone also spoke? Di Nolfo had no doubts: "the fact that we have been deceived by the Fascism-capitalism identity" has made it impossible for us "to plan the future":[18] that future which others would have to construct. And to succeed they would have to bring about the defeat of militant antifascism.

That deception referred to by Di Nolfo explains not only why other hands than those of the Left had to lead Italy toward the future, but also constitutes the main reason for Togliatti's extraordinary success in rooting the PCI so profoundly in the social, cultural, and political fabric of our country. The widespread anticapitalist prejudice meant that the non-Communist left was unable to block that plan effectively, and in fact drove it, more or less knowingly, more or less voluntarily, to cooperate with it. It was inevitable that Stalinist Communism would appear as a lesser evil than the "profound iniquity of capitalism," even to those who were totally unaware of the crimes or who were gradually discovering them; because of the particular nature of the development of socialism in Russia it was also understandable. One thing that Stalin did that cannot be denied was to suppress capitalism radically and forever, while even Lenin, after having got rid of it, partly resurrected it with his New Economic Policy. It was such a deep-rooted prejudice that it remained with Nenni until his death, despite the clear break with Communism in 1956 and the long participation in the center-left governments. In his last interview, Nenni in fact declared his admiration for the "two world-scale revolutions, the Russian and the Chinese," which had had the eternal merit of achieving "one of the fundamental postulates of socialism with the suppression of the private ownership of means of production and trade."[19]

And yet after Fascism, despite that prejudice, Italian domestic circumstances and the very orientation of the working class were not sufficient to guarantee the success of Togliatti's attempt to root the PCI in society, or at least not enough to guarantee it to the extent it achieved later on. This was recognized, among others, by a protagonist and faithful witness, Lelio Basso, founder during Fascism of the Proletarian Unity movement

—the reason why the PSI returned to the Italian scene with the name of PSIUP (Italian Socialist Party of Proletarian Unity), with a program that explicitly aimed to "achieve the merger of Socialists and Communists on the basis of a clear awareness of the revolutionary goals of the workers' movement."[20] In 1960, during a series of lessons on Fascism, Lelio Basso declared that: "after semilegality was achieved on 25 July, militant Socialists sprouted everywhere like mushrooms, linked to the memory of the past, but we had not yet had any contacts with them. . . . It was immediately clear after 25 July that, despite our efforts and dynamism, we were overwhelmed by the PSI's spontaneous organization, occurring almost everywhere."[21] So Aquarone's thesis also applied to the PSI: How many in the party, during Fascism, had continued to keep the socialist idea alive by looking to the "past," thinking to re-create the old party? Were these people not therefore extraneous if not hostile to the Leninist-model party and to the merger with the Communist party, desired by Basso, Morandi, and Nenni? And here we have the testimony of Nenni himself. His diaries reveal that the more he realized that the Socialists were reluctant to embrace the Communists, the more he was convinced that he must not support this reluctance, but repress it and cage it in. Thus in August 1945 he noted: "The party is almost unanimous in accepting me as its leader, but it is not convinced of the need to march with the Communists. This is something that must be borne in mind. In the end, it involves bringing back a class concept of politics to socialism, for which it has lost the habit."[22]

But let us be quite clear, this spontaneously reborn socialism was just as against the system as the PCI itself, or anyway just as reluctant to see its own horizon ending in the sphere of a liberal democracy, however advanced in terms of social policy it might have been. It aspired to the myth of collectivism with a human aspect, so that it was not Marxism that separated it from the PCI but Stalinism. This meant that, even if it had prevailed inside the PSI, even if it had managed to force the stubborn pro-Communists to a schism, instead of finding itself obliged to split at the last moment, it would certainly have been able to reinforce and condition that decisive contribution which Saragat gave to De Gasperi's plan for democratic rebirth. However, it would never have been able, or known how, to take the initiative and the leadership of that rebirth. Nor, if we think of economic renewal, without which no democratic renewal was possible, was it desirable that it would succeed.

The recently published documents from the Faravelli archive give significant proof of this. Giuseppe Faravelli was the Socialist who, behind the scenes, was mainly responsible for persuading Saragat to make the schism, so that the editors of the publication have justly defined him as its "principal instigator." However, Faravelli's papers also show that it was Saragat who—once he had got over his own perplexities and not without sometimes very bitter conflicts with the co-founders of the party—played an indispensable role in taking the party along the route that encouraged cooperation with America in the international field and with the DC in the domestic one. It was also Saragat who incited the party not to put "doctrinal subtleties" before the "life of the gasping nation," an invitation that Vanni Montana, one of the Italo-American trade unionists who had striven to save the autonomy of Italian Socialism, was already making to his friend Faravelli in the months following the schism.

However, Faravelli evolved in the opposite direction. Aware of the indispensable role played by governments led by the DC in the defense of democracy up to September 1948 (that is, until the Communist threat looming over Italy seemed to have passed), he also supported cooperation, albeit as a state of necessity. Then he suddenly had the impossible dream of the "third way," which led him to break with Saragat and to struggle for a Socialist reunification that would occur on the platform of opposition both to the PCI and DC and to Stalinist totalitarianism and democratic capitalism, to prepare one day—as he wrote on 28 October 1950 to the Russian Menshevik Abramovich—"the victory of revolutionary Marxism." All this in the conviction "that one can only defeat Bolshevism by fighting it from Socialist [Marxist] positions"; otherwise "one ends up playing its own game, that is, reinforcing it." [23]

So, summing up, we can say that the only realistic alternative to how things actually went would have been for the Left to have managed to circumscribe to a considerable extent the PCI's electoral success. The person who did everything he could to thwart this possibility, which would have required the Socialist leadership to support the spontaneous diffidence of its members toward the Communists and construct a policy on it, was, by his own admission, Pietro Nenni. Collective prejudice certainly also had a role in this choice, which in Nenni's case served perhaps mainly as a rationalization; that is, to hide, even from himself, a decision really made from a combination of two bad motives. The first was misguided resignation: Communism was destined to win in Italy, whomever the PSI aligned itself with. The second was cowardice: the first victims of the Communist regime would be the companions who opposed it. Antonio

Gambino, on the basis of extensive testimonies, proposes the thesis that "behind" Nenni's "subjection" to the Communists during those years "there was the firm decision not to lay himself open any longer, as in the past, to the frontal attacks and insults of a party that had the growing influence of the USSR behind it and was, in his opinion, destined to gain power." Among the testimonies Gambino uses, the most impressive is Scelba's. He refers to a conversation between Nenni and De Gasperi, in the presence of Scelba, after the elections of 1946. When the prime minister reproached him for having made "a DC-PSIUP government" impossible with his pro-Communism, Nenni retorted that it had been expected that the left-wing bloc would have come out of the elections with a clear majority: "Seeing how things were going, I wanted to find myself on the winning side. Moreover, in the case of a Communist success, my fate would have been very different from yours: at the worst, they would have put you, as traditional enemies, in prison; but I, as a betrayer of the working class, would have had my head cut off."[24] On the basis of a report of a conversation in October 1944 between Nenni and an officer in the American Secret Service, the historian Michael Ledeen comes to the same conclusion: "Nenni was completely wrong in his calculations on the political future of Italy," underestimating the political and financial commitment the United States would have been prepared to make "to prevent a Communist triumph in Italy"—a triumph that, without that commitment, seemed inevitable in 1944.[25]

The fate of a modernization of the Left (and with it, that of Italy's full alignment with the liberal democratic model of the West) or the possibility of our finally becoming "normal"—as Silvio Lanaro writes in his latest book[26]—was thus definitively decided in the very brief span of a year or two after the fall of the Fascist regime. The failure to make good this lapse is proved by the confusion and torment the entire Left is experiencing after the collapse of Communism and by the serious crisis affecting all the historic parties, and therefore democracy itself.

It is true that a formidable obstacle to a happier ending to the drama was represented by the inheritance of a large part of all the Risorgimento, post-Risorgimento and Fascist past, existing within the Left itself in various forms, and of which Togliatti made very shrewd use. It is also true, however, that the international economic crisis in which Italy found itself after Fascism was one of the most fortunate possible. By now all historians are unanimous in stating that not only was the United States not responsible for the Christian Democrat hegemony (which in fact it submitted to *faute de mieux*) but it had in fact greatly courted the leaders of the non-Communist Left in the attempt to persuade them to take a leading role in establishing a democracy open to the most advanced reformism, considered the best for coping with the dissemination of Communism. It thus seems impossible to deny that, if any possibility of a less negative outcome had existed, then it went through Nenni's hands, who refused to use it for the reasons that have been given.

Notes

1. Quoted from S. Telmon, *Ugo la Malfa: Il professore della Repubblica* (Milan: Rusconi, 1983), 71.
2. A. Aquarone, "Violenza e consenso nel fascismo italiano," *Storia contemporanea*, February 1979, 145–55.
3. In *Il fascismo e gli storici* (Rome: Laterza, 1989), 104.
4. In P. Nenni, *La battaglia socialista contro il fascismo* (Milan: Mursia, 1977), 290 and 296.
5. P. Nenni, *Storia di quattro anni (1919–1922)* (Turin: Einaudi, 1946), 139.
6. See C. Rosselli, *Scritti dell'esilio, 1929–1934*, edited by Costanzo Casucci (Turin: Einaudi, 1989), 271.
7. Quoted by S. Setta, *Croce il liberalismo e l'Italia postfascista* (Rome: Bonacci, 1979), 58.
8. U. La Malfa, *Scritti, 1925–53* (Milan: Mondadori, 1988), *passim*. Only in January 1949, arguing with Pietro Nenni, did La Malfa call the idea of neutrality "puerile."
9. P. Nenni, *Tempo di guerra fredda: Diari 1943–1956* (Milan: SugarCo, 1981), 96.
10. P. Nenni, *La battaglia socialista contro il fascismo* (Milan: Mursia, 1977), 578.
11. P. Nenni, *Vento del Nord, giugno 1944–1945* (Turin: Einaudi, 1978), 281.
12. Quoted by A. Gambino, *Storia del dopoguerra: Dalla Liberazione al potere Dc* (Bari: Laterza, 1978), 311.
13. G. Saragat, *L'humanisme marxiste*, E.S.I.L. (Marseilles, n.d.), 157–58 and 124.
14. R. Vivarelli, *Storia delle origini del fascismo: L'Italia dalla grande guerra alla marcia su Roma* (Bologna: Il Mulino, 1991), 109, 132–33, 754, 857.
15. G. Saragat, *Quarant' anni di lotta per la democrazia* (Milan: Mursia, 1966), 17.
16. G. Saragat, *L'humanisme marxiste*, 152.
17. G. Saragat, *Quarant'anni di lotta per la democrazia*, 338.
18. *La sinistra europea nel secondo dopoguerra* (Florence: Sansoni, 1981), 116, 16, 20, 303, and 309.
19. P. Nenni, *Intervista sul socialismo italiano*, ed. G. Tamburrano (Bari: Laterza, 1977), 150.
20. See in Carlo Vallauri, ed., *La ricostituzione dei partiti democratici, 1943–1948* (Rome: Bulzoni Editore, 1978), 1222.
21. *Fascismo e antifascismo (1936–1948). Lezioni e testimonianze* (Milan: Feltrinelli, 1962), 469.
22. P. Nenni, *Tempo di guerra fredda*, 135.

23. P. C. Masini and S. Merli, eds., *Il socialismo al bivio: L' archivio di Giuseppe Faravelli, 1945–1950* (Milan: Feltrinelli, 1990), 432 and 404.
24. A. Gambino, *Storia del dopoguerra: Dalla Liberazione al potere Dc*, 144 and 179.
25. M. Ledeen, *Lo zio Sam e l' elefante rosso* (Milan: SugarCo, 1987), 25–27.
26. S. Lanaro, *Storia dell' Italia repubblicana: Dalla fine della guerra agli anni novanta* (Venice: Marsilio, 1992).

12

POSTWAR REALITIES

Carlo Vallauri

One observation of Settembrini's essay is especially worth pointing out: the observation that, after the fall of Fascism and the return of democracy to Italy, most of the antifascist political leadership had the same themes and weaknesses and made some of the errors that led to the fall of liberal institutions and the victory of Fascism after World War I. I find it difficult, however, to believe that the representatives of the Left really intended to abolish private property and implement radical solutions. Many declarations cited by Settembrini refer to the 1930s, when the bitter struggles against dictatorship could lead to identifying capitalism with Fascism, encouraging the idea of destroying the capitalist system after the Fascist one. Nenni, Saragat, and Morandi's affirmations in the 1930s cannot be taken as the platform of action that the reestablished Italian Socialist Party (PSI) intended to carry out from 1945 on. Indeed, Saragat, albeit urged to do so, never wanted to republish his *L'humanisme marxiste*, which set out theses he had abandoned in the 1940s.

Nenni certainly considered that the Italian Communist Party (PCI) would have taken the Left to power along with it, and his party and all of Italian democracy paid dearly for this error of judgment. While waiting for the great upheaval, neither Socialists nor Communists were much worried about what was happening in 1946, 1947, and 1948, since a "second wave," in which the parties of the proletariat would have been victorious over the bourgeoisie, seemed almost inevitable—an October revolution after the February one with a longer time interval.

I think it was precisely this minimizing of events while awaiting this

"second wave"—already considered certain by the more militant representatives of the Left because of a kind of "historic providence"—that
caused the PSI and PCI's estrangement from the government in May 1947
to be taken less seriously than it should have been. You only have to read
the newspapers and the documents of those weeks to realize this. The
important thing at that time was to obtain a constitution that affirmed
certain general lines and a pluralism that guaranteed absolute freedom of
action for parties that could otherwise be accused of being antidemocratic.
Togliatti was to be implacable in blocking the jurist Mortati's proposals
for a regulation ensuring the respect of the *internal democracy of the parties*.
Having obtained this result, the masses had to be mobilized against the
conservatives: De Gasperi himself was accused of supporting the reaction
of 1948.

I am giving these details because two serious errors of judgment can be
inferred from them. The first is the already mentioned one of the *un-
awareness* of the actual situation in the nation, its humors, the changes that
had occurred in its structures and its mentality in the long journey through
Fascism, and also in the political conscience during the war years and
those of the fight for liberty. You only have to consider the neglect of
Catholic women, who were one of the main reasons for the Christian
Democrats' (DC) victory of 18 April 1948. Moreover, during the civil war
against the Fascists, and especially during its most savage phase, it began
to be realized in many Catholic and moderate spheres that only a specific
commitment and mobilization could stop the last dictatorship being followed by another one. Last but not least, Italian economic structures
(albeit with monopolist practices and rather backward) had their own
vitality, with a shrewd business ability that the left-wingers either ignored
or accused out of hand.

This mistaken idea of the real situation was accompanied by the conviction of the leaders of the Left that one only had to step on the accelerator
(verbal threats, extraordinary promises, collective organizations) to obtain
the greatest possible votes in the nation. At the same time, however, there
were economic and political powers emerging that were challenging the
tide of the Left. Since a reformist project was effectively lacking (except
for the short-lived one of the party of action in Calamandrei's institutional
and Riccardo Lombardi's economic-social proposals), and faced with the
fear of success of that kind of Left from which very few positive things
were to be expected, great sectors of society considered supporting a
moderate line. Once the season of liberalism was over, moderates saw

the Christian Democrats as the greatest bulwark, backed by the Catholic Church and the Confindustria, because it was the only party able to stand up, en masse, to the Socialist and Communist impact on the various classes in the nation.

A moderate, Catholic-led affirmation, even though termed "clerical" by its adversaries, seemed outside any logic and perspective; all that could be seen was an opposition between right and left in the most antithetical terms, a reflection of the class struggle. If the DC moved increasingly to the right, the Socialists considered it logical to remain firmly compact alongside the PCI, the strongest, most weathered people's movement, fortified by the approval of many intellectuals ready to submit to the new master, as they had earlier to Fascism. Even the social factions of the DC seemed to have no stratagems against De Gasperi's leadership; thus Nenni, Basso, and Morandi, albeit with different positions, could do nothing but reinforce the people's bloc in the opposition, for which an electoral success was anticipated outside any international complications.

I therefore think that the postwar period in Italy cannot be examined without analyzing how the protagonists lived through these events and, therefore, by trying to understand how the Socialists made such serious errors of judgment—on this I agree with Settembrini—even if (and Settembrini points out that Nenni was well aware of this) there was in fact no unanimity in the decision to "march" with the PCI.

At this point I put forward another point. In the bourgeois-proletarian party contest, these latter would never have been able to take a leading position on the basis of their organization during exile. They were only united in the fight against Fascism during the last stages of the war (the new DC only made contact with Communist emissaries after the Comintern had been dissolved in the spring of 1943); nationwide the real strength of antifascism rested on two factors. The first was the unity among representatives of different classes; if that unity were to crumble, it could only weaken the so-called proletarian parties to the benefit of the bourgeois parties (which that part of the nation that had been Fascist would certainly support at the decisive time). As Andreotti noted, De Gasperi decided to break away from the Communists after the great administrative electoral victory of the "man in the street" *(uomo qualunque)* in November 1946; the victorious formation of 1948 was being established along this new line.

The other determinant factor in favor of antifascism was the allied military victory on the Italian front. Without the Anglo-American armies,

Fascism and Nazism would not have been defeated, but the great ethical value, the spontaneous mass outbreak of new groups lined up against Fascism and Nazism made the left-wing representatives returning from exile believe that the victory of the liberation had been achieved only with internal forces. This was a great mistake. There was also an underground Fascism in Italy that would soon spread in revised forms, with a specific anti-Communist slant.

Social unrest was based on a condition of serious intolerance, above all in southern Italy, and the left-wing parties were forthright in their attempts to channel these energies against reactionary interests, old and new Mafias, and strongholds of local power. They paid dearly for this action (witness the dozens of Socialist and Communist trade unionists killed or attacked in the south). The trade-union leadership had a very realistic idea of things and, starting with Di Vittorio, followed a different road from the more combative and revolutionary one (in words) of the Socialist and Communist leaders. Forces for renewal were collecting around the trade-union movement, the Red and White associations, with a very different line of action from that of the left-wing parties: it was not waiting for zero hour, but worked day by day to improve labor relations and living conditions of the various workers in the factories, on the land, and in the offices. The Socialists were undeniably under the Communists' leadership; yet if we look at the behavior of the parties year by year compared with that of the main Italian trade-union (CGIL), we note attitudes and choices closer to the real situation. In fact, the most extreme positions tended to tone down in later years as improvements were gradually made, and the trade-union movement became stronger precisely because more and more of the masses became aware that it was the greatest point of aggregation for limiting the influence of conservative interests.

I have already indicated a lack of political awareness in the leaders of the Left. To be frank, after an initial tendency toward a renewal of concept (as proved, for example, by the magazine *Socialismo*, by the creation of the Socialist Institute of Studies—soon abandoned—and in ideological debate) when the schism of Palazzo Barberini occurred, in which the Social Democrats split off, the Socialists lost all their initiative, and the attempt of numerous intellectuals to stress the difference between the Socialist and Communist perspectives failed. From 1947 to 1952 the PSI was a slavish follower of the PCI, taking from the latter all its organizational formulas and patterns. Thus Italian democracy was deprived of the support of an original, authentically socialist point of view, along lines that we can only find in isolated writings, such as those of Silone, and not in practical action.

I think that the sacrifice of socialist ideals and objectives was the consequence not only of wrong judgments but also of an opposition in economic and political matters that the victorious moderate side had caused in Italy by refusing a reformist line. In the Christian Democrat Party itself, first Gronchi's position was sacrificed, then the more innovative one of *Cronache sociali*, potentially more important. In this context I can affirm that Italy did not miss a revolution in the post-World War II period, in the sense that the conditions did not exist for it: the regime was overthrown mainly as the result of the Allied military victory. The majority of Italians were working to restore "normal" conditions, so that a left-wing opposition could only aim at the long term, but the country lacked a reformist line. On this level the Socialists failed badly, as they were to have been the supporters of this line. Instead reformism remained the prerogative of Saragat's small group, and later even became the banner of Christian Democrat moderation. A systematic analysis on how the different movements behaved in the economic sphere would further support this opinion.

13

WOMEN AND MASS POLITICS IN THE REPUBLIC

Margherita Repetto Alaia

A century after the first strains of a socialist movement in Italy coalesced into an organized force, there is a need to address the question of whether in Italy, in Europe and in the world there is a future for the socialist idea. This question implies taking a decisive step toward a comprehensive reconstruction of the history of socialism. This means using a methodology that will allow insight into the choices, expectations, actions, and self-image of those women led by socialist ideals and acting as historical agents for change between the last decades of the century and the second postwar period. Italian historiography on the socialist movement has not been conducive to that type of reconstruction. Traditionally the object of interest has been institutional (i.e., a profile of the movement's relationship to the state and to other political and institutional entities); alternatively, when ideological orientations have been under scrutiny, sexual politics and the gender conflict have never been included as components of the revolutionary perspective. And yet, generations of socialist women have labored around these formulations. Finally, Italian historiography still lacks a tradition of biographical reconstruction, regarding both single personalities and homogenous social groups—as illustrated in the introduction to a collection of essays presented at a 1976 symposium on Anna Kuliscioff and the "reformist age" (*Anna Kuliscioff* 1978). Ironically, English-speaking historians have recently taken the lead toward a new historiographical direction on this question.

Which circumstances account for the invisibility of women in the socialist movement? One factor may be in the passage from the earlier "indirect" form of organization—that of the workers' sodalities and mutual aid societies, where women abounded—to the "direct" organization, which led to the formation of a Socialist party in 1892, as emphasized by Giorgio Galli and Leo Valiani, among others. Valiani stressed that from 1891 Turati spent most of his time "politicizing" the Workers' party and workers' societies. The *direct organization*—the political party geared to political representation—calls for individual participation and militancy. The immediate consequence is that women are cut out and their participation restricted to a proxy of the politicized male; they become politically marginalized and to a great extent historically invisible. Thus women's political marginalization proves to be organic in the formation of modern political parties. From this viewpoint one should also evaluate two major reformist goals of the Socialist party between 1890 and World War I: (1) social legislation, a recovery of workers' protagonism through mobilization; and (2) universal male suffrage, which reduced the gap between individual participation and institutional representation by giving the working male more access to the political process. When we look at women in light of these goals, we find that social legislation meant protective legislation for women and children in 1906–7—a factor discriminating against women in employment, and, ultimately, a demobilizing factor from the viewpoint of women's participation in workers' struggles. Furthermore, socialist diffidence toward women's right to vote proved to a large extent responsible for the widening gap between women and politics and for the split that occurred within the women's movement after 1908.

It is significant that while these two issues have been the object of very intelligent and deep scrutiny in the last few years in *women's studies* by women historians—starting with the invaluable pioneering work by Franca Pieroni Bortolotti—mainstream academic and political historiography has hardly scratched the surface.

From the point of view of women's political participation in Italy the second postwar period opens up with a decisive novelty. Women—including Socialist women—had actively campaigned for the vote since early fall 1944, and the decree recognizing that right was issued in January 1945 when the country had still not been liberated. It is natural to ask to what extent this institutional novelty made women and specifically Socialist women, politically visible. Paola Gaiotti, who has focused on this issue more intensely than any other woman historian, places the decree in its proper social and cultural context. She emphasizes a context characterized by a "sense of necessity," or a "democratic obviousness." She also points to the *passive* nature of the process of feminization of society, which had begun during the Fascist regime, and concludes that the growing feminization of society and "its apparently painless, 'unthinking' nature conspired to give the impression of a nation of tranquil, reconciled women, untroubled by any rash or uncurbable wants or needs" (Gaiotti 1993, 223–25).

The Socialist party shared this general agnosticism. Some additional factors, however, account for the relationship that existed from the beginning between Socialist women and the party. First, the January 1945 decree was approved by a government that did not include the Socialist and Action parties. Besides being an undeserved retribution for the efforts that Socialist women had made along with others on behalf of the vote, this exclusion put the Socialists at a disadvantage. Again Paola Gaiotti identifies three strategies, Togliatti's, Pius XII's, and De Gasperi's, while pointing to a class-oriented proposal on the part of the PSIUP executive committee in May 1944 in which there was no room for any gender-based political category (Gaiotti 1993, 231). Eventually this strategy became identifiable with Rodolfo Morandi's leadership and his increasing grip on the organizational structure of the party.

From all it is possible to know of these formative years, I believe that one should credit Pietro Nenni with a strong personal conviction of the relevance of women's contribution. As secretary of the party speaking at the Congress of UDI (Unione Donne Italiane) in 1974 he used strong words against what he called "i 'mezzi dottori' delle nostre sezioni, dei quali Giacomo Matteotti parlava con tanto disprezzo," recalling how they had resented the burden that the UDI grassroots organization put upon their time and efforts, and insisting upon the high political value of women's mobilization. I believe that he had developed this attitude of respect for women's political capacity from his exile experience (which, in this regard, puts him very close to many other men of the Socialist and Communist leaders of the older generation). Nenni's emphasis—and that of Morandi—fell on the emancipatory value *per se* of women's participation in political movements on an equal footing with men. However, they failed to perceive the political value of women's specific needs; Morandi would deny such value, and Nenni did not make the point clearly until much later.

Before closing on this point, one needs to recall another powerful factor: the long-lived diffidence toward women due to their supposed dependence on the Church and priests. This was no sole prerogative of Socialist men. It was to be found in the Left at large, Communists, actionists, and other radicals and lay anticlericals. This important point deserves closer and less prejudiced scrutiny than it has usually been given. So far there are only a few works by women which examine this point (Gaiotti 1993, 233ff.). As for the Communists, Togliatti personally had to chastise party officials who believed that women's suffrage had been a clear loss to the party. On this point the attitude of the Socialist leadership clearly differed because there was no effort spent in contesting that reaction at the party's grassroots.

When speaking of Socialist women after World War II, it is necessary to examine the continuity of a Socialist political tradition among women between the pre-Fascist period and the years 1943–45. During World War I, the Socialist women's organization was clearly on the rise: the Union of Socialist Women numbered more than one hundred groups nationally; the debate on the contents of women's demands had reached a high level of maturity, and so had awareness of the difficulties encountered within the party itself; circulation of *La Difesa delle Lavoratrici* exceeded 100,000 in 1919. After the war, however, the split on the right caused by the interventionist stance of prominent leaders such as Labriola, Regina Teruzzi, and Margherita Sarfatti—active in discrediting the emancipationist tradition among middle-class women—was followed by the secession on the Left of the Ordine Nuovo group. Here we lack a sufficient critical reconstruction of the developments in those years that might tell us to what extent the women's organization was weakened by division among the leadership or rather by the lack of support by the party for the struggles of women factory workers against layoffs following demobilization, as well as by the party's belated and ineffectual stance on the issue of suffrage.

Research regarding the years from 1919 to 1927 sends us contradictory messages. Where middle-class women are concerned, the history is somewhat better known. The 1919 Legge Sacchi abolished the "marital authorization" and opened to women access to all professions except those linked to the exercise of political rights. But a government administrative ordinance in 1920 called for the exclusion of women from all ranks and jobs in the public sector. Much less known in their historical significance are frequent episodes of struggle by women workers, especially in the textile industry where demobilization had not resulted in the expulsion of all female workers, and among women agricultural laborers. The episodes go from 1919 to 1920 until 1926 (Pieroni Bortolotti 1987, 265ff.). We do not as yet have an interpretive key allowing us to read how politicized was the nature of frequent mass rebellions by women in the years of the regime. The lack of a historiographical effort to trace a political continuity among women has caused once again a blank-out of women's political visibility. We know a little bit more today thanks to some historical reconstructions and especially to personal memoirs of what happened to the leaders and militants of the new Communist party in the interwar period; but we know very little of what happened to the many socialist groups still active in 1921 after the Congress of Leghorn. One thing is clear, between 1922 and 1926 the feedback between collective action and leadership was broken, thus preventing further formation of a female leadership. Significant Socialists of the old generation of women died in the decade following Fascism's ascent to power. In the biographical dictionaries of the antifascist and Resistance movements we encounter a few names, such as Maria Giudice (executive secretary of the Socialist party chapter in Turin until the outbreak of World War I) and Alda Costa (repeatedly arrested and sent to confinement by the regime), whose presence and activities project themselves into the World War II years. Angela Merlin is the only personality of the prewar generation whose political activity extends itself through the 1950s.

Since 1970 historical investigation of local activity has uncovered a wealth of data, but we lack sufficient conceptualization of the work of these Socialist women and of the continuity between old and new generations. In fact, the formation of new cadres of politically active women militants and leaders in the postwar society still remains a problem. In the case of Socialist women this is even more uncharted territory. A few months ago I tried a small investigation of my own. I discovered that during the regime a socialist tradition in many working-class families survived, especially in the north, but also in some areas of the south. In the center and north, young women who participated were not usually affiliated with any party. The choice came later, at the end of the war, and it was between the Socialist party and the Communist party. Family tradition had an influence, but so did personal experience. Especially in the middle class there were male influences—a brother, a boy friend, a professor. Middle-class youths of the late 1930s and early 1940s enjoyed a freedom of movement unknown to women. This discrimination was a recurrent motivation among women of the urban and well-to-do middle class. Thus the drive to share experiences with their male comrades found an ideal justification in the participation in initial antiregime activities, which took on a more serious character in 1943. Finally, many women in the center and especially the south—cut off from active resistance—came to political activity from their experience in the teachers' unions, which witnessed a revival of the prefascist Socialist tradition in 1944–45.

Some points are worth considering in reconstructing the history of women in the socialist movement after World War II. First, the approach by these women to their problems appears less rigid, much more unstructured, as compared to Communist women's. The July 1944 premiere issue of *La donna socialista* (circulated in the liberated part of Italy) stressed the need for women to involve themselves in politics. In the following months, the newly reconstituted Centro Femminile Socialista started a new publication, *Lettera alla donna*, to which Umberto Calosso contributed a column dealing humorously with housework, as part of a campaign aiming at the reshuffling of social roles (Alloisio and Ajò 1978, 86). The editor was Carla Cartasegna, one of the young leaders of the central group of Socialist women; later, in January 1946 Lina Merlin replaced Calosso as co-editor. Calosso was in fact ostracized, as Paola Gaiotti points out, for "constantly referring to the Scandinavian model of family relationships and for introducing issues such as divorce and free love into the political debate" (Gaiotti 1993, 225). Some of the issues that continued the socialist cultural tradition—first of all, divorce—contrasted sharply with the policy of unity of the Left as it shaped up in 1945–48. Anna Franchi, the author of the 1904 book *Viva il divorzio!* published in 1946 a book recounting to the new generation of Socialist women the story of the struggles of the early century (Alloisio and Ajò 1978, 89–90). Socialist periodicals in 1946–47 featured numerous articles by women such as Bianca Bianchi, elected to the Constituent Assembly, which consider divorce and the family (Ruffilli 1979, 158ff.). The climate in which options still appeared open seems to have been well exploited by Socialist women, but 1947 marked the end of such experimentation.

A second important point is the continuous resurfacing among Socialist women of the need for their own organization within the party. Inevitably this debate carried with it another issue, that of whether Socialist women should participate in UDI. This debate began in 1945, when Socialist women from the north met their sisters from the center-south during the first national convention of the PSIUP. This issue reflected to some extent the strain in the relationship between the two parties of the Left, but there was much more to it. The debate on whether to form a separate organization was common to women in both parties because both Socialist and Communist women resented the patronizing attitude of the men in their parties; with few exceptions leaders and militants alike looked at women as a subordinate component whose main task was to gain the consensus of women at large for their parties. The intermediate party cadres, especially at the local level, made no mystery of the goal: to pull women "away from the priests"—and from the Christian Democrats at the polls. Of course, they stopped short of saying that so-called *general* politics was none of women's business. Leftist women have long been aware of this undervaluation and estrangement, the other face of which was that the strategy of the Left did not consider at the time nor later any of the problems "implicit in the inclusion of women in the modern system of civil liberties" (Gaiotti 1993, 225; she applies this criticism to the Italian party system as a whole). For this reason women in the PCI as well as in the PSI were divided as to whether they had to form the so-called women's section or women's bureau. Some women (such as the PCI's Teresa Noce) were decidedly against this position because they felt that women had to involve themselves in party politics on an equal footing with men and should refuse to be confined to dealing with women's issues. Opponents of this view maintained with good reason that unless women worked together to bring them up, women's issues would never surface in the party's strategy. This fact proved true over and over again. Where Socialist women were concerned, the overlapping of the function of women's organizations within the party and that of mass organizations was less likely to occur because the presence of women at the local level never reached mass consistency. In the PCI, however, the women's party organization assumed a competitive attitude with respect to UDI.

The misgivings of many women in the leftist parties with respect to specific work on women's issues were linked and made more acute in the case of Socialist women by the existence of factional struggles. Elena Caporaso, head of the Women's Bureau, summarized in 1954 developments starting from the 1947 Saragat secession: "Our best sisters, who had spent their energies in factional struggles [i.e., to contain damages] were unwillingly bending to devote their activities to women's issues. They wrongly regarded that task as a diminution of their status in the party, not realizing that it is in fact a difficult, delicate and important task" (Ascoli 1978, 131). Women were acutely aware of how internal factional struggles restricted their breathing space in the organization and how these internal struggles had worked as a double barrier to their being given recognition and leadership responsibilities—being up for top office in the party structure, being in the party electoral lots, etc. The situation, however, never really changed from this point of view; the slight improvement between 1954–55 and the early 1960s was rapidly eroded by internal dissent over the center-left and the subsequent secession. In 1974, Maria Magnani Noya at a congress devoted to Socialist women from 1924 to 1974, pointed out how history proved that the most fruitful periods for Socialist women had always coincided with times when internal differences had fueled political debate without degeneration into personal factionalism (Provisional Proceedings: 30 November 1974, 97).

How many women, at any rate, were members of the Socialist party over the years? And how many held offices in the party and/or were elected to local assemblies and to Parliament? Reliable data are very difficult to come by, aside from the organizational archives of the Socialist party. I remark that until the early 1970s all parties were reluctant to break down their organizational statistics by gender. A good example is the survey conducted in preparation for the PSI organization conference of February 1975, which has been a source of great frustration because there are no cross-references broken down by gender exactly where you would expect to find them. But because women held their own national conference in December 1974 in preparation for the 1975 conference, I can produce a few data as a result of cross-checking. I have not been able, however, to do that for the years prior to 1969. Where the party membership is concerned, I came up with the following numbers:

1969: 109,418 women (no total membership figure is available
for that year. However the total was 633,000 for 1967)
1970: 73,042 women out of a total of 537,000 (13.8%)
1972: 88,250 women out of a total of 575,000 (15.3%)
1973: 65,446 women out of a total of 463,000 (14.1%)(there is a
discrepancy on the total figure between the report at the
women's conference (485,652) and the official publication
of the 1975 conference).

The 1975 publication traced back the membership to 1961 when the total figure was 465,000. Since the percentage of women appears fairly constant, we can conclude that women represented over the years approximately between 12% and 13% of the total membership. The most striking feature was, however, their marginalization in the party, evidenced through the following figures at the women's conference: in December

1974 out of 4,653 men in the executive committees of the party's federations, women were only 51 (1.09%). In the regional committees, women were 16/962 (1.55%); in the central committee (and corollary bodies) only 5/225 (2.2%).

This grim picture was confirmed in the comment to the 1975 Conference publication, which concluded: "(a) women's participation in party management is totally marginal: of over 3,409 cadres surveyed, women are only a hundred and constitute 3.7% of the total; (b) women have a lower average seniority than men: 71% of women have a membership seniority lower than 10 years as compared to 47% of men in the same category." There was also a discrepancy with men where the professional/work status and the level of education were concerned (*Il Partito Socialista* 1975, 322). The subject of women's participation and politicization in the Repubblica dei partiti of the postwar years clearly deserves study. I conclude with one reminder: the situation was confronted in more recent years by women of both the Communist and the Socialist parties; both fought for a quota system, which considerably changed but did not resolve the situation. The following quote is from Samuel H. Barnes's work on an Italian socialist federation (the federation was Arezzo). Having surveyed the relationship to the party of the Socialist Youth Federation, he concluded that "it functioned effectively if not spectacularly as an auxiliary of the Party" (Barnes 1967, 87). He goes on to say:

> The same could not be said of the Socialist Women's Movement. While not even on paper granted the autonomy and importance of the youth organization, the women's organization was nonexistent in the province. With thirty-nine women forming 13 percent of the sample, only two of the militants were women, while seventeen of the women were nominal members only. Except for several outstanding individuals (including one of the two women secretaries of sections in all the PSI), women played a very small role in either the activities or the concerns of the party. The woman secretary of the section referred to above was also the nominal head of the provincial women's organization. But she was opposed to treating women's movement through inactivity. (87)

This rather crude description—which is only to some and not very substantial degree peculiar to the Socialist party—brings me to the last part of this essay where I intend to deal with Socialist women's participation in and contribution to mass sexual politics in postwar Italian society. I can only deal with this subject in a very restricted fashion, and I shall limit my focus on Socialist women in the politics of the Communist UDI as the major organization of leftist Italian women from 1944 to the late 1970s. Since I shall also limit my analysis to the 1950s up to the early 1960s, I must refer those who are interested in postwar Italian women to the few but significant works that exist.

I divide these years as follows: from the immediate aftermath of the war to 1953–54 and from then to 1959. I shall stop here at the threshold of a third period, 1963–64, when the center-left coalition took off. In the first period the PSI focused on training internal unity after the 1947 secession. It emphasized unity of action, considered necessary to carry on mass opposition to the DC-led government from which the Left had been ousted. Elena Caporaso was appointed head of the women's bureau by the PSI Congress following the 1947 secession. In October of that same year at the second UDI congress, the Communist M. Maddalena Rossi was elected president and the Socialist Rosetta Longo secretary general. The UDI executive committee included Socialist women who would be elected to Parliament or significant party offices: Giuliana Nenni, Elena Caporaso, Tullia Carrettoni, Marisa Passigli, and Anna Matera. When in January 1948 the executive committee of UDI met to decide UDI participation in the Popular Front, the only dissenting opinion came from the representative of the lay and Action party forces, Maria Calogero (who subsequently withdrew from the organization). In June 1948 Rosetta Longo read at the national meeting a report acknowledging the burning defeat suffered as part of the "women's alliance" of the Front and presented the agenda of the organization in the new cold war scenario. Among Socialist women the debate and the reshuffling of internal offices followed the curves defined by factional struggles that now once again flared up. When the leftists, which included Nenni, Morandi, Pertini, and Basso, gained the majority and the unity of action pact with the PCI was confirmed, Elena Caporaso was renamed head of the women's bureau, which she had left following the Front defeat. The majority of young leaders, women and men alike, were followers of Morandi, who exercised a particular fascination on young militants. Morandi invested considerable energies in the creation of a group of women leaders in the party, stressing the importance for Socialist and Communist women to collaborate. Morandi called for maximum involvement of Socialist women in UDI so that the association could respond to the widely diversified needs of women in society and mobilize them in social struggles. This line brought about the dispersal of UDI's efforts and did not allow it to concentrate on women's issues.

Between 1950 and 1951 many Socialists and Communists in UDI understood that the course was proving disastrous. The association was losing any specific profile, having given up in its mobilization and its appeal to women its own specific reason for existence. Still, well into 1952 the activities of Socialist and Communist women and of UDI appeared to develop along the same lines. The mobilizing efforts were spent in solidarity with factory women (and men) fighting against industrial restructuring and in the peace campaigns. A fresh and more significant issue was the campaign to force mayors to enlist women as jurors, which the mayors refused to do, in violation of article 51 of the Constitution.

A political debate gradually opened up among Socialists and Communists in UDI. Among Communist women, the undisputed leader since 1947 had been M. Maddalena Rossi, under whose leadership the association's policy had closely followed the lead of the Federation democratique des femmes dominated by Moscow. To confront M. Maddalena Rossi was now another Communist, Nilde Jotti, who in her speech at the 1953 UDI congress skillfully reintroduced elements for a radical change in policy of the UDI targeting the implementation of women's rights as outlined in the Constitution. The newly formed secretariat included two key figures who signaled the surfacing of an internal opposition: the Communist Nilde Jotti and the Socialist Giuliana Nenni. Meanwhile a significant evolution also took place in the political scenario. When the attempted passage by the government coalition of the "swindle law" offered the two leftist parties the opportunity of escaping political isolation, Pietro Nenni grabbed the moment. At the same time the *détente* following Stalin's death and the end of the Korean conflict removed the most compelling reasons justifying socialist "unity of action" with the Communists.

The elections of June 1953 were a success for the Left and specifically for the Socialists. Elena Caporaso, Anna Matera, Maria Vittoria Mezza, and Giuliana Nenni were elected to Parliament: a brilliant group committed to following a new course in mass politics concerning women. Angela Merlin was elected to the Senate. She introduced into Parliament two significant proposals: one intended to make it illegal to fire women when they married, and another for the abolition of the law regulating prostitution. Between 1954 and 1956 women in the two parties who maintained that women's emancipatory struggle was a specific component of the struggle to build a socialist society progressively gained ground. But women in the Socialist party came out in the open first. Pietro Nenni encouraged Socialist women to launch UDI onto the new course. In 1954 at the National Conference of Socialist Women, Elena Caporaso defined emancipation as an issue common to all women, cutting across class lines, and therefore of interest to all political parties. The words are Togliatti's in 1944, but neither the Communist party nor the Left had paid but lip service to them. Now Pietro Nenni reminded Socialists that "the party is not all, it is only the means, the testing ground is outside the party, in the mass organization. . . . The women in our country have created a great and original mass organization which is the Union of Italian Women" (Alloisio and Ajò 1978, 99–100).

Following the Congress of Turin in the spring of 1955 and Morandi's death in the summer of that year, Nenni's leadership grew stronger. Also the organizational structure of the party was now more solidly in Nenni's hands. This reflected on the women's bureau: Anna Matera replaced Elena Caporaso. Matera had led Socialist women's groups in the south since 1944; she had been active in the teachers' association and recently elected to Parliament in one of the Apulia districts. As head of the women's bureau she also became a member of the executive committee of the party. Having no less energy than her predecessor and acting in a climate conducive to bringing into the open those disagreements with the PCI that had been for so long dealt with away from the public eye, Matera led Socialist women throughout the years when the Socialist party displayed considerable political dynamism. The PSI was indeed in those years at the center of Italian political life. It progressively became the focus of the hopes of reformists on the Left who had been frustrated by the nature of the political and social reconstruction that had taken place since 1945 as well as by the lack of a viable opposition to Christian Democracy. For a while it looked as if the PSI could fill these hopes. The turning point required was, in the eyes of many, that the PSI should progressively pull away from the PCI by developing its own strategic and policy choices. The opportunity was offered by the events of 1956 and especially by the Hungarian crisis.

Where Socialist women were concerned, the new dynamic course had developed with some anticipation with respect to these events. Following the Turin congress an effort was made to address those issues that at the time were identified as "mentalità e costume," which today we would call gender relations and sexual politics. A weekly page was dedicated to women in *L'Avanti*. It included a tongue-in-cheek column entitled "Detto tra noi" (Between us)(Alloisio and Ajò 1978, 105). Thus, by tackling issues more directly related to gender, Socialist women were also filling a void.

Since 1945, UDI had not taken up issues that would call for an open denunciation of the existence of a gender conflict in society. The Charter of Italian Women, as the agenda approved at the 1953 UDI conference was called, included issues concerning economic and civil equality, reform of family laws, and equal rights for children born out of wedlock. But the association encountered political difficulties in developing a strategy based on its agenda, because of men and women who considered the organization justified only if collateral to the traditional battles of the Left. This discourse was hosted especially (though not exclusively) in that part of the Communist camp which resisted "destalinization." Thus the Socialist women's critical attitude toward UDI, which developed especially from mid-1956, spurred debate inside the organization and ultimately lent support also to that part of the Communist UDI leadership that had favored change since 1952–53. A first significant sign of change was the replacement of Maria Maddalena Rossi with Marisa Rodano (close to Nilde Jotti) as president of UDI at the fifth congress of the organization in April 1956. A second crucible was the radical criticism that the executive committee of UDI expressed in a meeting in June 1956 with respect to the policy followed by the organization in the preceding decade. The meeting came only a week after the full disclosure by Togliatti of the Khruschev report. At the meeting Giuliana Nenni and Elena Caporaso were especially outspoken. They pointed out how the emancipation agenda, which had been put together by UDI at its first congress of 1945, had later been abandoned, so that the association had been engaged in "transposing in feminine terms the agenda of the left" (Michetti et al. 1984, 181–82). They also branded as a mistake UDI's failure to take a stance in favor of birth control and divorce and to have given lukewarm support to Merlin's proposal on prostitution.

Where UDI is concerned, 1956 was a point of no return. The critical process that took off then brought (1) a drastic realignment of the leadership at the 1959 congress; and (2) a pattern of internal political debate and at times confrontation between the Socialist and the Communist components. Starting in 1959 the UDI leadership widened very significantly, including once again well-known female figures of Italian intellectual and professional life, many of them women belonging to no party who contributed their expertise to the battles for equality fought from 1958 to 1963.

Other indicators illustrated this shift. Socialist women worked for the introduction of legislation on divorce, nullification of articles that considered birth control and the dissemination of birth control information a criminal offense, the rights of children born out of wedlock, the abolition of the so-called "delitto d'onore," and for a reform of family law based on equality between the spouses. Most of these issues (not divorce) had moved back into the UDI agenda, but the organization was still not aggressively and actively campaigning on them. Whether the reason was not to jeopardize an initial dialogue that was reopening after the cold war with Catholic women, or the opposition coming from many areas of the organization itself, the fact remains that those demands did not then reach the top of UDI's agenda. On the other hand, Socialist women focused on these issues in party congresses, meetings, and in the press wherever possible. Some of the issues were also included in the electoral platform starting in 1958. Following the congress in Naples in 1959, Tullia Carrettoni, appointed head of Socialist women, methodically and passionately made these issues a priority for which Socialist women held accountable first of all the men in their own party.

Another interesting development is the one concerning the dispute in which Socialist women engaged in regarding the role of the emancipatory struggle in party strategy. One of the first notes in this direction was struck by Anna Matera at the Venice congress in 1957 when she rebuffed the conception that the solution of women's issues was to be expected from the "structural reforms" that then encompassed the strategic line of the "opening to the left." As Matera pointed out, no change was to be expected unless the energies of half of society were mobilized to secure it. This concept emerged as the basic motive of all conceptualizations that leftist women presented to leftist men. Socialist women deserve the credit for having initiated a confrontation in open terms with a frankness then unmatched on the Left.

Finally, Socialist women reconstructed their own past. Significant among many other examples is a booklet published in 1956 to commemorate the tenth anniversary of the first vote cast by Italian women. It contained references to women in the Italian Risorgimento and illustrated the emancipationist tradition in Italy, focusing especially on Anna Kuliscioff. Significantly in 1961, when the PCI had weathered an internal crisis and was on the move again with regard to women, *Rinascita* published a monographic issue on women on the occasion of the one-hundredth anniversary of Italian unification. The main article by Nilde Jotti was entitled "Da Turati all'elaborazione del PCI." The article suggested that the Italian Communist party had somehow inherited the emancipatory tradition of Italian Socialism, thus ensuring the development of its potential.

To conclude, I believe that Socialist women deserve full credit for having played a significant role during, according to some observers, "one of the best seasons of socialist culture in Italy" (Galli 1980, 223). These years were also some of the best for UDI and for women's politics. By 1963 the organization could claim an impressive record of results: equal pay, laws forbidding firing of women because of marriage, and abolition of all discrimination in public office and on the job, while also suggesting significant proposals for legislation regarding men.

In the wake of this successful mobilization, UDI's seventh congress, held in 1964, also moved to conceptualize the "woman question" in the context of Italian economic and social changes. It marked the understanding that a new phase had begun and it called for realization that women represented an anthropological and cultural crucible; society had to plan for their inclusion and for the potential they represented. The awareness that change was taking place demonstrated the cultural maturity of several thousand women and counterbalanced that "numbness" and "obviousness" that I mentioned earlier and that surrounded Italian women's official entry into full citizenship in 1945.

The 1964 congress was however held during a low point for the left. The UDI had felt the strains in the relationship between Socialist and Communists, and this time the factional divisions split the PSI and gave rise to the PSIUP and hit close to the heart of UDI's Socialist component. The debate during the 1964 assembly was polarized around two issues that turned into political symbolism. One was the ratification of UDI's withdrawal from membership status in the FDIF (Federation Democratique Internationale des Femmes, i.e., the International Democratic Federation of Women) the second was a resolution binding the association to back a proposal introducing divorce. On the first issue, the national leadership, Socialist and Communist, was almost unanimous: a consequence of the June 1963 Moscow FDIF conference, when the UDI delegation had abandoned the conference hall to protest against the undemocratic procedures followed by Soviet women running the meeting. There was no agreement on divorce, and a compromise was reached by launching a referendum among women on the reforming of family laws, including divorce. In the following year the political malaise affecting UDI following the entry by the PSI into the government coalition resulted in a decision by Socialist women to leave the membership up to individual choice. This meant that the Socialist party no longer supported the association.

In the following years, Socialist women tried to influence society through cultural activities promoted either through the Anna Kuliscioff

Center (founded in 1964) or through their own party organization. A main focus of activity was the reform of family laws, on which seminars and conferences were organized and bills introduced. Efforts were also made to include women's issues in the much-discussed economic planning, a proposal that did not get off the ground. Communist women also focused on these issues, but set their priorities on economics. On the whole, those years marked the withdrawal of both Socialist and Communist women into the compound of their parties' politics. In this competitive climate, UDI struggled to achieve a mediating role, but this policy seriously curbed its capacity to send out its message to women in general. Indeed the women's movement on the whole was weakened by the developments producing the center-left coalition. An opportunity was lost when intelligent, committed women, more aware than were men of changes taking place in society, failed to be on top of party politics and thus failed to capitalize on that initial realization of the autonomous character of the gender issue, which had been slowly and painfully accruing during the previous decade.

References

Alloisio, M., and M. Ajò. 1978. *La donna nel socialismo.* Cosenza: Lerici Editore.

Anna Kuliscioff e l'età del riformismo. 1978. Atti del Convegno, Milan, December 1976. Mondo Operaio, Edizioni Avanti.

Ascoli, G. 1978. *L'Udi tra emancipazione e liberazione (1943–1964): La questione femminile in Italia dal '900 a oggi.* Milan: Franco Angeli Editore.

Barnes, Samuel H. 1967. *Party Democracy: Politics in an Italian Socialist Federation.* New Haven: Yale University Press.

Gaiotti, P. 1993. "The Impact of Women's Political and Social Activity in Postwar Italy." In *The Formation of the Italian Republic,* edited by F. Coppa and M. Repetto-Alaia. New York: Peter Lang.

Galli, Giorgio. 1980. *Storia del Socialismo Italiano.* Bari: Laterza.

"Il Partito Socialista." 1975. *Socialismo oggi* 3.

Michetti, M., M. Repetto, and L. Viviani. 1984. *Laboratorio di politica delle donne.* Rome: Cooperativa Libera Stampa.

Pieroni Bortolotti, F. 1974. *Socialismo e questione femminile, 1892–1922.* Milan: Mazzotta Editore.

———. 1987. *Sul movimento politico delle donne: Scritti inediti.* Edited by A. Buttafuoco. Coop Utopia.

Ruffilli, R. 1979. *Cultura politica e partiti nell'età della Costituente.* Bologna: Il Mulino.

Valiani, L. 1980. "Il movimento operaio socialista." In *L'Italia unita nella storiografia del secondo dopoguerra,* edited by N. Tranfaglia. Milan: Feltrinelli.

14

SOCIALIST CONSTRAINTS FOLLOWING THE WAR

Simona Colarizi

The reconversion of the mass bases of Fascism into new democratic channels was the main problem facing the antifascists after 25 July 1943, when the whole edifice of Fascist dictatorship fell with the king's coup d'état and the removal of Mussolini. In the scenario of the pre-Fascist epoch, the political powers capable of ushering the masses into the new democratic state—still totally to be reconstructed—were the Socialists and the Catholics. Already structured as modern parties for mass integration in the liberal political system, they each had deep roots as the two main subcultures in Italy. Before Fascism stormed onto the scene, they each had a nationwide organization and could rely on a series of parallel centers of aggregation, especially the trade unions. One of the most glaring anomalies of the Italian state was the absence of a modern, middle-class party. The Liberal party, locked in a nineteenth-century model of individual representation, was the expression of the ruling class and elites in power. It did not constitute a suitable channel for the upwardly mobile middle classes, who felt such a lack of representation compared not only to the upper bourgeoisie, but also to the working class and the rural world, all with their own political referents, that they rushed to support Mussolini's newly created movement.

The dictatorial vocation of Fascism put a violent end to this first cycle of politicalization of the Italian masses. Once the previous political system was destroyed and all the parties outlawed, the Fascist regime regimented the entire population into its organizational structures, legitimizing the

Fascist party as the only center of political—to a large extent forced —aggregation. Behind the facade of a permanent political mobilization, Fascism gradually managed to shatter the network of civil society. When the regime fell, the Italians, their bonds of spontaneous collective solidarity broken and deprived of any civil and political responsibility, had to find their identity as citizens again. And this time the recovery of political rights, denied for twenty years, also involved the world of women, always excluded from political life. It is symptomatic of the historical turning point marked by the Resistance that not one voice was raised among the antifascist forces against this step, too long postponed. The democracy that the antifascists were founding had to make a clean break with the Fascist and pre-Fascist past. Above all it had to be a democracy of the masses, a full expression, finally, of the will of the entire population—male and female—that symbolically and radically renewed the social contract in 1945. The first proof of the democratic maturity of the new antifascist political class, paid for by twenty years of dictatorship, a harsh civil war and national liberation, was this recognition of a right once only claimed by the leftist minority, now also acknowledged by the more moderate elements. But the apparent facility with which women were being granted their political rights pushed to the background the problems that centuries of inequality had produced. The parties were not pursuing the main goal of gaining women's votes and there were no specific themes involving the world of women. Women were not considered by the parties as equal entities with distinct needs; they were only paid attention as minority citizens; that is, on a lower ranking than men in the politicalization process.

The only reference parameter for the political recruitment of women was the fact of their belonging to a specific sector of society, classified on the basis of economic criteria. What was relevant was their place in the family, in a preordained socioeconomic sphere or, at the most, for the minority of women inserted in the labor world, their status as "workers." The only, so to speak, suprastructural element considered with any greater attention was religious faith, more widespread among women precisely because of their ignorance and their educational "inferiority." This was a general attitude in the political world of the time in both the moderate and progressive parties. Even if the Left appeared more sensitive than the Right to women's issues, in my opinion these were preoccupations (with certain exceptions) of an entirely political character. The competition of the Catholic party—which mainly relied on the church to find supporters in Italy—in the matter of women's votes was feared. Even in proletarian families—Socialist supporters or militants—the priest's authority often prevailed over that of the father, husband, or brother, who it was taken for granted imposed the choice of vote on their women.

On the other hand, the structural element in such a rigidly class-bound Italian society as that of 1945 is the key for reading the entire process of reaggregation of the masses in the parties after Fascism. In this process of civil and political reform the antifascist parties were all committed to seeking the traditional mass bases and new votes that could give them the necessary weight to ensure the leadership of the constituent Italian political system. The Catholics were heirs of the old pre-Fascist Italian people's party with their interclass nature and their moderate programs. They were proposing themselves as a political reference pole for the middle and lower rural and urban classes, although also aiming at the capitalist bourgeoisie and those middle classes deprived of their own party after the fall of Fascism. The Socialist party, on the other hand, aimed at the workers and peasants, at the progressive urban classes, pushed to the fore by the growth of capitalism in the big industrial cities of northern Italy—the sectors of society that have always represented the breeding ground for socialism. However, the PSI had the fierce competition of the Communist party which, born in 1921 as a revolutionary avant-guard party, was now changing into a party of mass integration, challenging the Socialists in those same areas where the Socialist subculture had spread.

The Communist challenge, which soon made the Socialists lose their hegemony over the Left, heavily conditioned the PSI's mass politics. In my opinion, this conditioning was behind the lack of evolution of the Italian Socialist party into a modern, reformist, and Western social democracy, similar to those present in France and Germany in this postwar period. With respect to its European brothers, Italian Socialism—maximalist, pro-Communist, anti-Europeanist and anti-Western, at least up to the middle of the 1950s—reflected the particularity of the Italian Communist party. This party was the only one in Western Europe to keep, and in fact gradually to increase, its supporters until it became the second political power of the system in the 1970s, almost equal in size to the Christian Democrats. In brief, the majority of the working masses and progressive forces that in the other democratic states turned to Socialism, in Italy had instead Communism as their referent, with the result of placing power in the hands of the Catholic party for fifty years without the possibility of an effective change. When the DC brought the Socialist party into the government in 1963, the PSI was a "minor" party with an electoral weight of less than 14% compared with the PCI, remaining in the opposition, which had about 25% of the country's votes. This proportion was destined to change later to the disadvantage of the Socialists, reduced to 9% in 1976, while the Communists had almost 35%.

There were many factors that helped, together with the problem of the Communists, to make the PSI miss the chance of becoming a modern, social democratic party in 1945, capable of guiding the ascent of the working masses and satisfying the aspirations of the progressive forces within a Western, democratic state, inserted in the American sphere of influence. Before examining them it is, however, necessary to establish if the PSI had the possibility of proposing itself for this hypothetical role with any credibility.

It has been said that in pre-Fascist times the PSI was deeply rooted in the country among the proletarian masses and a minority of progressive urban middle classes, attracted by the ideals of a socialism extremely variegated in its theoretical and practical points of reference. Marxism could not be said to be prevalent, not even at the time the party was established in 1892, albeit the leadership called itself Marxist after having broken away from the dominant anarchical element. Historians have stressed the pluralist nature of the Socialist mentality as it spread among the Italian masses where, as in a great melting-pot, Marxist, anarchical, humanitarian, egalitarian, and solidarity ideals fermented, experienced on a popular level almost more as a religion than an ideology. And these idealistic connotations explained the absence of a model of a rigid and centralist party. Although the PSI was inspired in its party organization by the German Social Democratic party, the Italian party was deeply divided at the top between reformist, maximalist, revolutionary, and anarchist-syndicalist union trends. These differentiations spread into the collateral bodies, trade unions, leagues, and cooperatives, almost as if reflecting the nonhomogeneous nature of the working classes, the mirror of an Italian economic development that was anything but harmonious.

The limits of such a marked pluralism were compensated by Socialism's capacity of penetration, bending and adapting to the different social situations, recruiting an ever-increasing number of votes, giving it a significant presence in Parliament and nationwide before the advent of Fascism. Moreover, the constant presence of two "strong" minds—reformism and maximalism—alternating in the party leadership, oriented Socialist strategy not only toward satisfying the requests of the proletariat (still in semifeudal living and labor conditions) and the working and peasant classes, already inserted in the capitalist productive process, but also toward those of a democratic-progressive urban middle class. The Bolshevik revolution of 1917 and the creation of the Italian Communist party had begun to upset this fertile equilibrium, provoking serious divisions within the PSI.

The unity the party leadership regained during its twenty years of exile rested on a delicate compromise between ideological issues and tactical choices: the PSI called itself democratic, but as a class representative it chose the Communist party as its main ally in the antifascist battle. The fragility of this Right-Left balance was still a point of strength for the PSI during this phase, and it was to remain so as long as the Socialists were able to keep their pivotal position in the line-up of antifascist parties reunited in the National Liberation Committees, which included all the oppositions: liberal, democratic, Catholic, and Marxist. A reflection of the international alliance between the Western democratic powers and the Soviet Union in the war against Hitler, the great antifascist coalition in Italy remained after the conflict when the pressing problems of giving the country a democratic-constitutional basis and of signing the peace treaty meant that the parties were forced to unite. Thus, in 1945, the PSI could again play a political role, asking for support both in the name of a socialist-reformist democracy and that of a revolutionary socialism based on class. In theory it had all the potential for collecting a large amount of moderate and revolutionary votes, while still undecided about its final strategic choice.

The determinant factor for this choice, however, soon appeared, when the cold war began in 1947, putting an end in Italy to the united government coalitions of Catholics and the Left, and forcing each political power to line up on the international scene. The East-West alternative, in its character of contest without possible mediation between two systems with contrasting values, put the PSI—in its pivotal role between the moderate Right represented by the DC and the revolutionary Left led by the PCI —in a difficult situation. The drama of Italian Socialism came to a head in the Rome congress of 1947, when the schism of Palazzo Barberini split the Socialist party into two branches, reformist and class-based. Much has been written on that rupture, considered by all to constitute a crucial moment for Italian Socialism. To summarize the terms of the conflict with reference to the mass politics, I shall briefly illustrate the points of view of the two great leaders, Saragat and Nenni. It was they who had taken over the party and had reunified it in the years of exile, as heirs of reformism and maximalism respectively.

The defeat of Fascism convinced Saragat of the need to bring the working class out of its isolation. Alone, the proletariat was not able to set itself up as a feasible alternative to the capitalist bourgeoisie in power unless it chose the way of Bolshevik revolution passing through proletarian dictatorship. This path being excluded, to found a Socialist democracy the proletariat had to ally itself with the democratic and progressive middle classes who were also hostile to privileges and inequalities and personally interested in a social and economic renewal of the system. Only this great bloc could stop other authoritarian turning points in the country and continue the antifascist revolution begun with the Resistance. Nenni partly shared Saragat's ideas, albeit his class concept of politics led him to concentrate on the problem of which of the two members of the alliance was destined to exercise political hegemony. And the response, naturally, was that the proletariat was the fulcrum of the coalition.

At first, the strength and capacity of the working class to propose itself as leader of the democratic revolution, bringing with it the more advanced sectors of the middle classes, was based on the unity of the proletariat, which had already been upset in 1921 with the appearance of the Communist party on the political scene with all its tragic consequences. In 1945 the workers' front had to be shored up to prevent any possible return to Fascism. The fracture that Communism had made in the Socialist movement was thus mended, and because it was not possible to have a systematic class reunification it was all the more indispensable to keep the bond strong between the PSI and the PCI, sanctioned by the unity of action pact. Unlike the other leftist representatives in the openly fusionist party, Nenni did not believe it was possible to overcome the schism of Leghorn of 1921. Despite Togliatti's new democratic strategy, the ideological gap between the two parties now seemed impossible to bridge, and the double track of Communist policy—progressive democracy and revolution— aroused not a few doubts about the PCI's effective renewal. There was thus all the more reason to keep the dialogue open, to make the PSI the guarantor of the democratic development of the class movement, against any extremist-revolutionary temptation.

This approach, even though not shared by Saragat, did not encounter any open opposition from the right of the PSI as long as the three-party (DC, PSI, PCI) government lasted. The central position that the Socialist party held in the government coalition offered it all the advantages of the role of mediator between Right and Left, while at the same time the unity of action pact ensured the preeminence of the forces of Socialist inspiration which, taken together, were greater than the electoral weight of the Catholic party. When, however, the process of polarization began in the Italian political system, the Communist issue exploded with devastating effects. Saragat explicitly asked that the special agreement with the PCI be broken, as it risked dragging the Socialist party into an opposition considered to be "unfair" and basically lacking the legitimacy to govern the nation. Only by finding a complete autonomy from the Communists could the Socialists protect their democratic legitimation and stop a dangerous bipolar balance being consolidated, destined to split the political system and the nation into two opposing line-ups of Communists and anti-Communists.

Nenni was not prepared to accept Saragat's ultimatum. The PCI did not only represent a small fringe of the politicized proletariat, it had become a great mass party, equal in electoral weight to the PSI itself, but stronger in the trade unions and in its organizational structures. The constraints of collective solidarity were so strong in the labor world that they went beyond party logic. There was the risk that a PSI-PCI rupture would not be understood, with the probable result of losing votes for the Socialist party when the proletariat turned toward the Communist party, regarding it as a bulwark against their interests being sold or betrayed by those (the Socialists) who wanted to link the destiny of the working class with that of the bourgeoisie. The class-based structure of Italian society, and especially twenty years of Fascism, certainly did not help to lessen the hostility of the proletarian masses who saw the middle classes as a servile appendix to the capitalist upper bourgeoisie.

The fear of Communism, spreading throughout the nation with the growth of international tension, immediately affected the white-collar elements, with the result of aggravating the old resentments of the blue-collar workers. In this climate, a Socialist policy for balancing the two sides became much more difficult. But faced with an ultimatum, Nenni decided to sacrifice the policy of alliance with the middle classes to preserve the class base of the Socialist party. The spreading anti-Communism vexed the Socialist majority, deeply influenced by the myth of the Bolshevik revolution and dazzled by the Soviet power that had stopped the advance of Nazism. Even those—like Nenni himself—who had already in the past expressed strong reservations about Stalin's dictatorship, were still attracted by the USSR. The fear of the spread of extremism among the masses who were becoming exasperated by the postwar difficulties was another important consideration that prompted Nenni to defend, even at the cost of an internal schism, the cooperation policy with the PCI. The memory of the two Red years and, above all, the ghost of Weimar were both essential for understanding Nenni's choice. A Socialist party that turned its back on the PCI could find itself in the same condition as German Social Democracy; that is, forced to repress the offensive of the extreme Left with bloodshed, as occurred in Germany with the Spartacist movements of 1920—and everyone remembered how the Weimar republic had ended. It was thus necessary for the Socialist party, precisely because it was democratic, to keep the Communist party bound to it, forcing it to be loyal to democracy. In this way it guaranteed the insertion of the masses in the life of the state on the basis of nonrevolutionary objectives.

Saragat did not agree: the PSI's renouncing its role as a pole of aggregation for the middle classes as well meant throwing the class back to the opposition and isolating it from the rest of the nation, with the sole result of encouraging the maximalist-revolutionary currents (as in fact had occurred in 1921). Saragat certainly perceived the scale of the worldwide Communist-anti-Communist rupture with greater lucidity than Nenni, who seemed to be unaware of the consequences of the international and domestic polarization. Most probably the choice of the alliance with the PCI ensured the PSI a large part of its traditional class votes, but it certainly deprived it of the support of the progressive lower and middle bourgeoisie ranks and even that of the reformist workers, all hostile to the Communist ideology and the dictatorial system of the Soviet bloc. In these sectors, twenty years of fighting Fascism and the experience of the Resistance had developed the values of democracy, which now seemed threatened by another terrible conflict.

The political tension arising in the nation, in the increasingly fermented climate of the cold war, did not allow the PSI to remain in an intermediate position. With the rupture of the anti-Nazi USA-USSR alliance (which in Italy meant the end of the governments of national solidarity) the PCI, systematically bound to the Soviet Union, lost its legitimation to govern the nation. In the new balances that were being prepared, the Italian Socialists—like their European brothers—still had the possibility of representing the forces of a democratic and progressive Left, loyal to democracy, able to aspire to the leadership of a democratic state inserted in the Western bloc. This is what the middle classes and reformist and progressive working sectors were demanding, worried as they were by the Soviet threat and fearing to lose the support of the United States, the guarantee of freedom and economic prosperity.

But Nenni and Saragat did not manage to come to an agreement. The Socialist party split in 1947 into two branches that never again managed to reunite. History was to prove Saragat right. Nenni's choice of forming a political front with the PCI, for the unity of the proletariat, opened the way to Communist hegemony. This led to a progressive reshaping of the PSI and the loss of its identity; above all, it meant that it was to be a long time before a reformist policy was able to be implemented. As Nenni predicted, the majority of the PSI's working base turned its back on Saragat, leader of a party that gradually lost its role as representative of the working class and took on the character of a party of the middle classes. Thus reorganized, the PSDI tried to compensate for its loss of power with a governing role negotiated with the DC from a subordinate position, which prevented it from carrying ahead an incisive reformist policy. On the other hand, however, the mass base that Nenni's PSI had kept was locked in the Communist policy of prejudicial opposition to the system; it could not be "spent" in a reformist action of the government—to which the PCI did not have access and which was also strictly forbidden to the PSI as long as it remained linked by the unity of action pact with the Communists and hostile to the international alliance of the Italian state.

What then would have happened if Nenni had supported Saragat's request to break the unity of action pact between Socialists and Communists and to line up the Italian Socialist party with the European and Western social democracies? The PCI's strong competition in recruiting the proletarian masses would have certainly brought about a great loss of class votes, as Nenni feared. However, the heart of the question lay in the extent of impoverishment predicted: in the case of a vertical collapse, the Socialist party would have found itself in the same circumstances as the PSDI, that is, deprived of the effective representation of the labor world. If the collapse was to be less serious, the PSI would be able to become an important pole of reference in the democratization of the Italian masses. This inevitable process occurred very slowly and went step by step with the process of social-democratization of the PCI, developing from the end of the 1950s with infinite rethinking and difficult wrenches in its international links. Presumably, the presence from 1948 of a strong Social Democratic party in the Italian political system would have at least hastened the maturation of a democratic and reformist awareness. When the PSI stopped its tendency toward forming a political front and began a dialogue with the DC for the center-left governments, it was too late to wrench the PCI's strong grip from the masses. At the same time, the Italian Communists—with a much greater farsightedness than their European brothers (and especially the PCF)—also started to invest in the future, aware of the inevitable fading of the revolutionary myths that had been a great binder for the masses in the ranks of their party. It was a different PCI, in a different international climate, that became the PSI's competitor in the 1960s, and once again in the duel of the Left it would have the winning hand.

15

SOCIALISTS AND COMMUNISTS

Luciano Pellicani

After the Second World War, throughout Western Europe the Socialist parties, which had already distanced themselves from their original revolutionary inspiration and, more or less explicitly, adopted a reformist philosophy and a Fabianist strategy, became poles of aggregation for all progressive political forces. The fact that they also gained experience of government in this period was to have a profound impact on the very specific configuration of representative democracy in Western Europe. Indeed, it was precisely due to this government experience of the Socialist parties that the external limit of the liberal state was further extended and the welfare state institutionalized: rights of citizenship (civil, political, and social) became universal and "outsiders" were integrated into the structure of modern industrial society. In short, the parties making up the Socialist International brought the laissez-faire era to an end by institutionalizing the so-called social democratic compromise between the state and the market.

But there was one exception. The Italian Socialist party (PSI) continued to be a minor left-wing party, with too few votes to take over the leadership of the progressive pole and transform it into a "historic bloc" strong enough to challenge the conservative pole. That this should have occurred in Italy is in itself remarkable since the Italian Left had always been strong both politically and culturally. However, this was under the hegemony of the Italian Communist Party (PCI), with respect to which the Socialists were in a position of permanent inferiority.

Clearly an analysis of the relations between Socialists and Communists is important for understanding why the Italian republic developed its own sui generis political system; indeed, why it is the only Western democracy that has still not experienced a government of the Left. The answer of course lies precisely in that hegemony of the Italian Communist party, that is to say the hegemony of a Marxist-Leninist party, that proudly proclaimed its "iron ties" with the Soviet Union and its belief in planned dictatorship as a superior form of social organization. Obviously the PCI aimed not so much at a change of government as at the introduction of a completely new system. This explains why Italian democracy was regulated by a so-called *conventio ad excludendum*, a pact between the Western-oriented parties to keep the PCI, an antisystem organization, out of government and away from power, lest it move Italy out of the Western sphere.

Thus for forty years Italian democracy was an anomaly, the typical expression of a particular political system referred to by Giovanni Sartori as (ideologically) polarized pluralism. The Italian Socialist party ended by being caught up in this system as if in a grip: it could either complement the Communist strategy or cooperate with the moderate bloc. Both alternatives were unappealing and forced the Socialists into a role in complete contrast with what they represented or aspired to represent.

The PSI came to be an anomaly within the anomaly. Not only was the PCI the strongest Western Communist party, in terms of strategy and political culture it was also the most open, the most ductile, and the closest to European social democracy. Admittedly the PCI had always proudly proclaimed its "diversity" and the fact that it could not be likened to any other party because of its internal organization (democratic centralism) and long-term goals (end of capitalism, formation of a "new type" of democracy, etc). But, at the same time, it presented itself as an energetic "people's tribune", whose ideal was to enhance democracy rather than eliminate it. Under Palmiro Togliatti, the typical ingredients of the revolutionary and reformist traditions were very cleverly mixed—so much so that in 1976, Alberto Asor Rosa proclaimed that his party could legitimately claim to be the heir of Lenin and Turati. Franco Rodano developed a subtle interpretation of Gramsci's *Quaderni del carcere*, in which Gramsci is considered to have invented a new form of communism combining the best of Western democratic tradition with the vital core of Bolshevism and the permanent values of Christianity. Thus, according to Rodano's theory of Gramscism, Italian Communism had every right to present itself as a more advanced synthesis and valid model for Italy and indeed the whole of Europe.

As we now witness the planetary ruin of Communism it is obvious that the synthesis, theorized by Togliatti and further developed by his epigones, was merely a cultural hybridization incapable of producing anything of worth. Communism cannot be commingled with other ingredients. It exists only insofar as it destroys its traditional enemies: liberalism, democracy, reformism, the market, religion, etc. Yet, during the ideological hegemony of the PCI, many believed that "Gramsci and Togliatti's party" had invented something truly original and progressive. Even the Socialists were intimidated, plagiarized almost, by the messages sent forth to Italian society by the PCI's "permanent persuaders" and activists.

There is another reason why the PSI was an anomaly within an anomaly destined to defeat and frustration. Even a very cursory glance at the history of Italian Socialism shows that it has always been dominated by an ideological dualism, that left no room for mediation or compromise: on the one hand, the "pathos" of rejecting the present for "a different society"; on the other, the tendency to come to terms with capitalism: its revolutionary soul and reformist soul were forced to coexist in a state of permanent conflict.

Even in 1921, when the revolutionaries decided to constitute the Italian division of the Communist International, in the wake of the slogan "Do as in Russia," the PSI did not overcome its moral quandary. Only one year later the Italian workers' movement split into three separate parties, just when the Fascists were starting to threaten liberal democracy. In the end the proletarian revolution aspired to by the Communists and the maximalists never did take place and the counterrevolution prevailed.

The two components of Italian Socialism—the maximalists and the reformists—joined forces to combat Fascism and a pact of united action was signed between the Socialists and the Communists. But as soon as the war ended, the ideological dualism came to the surface once more and relations with the Communists deteriorated. According to Giuseppe Saragat, Communism was foreign to Socialist tradition and a threat to the newly restored freedom; Pietro Nenni believed in the reunification of the European workers' movement in the illusion of building a bridge between the Left of the West and of the East.

These different, unreconcilable interpretations of the nature of Communism eventually led to the split of Palazzo Barberini, which had such catastrophic consequences. Some refer to this split as absolutely suicidal. Two completely different parties were formed: the PSI and the PSDI (the Italian Social Democratic party)—fiercely hostile to each other and both incapable of an autonomous political role. The PSDI soon became a minor component of the moderate bloc and never even developed a truly social democratic political culture. The PSI was never successful in performing that highly ambitious function that Nenni had dreamed of. In fact its ideology was no different from the Leninist version of Marxism and the leaders of the party felt duty-bound to sing the praises of the "fatherland of socialism" and Stalin, with the same rites as the Communists. In short, when it came to choosing between social democracy and Communism, the Socialists chose the latter, convinced that by siding with the Soviet Union they would be on the right side, and on the side of history as well.

Up until the end of 1956, the PSI therefore was little more than a complementary force of the European Communist movement. Of course this was suicidal because, if Communism had ever achieved its strategic objectives, the PSI would have been among the first to disappear. Yet, with very few exceptions, PSI leaders seemed convinced that they had made the right choice in deciding to sacrifice all initiative and be part of a strategy over which they had no control.

Nor did the revelations of Stalin's crimes in the famous secret report read by Khruschev at the Twentieth Congress of the CPSU (Communist party of the Soviet Union) shake their convictions. It was only after the brutal squashing of the Hungarian uprising and the invasion by the tanks of the Red army, that the principles accepted hitherto as a sort of religious dogma—a united workers' movement and, given the power relations that existed on the left, the PSI's subordination to the PCI—were finally questioned. And even after Hungary, a group within the party continued to side for the Soviet bloc. The Italian Socialist party of Proletarian Unity (PSIUP) was eventually founded in 1964 to defend the political and ideological cause of extreme sovietism.

In any event, the Hungarian revolt woke a good number of Socialist leaders out of their dogmatic dream. At least they began to realize that there was no room for freedom in the so-called socialist field and that everything was regulated by the brute force of a party-state that, in the name of the proletariat, was pursuing its own imperialistic ambitions. Pietro Nenni wrote some exemplary articles on the real nature of the Soviet Union, raising a number of vital queries disdainfully ignored by the PCI. It remained convinced that the October revolution had paved the way and showed humankind the route to follow to achieve a classless, stateless society.

The PCI's stance on Hungary prevented any kind of constructive dialogue between the Communists and the Socialists and eventually led to the final break. The umbilical cord between the two parties was cut once and for all, and, after a long and difficult labor, the PSI opted for the West. It abandoned its former identity (or, rather, nonidentity) because basically it had been little more than a bad copy of the PCI.

Unfortunately, this ideological revision was not taken to its logical extreme. Anticapitalism and distrust of liberal democracy continued to be the basic ingredients of the Socialist political culture. At least this is what emerges from the "unification charter" presented in 1966. Although the aim of the charter was a reconciliation with the political culture of European social democracy, ideologically it had very little to do with reformism. Reference is made to "a trend toward an authoritarian and dictatorial involution . . . that is ever present in capitalistic regimes" and liberal democracy is described as the institutional cover for the domination of the bourgeoisie and, therefore, basically, a system to be done away with as soon as possible.

Probably the radical Unification Charter did not reflect the basic convictions of the leaders of PSI and responded more to a desire to avoid presenting too moderate a picture of the new party formation. The charter was formulated under the pressure of Marxist-Leninist propaganda, which had fueled the idea among the left that the Socialist International was serving the vital interests of the capitalistic-bourgeois establishment.

Still, the ideology expressed in the charter could hardly be reconciled with the policy that Socialist leaders had meanwhile been conducting in institutions and government. Indeed it justified the general wariness vis à vis European social democracy—especially of the peripheral cadres and the militant forces—which, according to Marxist-Leninist ideology, was simply a rationalization of the domination of capital. Not surprisingly, hostility toward the social democrats emerged with renewed vigor after the 1968 elections, considered a strategic defeat.

The 1969 split marked the failure of Nenni's efforts to create a progressive pole autonomous from the PCI and therefore capable, albeit in the framework of cooperation with the government and the Christian Democrat party (DC), of having an impact on Italian society. Many concluded that there simply was no room in Italy for a reformist policy conducted under the flag of social democracy.

This conviction was further reinforced by the split between the PSI and the PSDI, coinciding with the start of a period of strong student protest, which was to leave a profound mark on Italian society. Marxist-Leninist ideology started to spread like a river that had overflowed its banks. It penetrated universities, schools, trade unions, parties, newspapers, and publishing houses. At the time, to belong to the Left meant one thing only: to be against institutions and the fundamental values of Western civilization; to fight to end a system on which history had expressed its final verdict. The psychological climate could be described as one of ideological terrorism. Whoever refused to identify with the revolution totally and without reserve was *eo ipso* branded a lackey of the bourgeoisie and a traitor of the working class.

In part by conviction and in part because they were intimidated, the Socialists followed the wave of student protest. They had been bitterly disappointed by their experience in the center-left government and by the failure to achieve unification. They did not want to be judged a moderate force and were tormented by the fear that they would never play a major role in Italy's political life. Thus, they embarked upon a journey that eventually proved to be a dead end.

The PSI reestablished close ties with the Communists, coining the formula "more advanced equilibria," meaning that basically it was at the service of the PCI (which meanwhile had raised the flag of the "historic compromise"). Much was written on the so-called historic compromise during the 1970s. Essentially it was interpreted as the acceptance by the PCI of the strategy and philosophy of Enrico Berlinguer's policy: it was perceived as the republic's only chance to avoid economic, political, and moral ruin. Newspapers and weekly magazines, ranging from the *Corriere della Sera* to *Panorama*, vied with each other to accredit the image of a PCI that had become completely Westernized (and therefore more than reliable as a government force).

The PSI seemed to be driven by one desire only: to disappear as an autonomous political force and immolate itself on the altar of a historical meeting between Communists and Catholics. Thus, for the second time, the Socialists revealed what can only be described as a disconcerting vocation for self-destruction. How else can we define the "more advanced equilibria" policy tenaciously pursued by Francesco De Martino? If the "historic compromise" had ever become a reality, inevitably the PSI would have lost any reason to exist.

What's more, true success of the "historic compromise" might have even meant the end of freedom. A harder look at the real meaning of the "historic compromise" reveals that essentially it was a lexical variation of Togliatti's "progressive democracy." The strategy was identical and especially its ultimate goal: the collective transformation of Italian society. Berlinguer made no mystery of the fact that his party's goal was the "exit from capitalism" and the PCI could not renounce that goal without losing its identity as a revolutionary party.

Nonetheless, in the 1976 elections the Communists did extremely well, and for the first time exceeded the barrier of a 30% share of the votes. The Socialists did worse than they had ever done. The PSI began to harbor two great fears of extinction as a party and fear of the extinction of democracy. In effect both were at risk. What would have happened if the Communists had got into power? How would they have gone about governing the country? What were their long-term goals? Were these goals compatible with the values and institutions of a pluralistic democracy?

These democratic queries were raised in a major political and cultural debate, mainly on the pages of *Mondoperaio*, the PSI's theoretical journal. Well-known scholars—Norberto Bobbio, Paolo Sylos Labini, Lucio Colletti, Luciano Cafagna, Giorgio Ruffolo, Giuliano Amato, Massimo Salvadori, Antonio Landolfi, Paolo Flores d'Arcais, Ernesto Galli della Loggia, Federico Mancini, Gino Giugni, Francesco Forte, Giuseppe Bedeschi, Giuseppe Tamburrano, to name just some—participated in this debate. The whole ideology of the PCI—from Marx to Lenin to Gramsci and Togliatti—was closely scrutinized and shown to be irrevocably totalitarian. This cultural revolution—for a revolution it was—put an end to the spiritual hegemony exercised over the progressive forces by Marxism for decades.

The PSI's psychological and ideological subjection to the Communists was to cease once and for all when Bettino Craxi (who had substituted Francesco De Martino as party secretary) published an article listing the objections of the non-Communist Left to Leninism. These were solemnly reiterated at an international meeting at the end of 1978, thus marking the formal and total break of the Socialists with the ideological tradition of the Third International. From then on, the PSI ceased to be a cultural colony of the PCI: its ideological autonomy was the essential foundation for its subsequent political autonomy.

The rejection of Communism that began to spread simultaneously throughout Western Europe contributed greatly to the success of the cultural revolution of the Italian Socialists. In France especially, the so-called new philosophers helped break the Communist spell by drawing the attention of the international Left to the cries of desperation coming from Soviet dissidents. A new ideological climate began to develop. For the first time Communist culture found itself on the defensive. Worrying reports were also arriving from China, Vietnam, and Cambodia. The only possible conclusion was that, intrinsically, Communism destroyed freedom.

By the early 1980s, at last, the PSI felt free of the unity of the Left imperative. Having got rid of the earlier mental reservations and inferiority complexity, it was able to walk confidently on the road to reform, strengthening the earlier (once "contaminating") ties with European social democracy. Once again it started to cooperate with the DC, this time with a dual objective: to create a kind of diarchic government to avoid becoming a force complementary to the DC; and, at the same time, to erode PCI support. In other words, it wanted to break away from the hold it had been ensnared in since 1947 and end the Italian anomaly.

Naturally this did not please the PCI. This was the second time that the PSI had shown signs of autonomy. The fight against Marxist-Leninist totalitarianism became the Socialist horse, and the values and models of reformism its political and cultural identity. Thus began the duel between Socialists and Communists for the leadership of the Left. It reached its climax in 1984 when Bettino Craxi, then prime minister, launched a bill for some controls on the cost of living index to curb inflation. The PCI's response was extremely harsh. Enrico Berlinguer called Craxi's government a "threat to democracy" and organized a mass protest movement. The bill finally became law. The outcome of the popular referendum held the following year, at the wish of the Communists, sanctioned the PCI's political isolation. This was a great victory for the Socialists and was further reinforced in 1987 when more than a million votes shifted from the PCI to the PSI. It seemed that the Italian anomaly would end by the end of the century and that Italy, despite an almost pathological delay, was on the point of being governed by a Socialist-oriented progressive pole.

But the "Socialist long wave" soon ended. Relations among the Italian Left forces precluded any Socialist leadership of the Left, as had occurred meanwhile in France. Nor did PSI support increase after the collapse of the Berlin Wall and the disintegration of the Soviet Union. The initial enthusiasm for European social democracy in the wake of these events was short-lived. The demise of Communism was to have a negative impact on the attitude toward Socialism in both Eastern and Western Europe.

Every party of the Socialist International is currently facing tremendous difficulties, having lost much of their traditional mobilizing capacity and being seemingly incapable of finding adequate answers to the specific problems of postindustrial societies. One can but wonder whether Ralf Dahrendorf was right a few years ago when he spoke of the end of the century of social democracy. Whatever the fate of European social democracy, one thing seems certain: the historic victory of the reformist culture over the revolutionary culture did not result in more votes for the PSI. Not even the split of the PCI into two separate parties—the Democratic Party of the Left (PDS) and Rifondazione comunista—did so.

There are many reasons that might explain why the PSI did so disappointingly in the elections; not least, the so-called moral issue, which was to explode with such violence immediately after the 1992 elections. The socialists' participation in the "management" of a corrupt economy ruined their image. The fact remains though that in Italy the duel between the forces of the Left has ended—an initial period of euphoria in which the Socialists seemed likely to win—with a possibly irreversible defeat of all the left.

Thus only one hundred years after the birth, as an organized political force, the Italian Left offers a somewhat miserable spectacle: it is split into four parties, none of which can claim for the moment to have the future on its side. Indeed one might even wonder whether there is a future for them as political actors of any influence. Whatever one's value judgments, we can only conclude that the Italian anomaly has not been eliminated because, as suggested by Arturo Labriola, Italian Socialism has always been "a mixture of political theology and practical opportunism."

16

TWO HISTORICAL MOMENTS

Carla Sodini

In his clear and concise paper, Luciano Pellicani cites as the root cause of the "Italian anomaly," the cultural aspect of the postwar PCI "hegemony" over the PSI. Italy is the only Western democracy that has never been led by the Left and that has excluded the extremes of the ideological spectrum from its national government (Giovanni Sartori uses the term *polarized pluralism*). Taking his cue from this interpretation and in the light of the most significant events of the past fifty years, Pellicani reviews the most important developments in the difficult search for Socialist autonomy and raises problems and questions of great interest.

To Pellicani's analysis on the PSI's long and troubled journey toward recovery of its political and cultural autonomy, I add some reflections on the historical conditions of two moments that were particularly important for the Socialists and that appear to provide proof of their disconcerting "self-destructive vocation": the one following the Palazzo Barberini split and the other linked to the 1968 developments in Italy and Europe.

As Pellicani justly observes, in the years following the war, the PCI was the most open and flexible Communist party of the Western world. Togliatti had succeeded in wedding the elements typical of the revolutionary tradition to those of the reformist matrix. To this initial reason for Communist supremacy must be added Socialist instability and the hard struggle between socialism's revolutionary and reformist souls. As pointed out by Antonio Landolfi, Giovanni Sabbatucci, and Giuseppe Tamburrano, the results were the Palazzo Barberini split and the Popular Front's defeat in the elections of 18 April 1948, which determined the Communist primacy within the left.

The total victory of Communist dogmatism was even more disastrous because it resulted in the rejection of values that had their origin in the tradition of Risorgimento socialism and it blocked the maturation of new ideas that—appealing to French Revolutionary experience—could have fundamentally influenced not only PSI history but that of the workers' movement in general. In fact, favoring the PCI, the Socialists reneged on their own generous efforts to amalgamate a socialist outlook with the development of European democracy and with the general growth occurring after World War II. They thus turned their backs on the concept of European cultural unity emphasized with such passion by Filippo Turati in his speech of 29 April 1919 to the Chamber and taken up again, even if with different accents, in the *Quaderni di Giustizia e Libertà* (Carlo Rosselli), in the production of the *Centro Estero Socialista* of Zurich (Silone), in the Ventotene manifesto (Calorni, Spinelli, Rossi), and in the underground press up to the Liberation. This theme was not extinguished and was temporarily renewed by intellectuals coming, primarily, from the Action party and gathered around the review *Il Ponte*. It is certain, however, that "Europeanist" feelings were overcome by being linked to divergent judgments regarding international alliances. What animated the postwar Socialist "Europeanism" of Emanuele Modigliani was the vision of a Europe united thanks to a proletarian-led revolution characterized by its third-force character between the contending blocs—neither Communist nor capitalist, neither Soviet nor American.

Contrasting the "European" thesis was the Morandian one of subordination and delegation of the defense of the international proletariat to the Soviet "guide" *(stato guida)*. This choice resulted not only in the greater subordination to the Communist party but in the renunciation of socialism's libertarian and democratic tradition; this selection set off other dangerous processes of degeneration and relegated the philo-European area either to the party's margins or to the ranks of social democrats.

International developments pulled the PSI toward choices that were more autonomous when in 1955 it accepted, in part, the Atlantic alliance and in 1956 took a position on the Hungarian turning point, reawakening from its long dogmatic sleep. In this way, the conditions ripened for a rapprochement with the "European" and Actionist souls, its principal referents being Lombardi and Codignola. But it was above all in 1957 that the polemics against the PCI took on greater significance when the PSI abstained in the parliamentary ratification vote on the Treaty of Rome, which established the European Community. Thus the history of these years of subjection is defined by two precise international choices, the second of which aimed at recapturing, also on the ideological plane, the original, traditional directives of Turatian Socialism.

On the other hand, the Palazzo Barberini schism presented the DC with a hegemonic possibility only slightly tempered by its choice of a governmental majority with the support of independents, liberals, and monarchists. In practice, not only the PCI but the DC took advantage of the Socialist rout to profit from the situation in order to build a homogenous, moderate, and centrist bloc supported by great industrialists and landowners, the middle class, farmers, and organized workers' groups, in addition, of course, to the church and the United States. It was also in those years that the myth of America was counterposed to that of Stalin and the PSI ended up in a subordinate position to both deployments. And the Christian Democratic hegemony remained intact also through the center-left, paralleling the PCI's cultural and political hegemony over the Left.

Let us also not forget that the economic problem (composed of old and new evils) of the immediate postwar period, consisting of heavy unemployment within a very heterogeneous social situation, had in the past frequently found in libertarian and democratic socialism the reference point closest to its views. The loss of these characteristics in favor of a more authoritarian and centralized structure conforming to the PCI image not only disoriented the party's base but drove it away from the party summit. This process resulted in PCI hegemony both in the Cooperative leagues and in the CGIL; that is, in the two largest organizations created by the Socialists at the end of the nineteenth and the beginning of the twentieth centuries. The loss of control of the cooperative and trade-union movements and subjection to the PCI resulted in extremely grave damage on the cultural plane. These were the years in which the organic Gramscian intellectual was born with the task of creating and preserving consensus in a situation in which force could not be used. Like the ancient philosophers of the platonic and utopian socialist tradition, this intellectual had the job of reigning over and governing the Gramscian party-prince.

The evolution that began in 1956 as a result of the PCI's internal crisis caused by de-Stalinization and the Hungarian events put the PSI at the center of political attention, not only with regard to possible new allies but, most important, with reference to its historic adversaries; it began a process of reconciliation of its two souls. It also provoked the resistance of the DC right, which reached its height in July 1960 and slowed down the center-left's course; as a result, the center-left became a model for government only in February 1962. During these years, the divisions between Socialists and their former Communist allies deepened, especially in connection with the idea of economic programming and the means of redistributing the wealth resulting from the economic boom. In this manner, the Socialists discovered themselves the protagonists of an extraordinary gamble that had its major moment in the Pieraccini plan. But they also found themselves isolated, on the one hand, by the PCI's radical opposition and, on the other, by the resistance of the DC and its governmental allies, with the exception of La Malfa. Within the party the battle was dramatic, and, even if former Action party members such as Codignola came closer to Lombardi's views, it led to the PSIUP schism. Nor did permanent results issue from a 1966 attempt at fusion between PSI Socialists and PSDI social democrats that aimed at recomposing the 1947 fracture.

Discouraged by this double defeat, the party confronted the storm of student revolt. Nineteen sixty-eight has passed into history as the year of missed opportunities: in the West, the French May; and in the East, the Prague Spring. The movement of 1968 accelerated the growth of Italian trade unions (unlike its effect in France and Germany), but it was on the cultural plane that the movement produced its greatest results.

It is important to recognize that the period opened by the movement of 1968 was difficult for all the political forces to interpret because of social problems expressed in the strikes of salaried and white-collar employees, in addition to the previously mentioned youth movements. There was a generic conflict with authority, but also widespread sentiment that national wealth needed redistribution. Nor should new, politically unrepresented products of the same kind of development be forgotten: for example, new immigrants to the north. The malaise that overcame the parties was absorbed in different ways. The Catholics had to deal with major changes in identity, which, however, paralleled internal hierarchical divisions. Leftists encountered greater difficulties, disconcerted as they were by the Czechoslovak invasion. Communists and Socialists drifted, searching for well-defined and clear international referents. There was born in this climate an extraparliamentary Left with indefinite and sometimes disquieting outlines, with an ideology oscillating between old-style Communism, pro-Chinese utopianism, American radicalism, and Western pessimism. The fundamental point, however, should not be forgotten: the trade union, even if affected by the above dynamics, served as a guarantor of continuing dialogue and as a coordinating element between the old and the new Left.

While the PSI was still racked by bitterness ensuing from the failure of the 1968 elections, which raised grave questions about the continuation of the center-left experience, the PCI succeeded, after a difficult initial phase, in channeling the protest into the party beehive once the most violent phase had passed. "Marxist-Leninist ideology began spreading like a river that had overflowed its banks," states Pellicani, emphasizing how that ideology succeeded in penetrating everywhere, in the universities, in the schools, in the trade unions, in the parties. Young people reacted against an alienating and repressive system at the same moment that Mao Tse-tung instigated the Red Guards to revolt against their own party, guilty of having betrayed the spirit of Communism. This is an interesting interpretation in which the disquieting emergence not only of that generic and westernized Marxism-Leninism but also the appearance of a disquiet-ing and ambiguous terrorism of Right and Left are united, immersed in the *Autonomia* phenomenon, which is also cloaked in darkness. It was these factors, in addition to the growing separation from the Soviet mono-lith, that spurred the PCI to seek more concrete collaboration with the DC, which was later translated into the experience of the "historic compromise."

The Socialists, divided by their involvement in the now-exhausted cen-ter-left governing formula and the attempt to present themselves as a focus for revolutionary aspirations, made (with great contradiction) the cause of agitation their own; they put themselves once again at the service of Communist strategy by means of their formula, the "more advanced equilibria." This was a suicidal choice implemented at the very time when the "Indian Summer" (as Pellicani defined it) of revolution seemed to contradict Daniel Bell's thesis of an imminent death of ideology. But it was a brief parenthesis; revolution had to submit not only because of capitalism's durability but because of the brutality with which, where Marxism-Leninism had affirmed itself, the most elementary rights of man had been trampled upon. The end of the revolutionary illusion coincided with a new and progressive understanding of the Left, and especially of the Socialists, that, once again, the reformist idea linked to the Enlightenment tradition was the only choice capable, in the long run, of producing the well-being and dignity to which the workers aspired.

Following the 1976 Communist electoral success and the decisions of the Socialist Central Committee in July of the same year, and taking its cue from the ideas mentioned above, the debate on the pages of *Mondoperaio* began. This debate made a substantial contribution to breaking the psychological and ideological submission of the Socialists to the PCI. Old and new Socialist protagonists participated in the discussion, including exponents of Actionist thought, confirming the survival of that tradition which has been recalled many times and which we still recognize today. And in the general project for a Socialist alternative themes and proposals reappeared that were crucial for the present but linked to the values of the past: the rediscovery of Western-style socialism, its characteristics, and the historical experience of the workers' movement; Eurosocialism, understood as a coalition of independent socialist forces from Russia to America; the long reflection on the themes of social democracy and world problems.

As in 1948 and 1956, so in 1976. The Socialists succeeded in overcoming a dangerous identity crisis by rediscovering their political culture and their tradition. This development demonstrates how, threatened with the loss of their identity and their autonomy, Socialists reacted forcefully by making radical internal corrections; perhaps it is worth meditating upon these solutions during the present difficulties.

17

SALVEMINI IN THE UNITED STATES

Spencer M. Di Scala

Gaetano Salvemini represents a rare breed in Italian history. Born in the agricultural region of Puglia in 1873, he managed to attend the University of Florence. He became a professor and an activist in the Italian Socialist Party (PSI). A convinced reformist, he abhorred "revolutionary" ideology and condemned Communism; nonetheless, his corrosive criticism of the reformists, especially on the southern question, and his battle with Filippo Turati at the beginning of the century remain legendary. In 1911, he left the party but always professed himself a socialist. He founded the extremely influential newspaper *L'Unità*, and with Leonida Bissolati advocated Italian entrance into World War I on a "democratic interventionist" platform. After the war, he sought a just peace on "Wilsonian" terms, drawing the fulminations of nationalists down on his head in the process —just as he had done earlier with his dogged opposition to the Libyan War. With the rise of Mussolini, he established one of the first opposition publications *(Non Mollare)*, and he became one of the earliest exiles from Fascism.

During this vast political activity, matched by an unbelievable outpouring of political publications, Salvemini also made an important mark in his chosen field of history with such fundamental works as *Magnati e popolani in Firenze dal 1280 al 1295, La rivoluzione Francese*, and a biography of Giuseppe Mazzini. Thus, when Fascism forced him into exile, his reputation as a historian preceded him and allowed him to earn a living— unlike many other Italian intellectuals—by following his profession. After living in France and England, he found his way to the United States where he became professor of Italian civilization at Harvard University. A number of Italian antifascist professors taught at other American universities, but none of them had the experience or prestige of Salvemini; in their attempt to mobilize American opinion against Mussolini, they acknowledged Salvemini as their leader.

Furthermore, the antifascist struggle was not centered only in the universities, and this dispersion contributed to splits in the movement. The antifascists vied with the Fascist government and its network of consulates for the hearts and minds of the Italian-American community. A complex interrelationship resulted, of which the Salvemini group was an intimate part. Salvemini's prodigious activity reflects an important aspect of the American and Italian history of the interwar period and gives the lie to biographer Gaspare De Caro's contention that Salvemini "isolated" himself in Widener Library.

Given Salvemini's travels after going into exile, and for the sake of clarity, it might be useful to recall the various "stops" in his long journey. At the age of fifty, Salvemini found it necessary to learn English, a language he never learned to speak very well. As we learn from his *Memorie di un fuoruscito* and from the reports by Italian officials preserved in the Archivio Centrale dello Stato, he spent the years from 1925 to 1932 primarily in England. He traveled frequently to France during those years and participated actively in the antifascist struggle in both countries. He was close to Carlo Rosselli, also from Florence, and co-founded *Giustizia e Libertà*, the best known of the interwar antifascist organizations. The most famous periodicals of both countries and small-circulation antifascist publications carried his articles. During the same period, he also published two important books on Fascism: *The Fascist Dictatorship in Italy* (U.S. edition, 1927; English edition, 1928), and *Mussolini Diplomate* (France, 1932).

In 1927 and 1929, Salvemini conducted two lecture tours of the United States. These trips allowed him earn the funds to continue his spartan existence and his struggle against Fascism. During his second voyage, he taught at Yale and at the New School for Social Research. He went to Cambridge, Massachusetts, to meet George La Piana, an Italian specialist on church history teaching at Harvard. Besides becoming "excellent friends," as Salvemini states in his memoirs, La Piana introduced him to some of the best American historians of the period, including Arthur Schlesinger, Sr., William Langer, and others.

Before leaving for Europe, a young man named Lauro De Bosis passed by to meet him. A young monarchist and Liberal (in the Italian sense), De Bosis headed the America-Italy Society, considered by Salvemini to be a Fascist front. De Bosis overcame Salvemini's reluctance to see him by explaining that he had dropped his early philo-Fascist ideas. During their conversation, De Bosis told Salvemini that he planned to fly over Rome to drop leaflets urging the Italians to end the Fascist regime. Salvemini cited the dangers involved, but did not discourage him. In October 1931, De Bosis carried out his dangerous mission. Leaving from Marseilles, he reached Rome but disappeared on his return flight to Corsica, probably having run out of fuel.

Following De Bosis's death, his fiancée, Ruth Draper, endowed a chair at Harvard University in De Bosis's name. Draper, an American actress and descendant of newspaper publisher Charles A. Dana, made certain that the chair would go to Salvemini. "It was the permanent solution to my economic problem," Salvemini commented in his memoirs. He remained at Harvard from 1934 to 1948, when he returned to Italy.

The Consulates Versus Salvemini

Besides economics and the opportunity to do research in history, a significant reason for Salvemini to settle in the United States was the large Italian-American population. He hoped that he would be able to counteract the influence of the Italian consulates and of the major Italian-American newspapers, especially of Generoso Pope's *Il Progresso Italo-Americano*, sympathetic to the Italian regime. The years before Italy's entrance into World War II witnessed an ongoing battle between Salvemini and the Italian Embassy in Washington, which coordinated the consulates in an effort to discredit Salvemini.

This attempt began early and proceeded at an intense pace. A telegram dated 11 August 1926, for example, informed the Italian police that the ambassador had sent a representative to the International Institute of Education to protest Salvemini's visit, which the embassy believed would be financed by the IIE. According to the embassy Salvemini's tour would be inopportune: even if he abstained from attacking the Italian government at the institute, nothing prevented him from doing so elsewhere. If this occurred, the embassy argued: "His activities would provoke disorder in the Italian-American community, which would ill-bear attacks against the Italian government." The institute secretary responded that

Salvemini's trip was uncertain, but at any rate the institute would insist upon the abstention from politics in any lectures.

Salvemini did not come to the United States under the institute's auspices, but through a manager, as noted by the New York consul-general on 2 November 1926, and as Salvemini himself stated in his memoirs. What is interesting, however, is that the consul-general had already contacted a certain "Professor Bigongiari" to show up at a Salvemini talk before the Foreign Policy Association to rebut him. Bigongiari refused because he had previously had a debate with Salvemini in Florence, but suggested Professor Bruno Rosselli, later identified as head of the Department of Italian at Vassar, as the ideal person to answer Salvemini's attacks on the Fascist regime. If Rosselli refused, Bigongiari promised to recruit someone else. This proved unnecessary because Rosselli agreed, becoming the consulate's adviser on this issue and Salvemini's chief gadfly during his lectures. During his time in the United States, the embassy organized a campaign against Salvemini so there was someone to rebut him everywhere he spoke.

At the same time, the Italian ambassador approached Secretary of State Kellog and other high officials in the State Department to deny Salvemini a visa. They responded negatively; since no legal reason existed, they argued, a scandal would result that would benefit Salvemini. In order to demonstrate the department's good faith, the officials informed the embassy that they had already conducted an investigation in Europe to see if Salvemini had any Anarchist or Communist antecedents, but were unable to find any. Admitting the State Department's valid position, the Embassy nonetheless believed it important to call the department's attention to the incidents that Salvemini's presence would certainly provoke in the Italian-American community, which held the highest admiration for the Italian government.

Consular and ambassadorial reports to the Interior Ministry during Salvemini's second tour of the United States make it clear that Salvemini stepped up his attacks on Fascism during this time. A telegram dated 6 June 1930, which reports on a talk given by Salvemini at the "People's House" in New York, explains why and how. Salvemini had earlier contended that the Fascist regime would be a long time in falling. Now, he said, he had changed his mind because of the magnificent organization of the opposition and the open unrest that had broken out in parts of Italy. In truth, the Depression had animated antifascists and fueled a burst of illusory optimism. What makes Salvemini's remarks significant, however, is the role he assigned to Italian-Americans in the future fall of Fascism, that is, to finance the revolution. He held out the Irish example, stating that while the focus of the anti-English struggle was in Ireland and England, the funds were collected in America. Salvemini concluded: "Like the Irish, the Italians in America must be the financiers of the revolution in their homeland."

Greater knowledge of the Italian-American community would soon disabuse Salvemini and his friends of the extent to which that community would sponsor the fight against Fascism. In fact, most Italian-Americans were hard workers, trying to succeed in a difficult situation, and they concentrated on economic activities. Furthermore, having been ill-treated and discriminated against in their adopted country, they appreciated the new prestige that the Fascist regime had brought to their homeland in American eyes. During Salvemini's talks against Fascism, bankers who had made loans to Mussolini's Italy were usually present to object that the Duce had transformed Italy, thus justifying increased American economic confidence. When Salvemini explained the corporate state to American labor union leaders, they cheered instead of being shocked. As Salvemini complained time after time, the myth was that everything was rotten in Italy until Mussolini had taken over, after which everything was beautiful. The constant refrain that the "trains ran on time" and that the Italians now had bathrooms exasperated him. The pro-Fascist orientation of American society and American leaders has been excellently described in John Diggin's *Mussolini and Fascism: The View from America*, and we need not go beyond these few examples.

Salvemini attempted to reverse the pro-Fascist American attitude, but he failed. This failure should come as no surprise. The point is that most Italian-Americans had emigrated from the old country for economic reasons. Many of those who wished to return—and there were substantial numbers—had already done so. In fact, in making his argument for giving the vote to illiterates at the beginning of the century, Salvemini himself had highlighted the returning American immigrants, who, he argued, should vote because they had learned practical democracy in the United States.

While attached to their homeland, Italian-Americans had concerns and views that were American, not Italian, and the Americans were strongly pro-Fascist. Salvemini had emigrated for political reasons, and his concerns were Italian, not American; he and other highly educated Italians wished to return to Italy once Fascism ended, even if some of them wound up not doing so. In short, the Italian antifascist exiles formed a sort of club separated by class, education, and temperament from the bulk of Italian-Americans. This went for Salvemini as well, born a poor southerner but whose elegant education spoke well for the Giolittian era he condemned *and* drove a wedge between him and his origins. In Italy, Salvemini attempted to maintain contact with those origins, but we must conclude that he did not really understand the Italian-American milieu, which is quite different from the southern Italian one. An abyss separated the refined and sophisticated Italian intellectuals and the majority of Italian-Americans; Salvemini and his fellow professors at the University of Chicago, Smith, and other institutions were no match for the consulates —and the church—in bridging the gap.

As might be expected, Salvemini got along much better with his colleagues at Harvard and other universities, and American liberals in general, than he did with Italian-Americans. Salvemini's correspondence during his Harvard period testifies to the close contact he had with American liberals. That correspondence also testifies to something else: his single-minded pursuit of persons he considered Italian-American Fascists, and his possible misinterpretation of their aims.

There is no doubt that a person of Salvemini's intelligence understood that only a small percentage of Italian-Americans were Fascists, and he said so in writing. Salvemini, however, practically ran a one-man investigating committee against people he suspected to be Fascists. There has been a running dispute as to whether or not his activities constituted a violation of civil rights or might have falsely branded some people of being Fascists. Without getting into that argument, and granting the meticulousness of his research, a dispassionate observer may recognize that there was something vengeful in his approach. He compiled the work on *Italian Fascist Activities in the United States* (posthumously published by Philip Cannistraro), designed to focus the attention of Congress on the activities of Italian Fascists, in which attendance at Fascist-inspired rallies served as one proof of strong Fascist sympathies. During World War II, he let the FBI have the manuscript.

We might cite another example of his views. In a letter to Hugh DeLacy, chairman of the American Committee for Protection of the Foreign Born, Salvemini refused to sign a open letter seeking to kill a provision of a bill allowing the denaturalization of citizens on the ground that a naturalized person's "utterances, writings, actions or course of conduct establishes that his political allegiance is to a foreign state or sovereignty."

Salvemini objected that such a provision was not bad, although he suggested its enforcement be entrusted to the regular judiciary. Informed that this vague provision was unnecessary because the Justice Department was already empowered to proceed against naturalized citizens who were disloyal, and that the section undermined the status of naturalized citizens, Salvemini answered crustily on 13 April 1942 that while it was difficult to prove a person had taken the citizenship oath in bad faith, "Vice versa it is not difficult to prove that the writings, addresses, activities of a man are inconsistent with his oath of allegiance, whether they precede or follow such an oath. I know a great many Italian born and naturalized who would fall under such a law. And I think that they would deserve to be deprived of their citizenship."

That DeLacy's organization was a Communist front does not justify the harshness of Salvemini's attitude, which indicates an emotional misunderstanding of the Italian-American experience, an insensitivity to civil rights, and a vengeful view. On the other hand, Salvemini's intransigence was not limited to this issue, or to this time; he had a history of cantankerousness and always expressed himself strongly and frequently immoderately, not only in the United States but in Italy. It was the flip side of a character that made him such a strong antifascist, but it was not calculated to win him friends among an Italian-American community that, ironically, hailed primarily from his own beloved south.

The Harvard Connection and World War II

Besides assuring themselves the support of the Italian-American community, Italian diplomats in the United States attempted to deprive Salvemini of influence in the intellectual community. In April 1930, the Boston consul-general reported that he had objected to Harvard for hiring Salvemini as a visiting professor. He reported that strong opposition to the move existed among Harvard's administrators and that, in part, ignorance of Salvemini's politics was responsible for the "gaffe." According to the consul-general's Harvard informant the administration "read him [Salvemini] the riot act," telling him that he was absolutely not to make any reference to present-day Italy in his course.

Other Italian documents make clear that the diplomats had strong contact with Harvard professors and that they believed that substantial opposition to an appointment for Salvemini existed. But on 29 April 1933 the Foreign Ministry requested information from the Interior Ministry on the circumstances of Salvemini's leaving Italy, whether he had really been a professor in Italy, and whether it was true that his mother had been a Yugoslav subject. The purpose: "to attempt to block, if we are still in time, Salvemini's appointment to Harvard University." Despite assurances to the contrary from their Harvard informant, the Foreign Ministry reported on 8 May that Salvemini had indeed been offered a chair. Italian officials attempted to sabotage the appointment by reporting that Salvemini had been implicated in a plot to kill the Duce by planting a bomb in Saint Peter's Basilica, but Salvemini challenged Mussolini to extradite him by bringing evidence in an American court, and the government dropped the affair.

Despite what appears to have been stiff opposition to Salvemini, the appointment had gone through. It represented a significant defeat for the Fascist authorities because from this base Salvemini was able to organize his antifascist activities not among Italian-American community leaders (who, much to Salvemini's chagrin, smoothly made clear their loyalty to the United States when the war began) but among Italian intellectuals in American universities and American liberals. These colleagues included G. A. Borgese at the University of Chicago, Max Ascoli at the New School, Michele Cantarella at Smith, and Arturo Toscanini.

Even after Italy's entrance into the war, the Italians followed Salvemini's activities very closely. The introduction of the racial laws into Italy stimulated the exodus of Italian Jews to the United States, adding to the antifascist ranks; the French defeat swelled the antifascist groups in America and added well-known personalities such as Carlo Sforza and Alberto Tarchiani. In order to influence future American policy toward Italy, to stimulate more opposition to the Italian regime, and to spur the birth of a republic, Salvemini inspired the foundation of a new organization in 1940. While Salvemini kept in the background in Boston, Ascoli became president of this new "Mazzini Society," and Tarchiani became its secretary.

Despite this hopeful beginning, the Mazzini Society soon split. As the war progressed, Salvemini became convinced that President Roosevelt had decided to leave determination of Italy's future configuration in the hands of Winston Churchill and the British, who favored continuation of the Savoy monarchy. In addition, Salvemini had always been anticlerical and had stepped up his attacks on the Vatican after the Lateran Accords of 1929, which created opposition to him among American Catholics. Furthermore, Salvemini divided the responsibility of the Italian people from Mussolini, who had stabilized his government by receiving crucial support from American and European conservatives. Such considerations led him to argue against any compromise with persons who had collaborated with Fascism for a favorable peace treaty, maintenance of Italy's frontiers, and Italian self-determination in choosing a form of government.

Mazzini Society officers led primarily by Sforza and Ascoli were reluctant to attack Roosevelt and Churchill frontally and advocated prudence. This is one quality Salvemini decidedly lacked. The result was that the society split between the Salvemini group and the followers of Sforza—a dispute that also involved certain State Department offices. Salvemini's opposition to American policy toward Italy produced the threat of the Justice Department's instituting denaturalization proceedings against him. According to Salvemini collaborator Enzo Tagliacozzo, Salvemini's fear that the Sforza group's attitude would compromise his campaign in favor of an Italian republic among Americans explains his adamant position on the issue.

The debate over this question of Anglo-American policy toward Italy led to publication of the book *What to do with Italy?* (with La Piana as its co-author). Written in Salvemini's customarily clear and uncompromising style, this book synthesizes the Salvemini group's position at the end of the Second World War with regard to a republic, the Vatican, and Europe's future. Most of all, however, it is a scathing criticism of British policy—a position that echoes Salvemini's correspondence during this period. Summarizing Salvemini's position, by blaming Mussolini alone and not the entire Fascist regime for the war, and by urging the Italians to get rid of "one man and one man alone," Churchill was telling the Italians "that what they should do is, merely, to substitute Fascism without Mussolini for Fascism with Mussolini and everything will be fine." This book and his support of the Resistance represented Salvemini's last battles on American soil. He resumed teaching at the University of Florence in October 1949 and died at Capo di Sorrento on 6 September 1957 at the age of eighty-four.

How shall we judge Salvemini's American experience? This is a very difficult question: while it is clear that he influenced American students who still speak about their experiences with him and though he lives on in his numerous articles and books of the American period and the significant introductory essay to A. William Salomone's *Italian Democracy in the Making*, his influence remains elusive. But this elusiveness is not restricted to the American period. Even in Italy, the same consideration applies. In both countries he was respected for his uprightness, his consistency, his logic, his analytical prowess, and his historical research. But Salvemini was not the kind of person who could leave a party or a "school," which probably explains the lack of biographies about him in Italian as well as in English and why a typical "party" view, such as De Caro's, is so hostile to him.

On the other hand, it might just be that Salvemini was the prototype of the "sophisticated rebel" of the late twentieth century described in a recent book by H. Stuart Hughes, an old Harvard colleague and friend: an intellectual unattached to parties, stubbornly resisting the will of powerful groups and governments, and somehow prevailing in the end.

18

UNDERSTANDING AMERICA

Philip V. Cannistraro

Spencer Di Scala has shown that Salvemini was not only an important figure in the Socialist movement and in Italy's political development, but a man whose active career (and especially the years between 1931 and 1943) reached into this country as a political exile from Mussolini's dictatorship. This is a phase in Salvemini's life that deserves to be better known; it was, and remains, a controversial period that continues to elicit conflicting interpretations.[1] The subject is tremendously important: beyond the specific issue of Salvemini's American career, it suggests that the origins of the Italian republic are to be found partially in the policies of the United States during World War II.

As Di Scala reveals, it is clear that the thesis presented by Gaspare De Caro some years ago, namely, that Salvemini isolated himself in the "enchanted island" of Harvard University and withdrew from active participation in the political struggles of the day, is untenable.[2] Yet Di Scala's view is that Salvemini's efforts in the United States must be judged a failure, if by that we mean his efforts to "reverse the pro-Fascist American attitude." Di Scala maintains that this failure was due to the inherent weakness of the *fuorusciti:* "The Italian antifascist exiles formed a sort of club separated by class, education, and temperament from the bulk of Italian-Americans. This went for Salvemini as well. . . . We must conclude that he did not really understand the Italian-American milieu." In Salvemini's case, this failure was compounded, argues Di Scala, by Salvemini's political rigidity, his inability to cooperate with fellow antifascists, and his moral intransigence.

While I agree with Di Scala's general argument concerning the *fuoru-sciti*, I see Salvemini's American experience—and especially his understanding of and reaction to the Italian-American community—in a different light. Salvemini was perhaps the exception to the rule. A closer examination of his role in the struggle to combat the influence of the Italian-American *prominenti* between 1940 and 1943 reveals, in fact, that no Italian exile better understood the nature of the power structure of the Italian-American community than Salvemini.

When Salvemini joined others in founding the Mazzini Society[3] in late 1939, he did so because he believed that by countering Fascist sympathies in the Italian-American community and in American society at large, the *fuorusciti* would be able to influence postwar U.S. policy toward Italy—their foremost goal. Salvemini's understanding of the importance of reaching the Italian-American community derived not from nostalgic solidarity with people of his own national background, but from an analysis of the American political system as it operated in the 1930s; namely, the importance of the ethnic vote in the political strategy of Roosevelt's electoral successes. He and the *fuorusciti* concluded that those who influenced Italian-American opinion and voting behavior—the *prominenti*—were the real enemy of the antifascist struggle in the United States, especially after December 1941. His exposé of Fascist activities in the United States, which he turned over to the FBI, was aimed against the Italian-American leadership that had supported Mussolini.[4] In this context, the principal target of the Mazzini Society and of Salvemini's efforts was Generoso Pope, the most influential Italian-American supporter of Mussolini in America. Pope was the millionaire owner of a construction supply empire, publisher of *Il Progresso Italo-Americano* and other widely read Italian-language papers, and a powerfully connected figure in Tammany Hall.[5]

Salvemini expected that in the struggle against the *prominenti*, the *fuorusciti* of the Mazzini Society would join forces with the older generation of Italian immigrant activists that included socialists, anarchists, and syndicalists. In Salvemini's mind, one figure stood out among these leaders as having the greatest potential to assist in the cause: Luigi Antonini, the social democratic head of the ILGWU's local 89.

Elsewhere I have argued that Antonini was in his own way as much of a *prominente* as Pope.[6] Both of them (like almost all the other *prominenti*) were naturalized U.S. citizens, whose lives, careers, and futures were tied permanently to the United States; for them Italy was a personal point of reference; but it was not the source of their power: that power was derived only from the ethnic factor; that is, from the existence of a compact mass of Italian-American immigrants who voted as a bloc.

In terms of the ethnic factor, Pope and Antonini held very similar positions. Personally, both men were ambitious, shrewd, and egotistical. Both controlled access to many hundreds of thousands of Italian-Americans through newspapers, radio stations, and employment opportunities; both wielded considerable financial resources, were well connected to local politicians, judges, and public officials, and were able to bring out the vote among their constituencies. The Democratic National Committee considered Antonini and Pope the linchpins of Roosevelt's election victories in New York. As a result, they were frequent visitors to the White House and exercised considerable influence on U.S. policy toward Italy. The only factor separating Pope and Antonini was that one was a Fascist supporter and the other an antifascist.

The weak link between Antonini and the *fuorusciti* was the fact that Antonini found it difficult to reconcile his role as an antifascist with his position as an Italian-American *prominente*. Political opportunism led him to collaborate with other leaders of the Italian-American community, regardless of whether they were antifascist or not. In 1934, after Antonini got the ILGWU to adopt an antifascist platform, he and Pope went to war against each other. The next year, however, both men decided that it was in their interests to arrange a truce: each agreed to stop all personal attacks. Thenceforth, they collaborated with each other when necessary, appearing together on the same platforms and both working on behalf of Roosevelt.

Salvemini and his comrades in the Mazzini Society soon discovered that, despite a relentless and bitter campaign to expose and discredit Pope, he would not easily be brought down. When Pope's back was to the wall in the summer of 1941 and the Mazzini Society was on the verge of seizing editorial control of his newspaper chain, Roosevelt came to his rescue. When Pope and the other *prominenti* reacted to Pearl Harbor by breaking with Mussolini and declaring their loyalty to the United States, Antonini welcomed them behind the war effort—and Salvemini knew the game was up.

Salvemini judged Antonini harshly, but not merely out of moral outrage over his refusal to join in the fight against Pope. He began to see that in the Antonini-Pope alliance were the roots of what became a broad and subtle struggle for control of U.S. policy toward Italy: a struggle between the Mazzini Society and the Italian-American *prominenti*. This realization,

I would argue, was the first step in Salvemini's separation from his colleagues in the Mazzini Society.

Di Scala explains that Salvemini became convinced that Roosevelt was prepared to allow the British to determine Italy's future, and that Count Sforza was ready to accept such an arrangement. The result would be, in Salvemini's mind, that Italy would have a postwar government run by former Fascists, Catholics, and the House of Savoy. My point is that even before he came to this conclusion, Salvemini understood that Roosevelt would allow the conservative *prominenti* to influence Italian policy in this same direction.

In December 1941, Antonini moved to take control of Italian policy through the formation of the Italian-American Labor Council (IALC), and invited a wide spectrum of Italian-American leaders (including those who Salvemini called "pre-Pearl Harbor Fascists") to participate in its activities. Salvemini now began to demand that the Mazzini Society keep its distance from Antonini. Alberto Tarchiani, the society's secretary, scolded Salvemini: "I beg you not to fantasize too much. . . . We must not forget that the only organization that has been capable of a *practical antifascism* has been precisely Antonini's. . . . I still see the need for us to get along with Antonini's organization and all other labor groups if we are to have the masses of New York behind us."[7]

Salvemini saw Tarchiani's point only too well. When some *fuorusciti* suggested splitting the Mazzini into separate groups, an Italian and an American, Salvemini supported the idea because he saw the Antonini-Pope relationship as symptomatic of the political ties between FDR and the *prominenti*; he became convinced that antifascism had to be free from the constraints of domestic American politics. "It is evident," he told Max Ascoli, "that between the chairman of the Democratic National Committee [Edward] Flynn, [Fiorello] La Guardia, [Edward] Corsi, Antonini, Pope and Co. there is an agreement to the effect that they have to control Italian affairs in this country."[8] When Sforza agreed to speak at a huge meeting of the IALC, an enraged Salvemini wrote to Antonini:

> I am deeply disturbed by your attitude toward such Italo-Americans as Pope and Corsi, who have contributed to poisoning the Italo-Americans with Fascist misinformation. I do not think we have to fight them now that they have changed with the wind. But we have to maintain that people who have been helping Mussolini for the last twenty years should not claim leading positions in the present political set-up. . . . I know that the administration wants us to put our-

selves at the service of Pope and Corsi. But I am not an agent of the administration, and the Mazzini Society ought not to act as a transmission belt of the administration.[9]

After America's entry in the war, Pope's rehabilitation in the government's eyes proceeded rapidly, especially as Pope began to raise millions in war-bond subscriptions. When the government sponsored a series of Italian-American Victory Councils in 1942, Antonini agreed to participate with Pope and the other "pre-Pearl Harbor Fascists." The next year, Antonini and Pope joined forces publicly in creating ACID (the American Committee for Italian Democracy), whose platform for postwar Italian reconstruction effectively expropriated the Mazzini Society's program. By the end of 1943, Salvemini and his friends had left the Mazzini and Ascoli had resigned as its president. Antonini then seized control of the organization and put his own men in charge, and the new leaders of the group endorsed a resolution supporting the Roosevelt-Churchill policy of collaboration with Badoglio and the monarchy.[10]

Did Salvemini, as Tarchiani asserted, "fantasize too much"? Perhaps, but his fulminations against Antonini and his own colleagues were not the ranting of an isolated intellectual removed from the real world. The history of the Mazzini Society from 1942 to 1945 suggests, to the contrary, that he understood only too well, and long before any of his more "realistic" colleagues, the dynamic of Italian-American politics. If anything, we may fault him for overestimating the degree to which the *prominenti* would be able to influence the State Department in a postwar world in which the ethnic factor would be less important that it had been, and perhaps also in having underestimated the strength of the resistance at home in shaping a new Italy.

Notes

1. On Salvemini in the United States see Gian Giacomo Migone, "A proposito de 'L'Italia vista dall'America' di Gaetano Salvemini," in *Problemi di storia nei rapporti tra Italia e Stati Uniti* (Turin, 1971), 95–156; Max Salvadori, "Salvemini negli Stati Uniti," *Archivio Trimestrale* 8 (1983), 621–25; Enzo Tagliacozzo, "Gli esuli in Inghilterra e negli Stati Uniti: Gaetano Salvemini," *Terzo programma* 2 (1962): 196–209; idem., "L'opera di Gaetano Salvemini negli Stati Uniti," *Rassegna storica toscana* (1974): 19–36; Arturo Colombo, "Cinque battaglie di Salvemini," in Antonio Varsori, ed., *L'Antifascismo italiano negli Stati Uniti durante la seconda guerra mondiale* (Rome, 1984), 229–47; Antonio Donno, "Gli Stati Uniti visti da Salvemini," in Gaetano Cingari, ed.,

Gaetano Salvemini tra politica e storia (Rome, 1986), 402–11; and especially Charles L. Killinger, "Gaetano Salvemini in the United States: A Study in Italian Anti-Fascism," Ph.D. dissertation (Florida State University, 1985).

2. Gaspare De Caro, *Gaetano Salvemini* (Turin, 1970). For a more positive view, see especially Ernesto Sestan et al., *Gaetano Salvemini* (Bari, 1959); Massimo L. Salvadori, *Gaetano Salvemini*, 2d ed. (Turin, 1963); Enzo Tagliacozzo, *Gaetano Salvemini nel cinquantennio liberale* (Florence, 1959); the essays in the special number of *Archivio Trimestrale* 8 (1983), "Gaetano Salvemini tra storia e politica."

3. No complete history of the Mazzini Society has been published. For a general survey see Maddalena Tirabassi, "La Mazzini Society (1940–1946): un'associazione degli antifascisti italiani negli Stati Uniti," in *Italia e America dalla grande guerra a oggi*, ed. G. Spini, G. G. Migone, and M. Teodori (Venice, 1976), 141–58, and Antonio Varsori, *Gli alleati e l'emigrazione democratica antifascista (1940–1943)* (Florence, 1982), 38–43ff.

4. Gaetano Salvemini, *Italian Fascist Activities in the United States*, ed. and intro. Philip V. Cannistraro (Staten Island, N.Y., 1977). See also Charles L. Killinger, "Gaetano Salvemini e le autorità americane: Documenti inediti del FBI," in *Storia Contemporanea* (June 1981): 403–39.

5. On Pope see Philip V. Cannistraro, "Generoso Pope and the Rise of Italian American Politics, 1925–1936," in ed. Lydio F. Tomasi *Italian Americans: New Perspectives in Italian Immigration and Ethnicity*, (Staten Island, N.Y., 1985), 264–88. On the Mazzini Society's struggle against Pope, see Philip V. Cannistraro and Elena Aga Rossi, "La politica etnica e il dilemma dell'antifascismo italiano negli Stati Uniti: Il caso di Generoso Pope," *Storia Contemporanea* (April 1986): 217–43.

On the Mazzini Society's attacks against Pope, see Lamberto Mercuri, ed., *Mazzini News: Organo della 'Mazzini Society' (1941–1942)* (Foggia, 1990), passim.

6. Philip V. Cannistraro, "Luigi Antonini and the Italian Anti-Fascist Movement in the United States, 1940–1943," *Journal of American Ethnic History* (Fall 1985): 21–40.

7. Tarchiani to Salvemini, 2 March 1941, Istituto per la Storia della Resistenza in Toscana, Florence, *Fondo Alberto Tarchiani*, f.55.

8. Salvemini to Ascoli, 12 February 1942, Immigration History Research Center, University of Minnesota, Max Ascoli Papers, file "Salvemini."

9. Salvemini to Antonini, 29 June 1942, International Ladies Garment Workers Union, *Luigi Antonini Papers* [now at Cornell University], box 17, file 9.

10. Salvemini's program for a postwar Italy was incorporated in his book, written with George La Piana, *What to Do with Italy.* (New York, 1943).

19

THE KENNEDY ADMINISTRATION AND THE CENTER-LEFT

Arthur M. Schlesinger Jr.

I find it entirely felicitous that this topic should follow a session on Gaetano Salvemini, for it is to that grand old patriot that I owe my long-standing concern with the fate and future of Italian democracy.

The ascent to power of Mussolini produced mixed reactions in the United States in the 1920s. Many conservatives and business leaders admired Il Duce. They thought he was bringing order and discipline to an unruly people, and they regarded antifascist Italians as troublemakers and radicals. Liberals condemned Mussolini as a dictator and tyrant and sought to help the antifascists. This was my father's view, and in 1929, as chairman of the Harvard history department and with the department's and the dean's backing, he sent a cable to Salvemini, then in exile in London, inviting him to come for a semester in Cambridge as a visiting professor.

After the invitation went out and before Salvemini replied, the president of Harvard, A. Lawrence Lowell, notified my father that an influential member of the Corporation, Harvard's governing body, strongly objected to the invitation and that it must be retracted while time still permitted. My father responded that, since the department had acted with proper authorization, the offer could not in honor be withdrawn. As my father wrote later in his memoirs, "Lowell may himself have had doubts about the proceeding. In any event he did not pursue the matter further."

Salvemini, a man of passion, wit, and unconquerable zest for life, quickly captivated Cambridge, and, after James B. Conant became president in 1933, the history department secured him on a regular basis. He was a familiar figure in our household when I was growing up. George La Piana was another friend of my father's, and I heard much talk when young of the hopes La Piana and Salvemini shared for a democratic Italy. Other antifascist Italian exiles passed through our house; so that, when war came, I followed events in Italy with particular interest while working for the Office of Strategic Services. By an odd coincidence, I rented a room in the winter of 1944 in the Paris apartment of Salvemini's second wife, from whom he had long separated and who was, by an even odder coincidence, the mother of Jean Luchaire, the notorious French collaborationist.

When I returned to Cambridge after the war, Salvemini, then in his seventies, was as vivid and vital as ever. I remember a wonderful evening when he dined at our house with Arthur Koestler, and the two survivors discussed in sardonic fashion the comparative merits of internment by Mussolini and by Franco. After he went back to Italy, I called on him in Sorrento. He fell sick in the summer of 1957 and died in September. I found in my father's papers Salvemini's last words as taken down by his friend Roberto Bolaffio. "To die smilingly," the old professor said, "this is what I should like. . . . I could not have foreseen a more serene death than this." He drifted off to sleep; then awakening a moment before he died, he said, characteristically, "I am not dead yet."

Well, the spirit of Salvemini is, I trust, not dead yet in Italy, nor is his dream of an honest, progressive, democratic republic; and I can well imagine what would have been the pungency of his reaction to the corruption of that dream in recent years. As one in deep sympathy with that dream, and ever hopeful, I have been now for many years an anxious observer of the fortunes of Italian democracy. In my effort to keep abreast of Italian developments, I must express particular gratitude to another Italian friend, this time of my own generation, Tullia Zevi, whom I first met in Paris in 1939 and saw much of when she and her husband, the architect Bruno Zevi, came to Cambridge, Massachusetts, in 1940. On my visits to Rome in later years, Tullia Zevi would often arrange meetings with leading politicians and journalists. It was at her salon that I first talked with Pietro Nenni and Giuseppe Saragat, and I owe much to her charm, wisdom, and generosity. I go into all this to explain why a historian of the United States who reads Italian with great difficulty and speaks it not at all become involved in U.S.-Italian relations during the presidency of John F. Kennedy.

In the immediate postwar years Italy had seemed one of the most vulnerable nations in Western Europe. An indisputably democratic country,

Italy yet had the largest Communist party outside the Soviet Union, and the most intelligent Communist leadership anywhere. It also had a Socialist party that was rich in tradition but, under Nenni's leadership, appeared to have aligned itself firmly with the Soviet side in the global civil war. Given the disquietudes that affected even Western Europe in the late 1940s, could one be sure that Italy would stay within the democratic camp?

I followed the Italian situation with keen interest, applauding the Partito d'Azione in 1945; cheering Saragat on when he led pro-democratic Socialists out of the PSI in 1947 and formed the Social Democratic party; approving too when the CIA intervened in the 1948 election to prevent a Communist victory; noting with disapproval Nenni's continuing attacks on NATO and American imperialism that in 1951 won him the Stalin Peace Prize. But a curious episode in September 1950 made me think that the situation might be more ambiguous than it appeared.

One day in London, that brilliant and iconoclastic Labour party gadfly Richard H. S. Crossman, the editor of that famed exposure of Communism *The God That Failed*, invited me to a dinner at the House of Commons. Among the other guests were Arthur Koestler, Raymond Aron, John Strachey, and assorted wives. Much drink was consumed, and after dinner the conversation became heated. Dick Crossman, who had just returned from Italy, argued that the Labour party should resume fraternal relations with the PSI. This roused Koestler to indignation that soon turned to fury. Nenni, he said, had sold out irrevocably to Stalin; Labour would fatally compromise itself if it tried to do business with him. Crossman responded with equal asperity. Finally Koestler arose, summoned his lovely wife and said, "This is intolerable. Come, Mamaine, we're leaving." Aron and I followed the Koestlers out into the corridor, begging Arthur to relax and not break his old friendship with Crossman; but he angrily declined and strode out into the night—a gesture somewhat complicated by the fact that the Koestlers were planning to stay with the Crossmans in Vincent Square. (Mamaine Koestler, however, solved that problem by phoning for a room at Grosvenor House.)

Crossman of course turned out in the end to be right. In 1952 Nenni began to favor independent PSI electoral slates, and in the spring of 1953 he indicated to the journalist Leo Wollemborg, from whose discerning and exceptionally well-informed dispatches and conversation I learned much in these years, that he was drawing away from the PCI. After the Soviet intervention in Hungary in 1956, Nenni gave back the Stalin Peace

Prize and gave the prize money to Hungarian refugees. By the late 1950s many observers were beginning to feel that a socialist breakaway from the Communist alliance was possible.

The American Embassy, however, refused to believe it. Ambassador Clare Boothe Luce, an intractable if charming antileftist, laid down a hard line against the PSI and refused to let the embassy staff meet with PSI leaders. When speculation arose about a reunion between Nenni and Saragat and even about PSI cooperation with the government, the Eisenhower administration made clear to Rome its profound opposition to any opening to the Left. It did not trust Nenni, believing him to be at best a neutralist, at worst a Stalinist dupe or agent; in any case it saw no urgent need for social and economic reform in Italy. In effect, the Eisenhower administration imposed an American veto on a center-left government in Italy. Mrs. Luce left in 1957, but her successor, James D. Zellerbach, while more easygoing in his attitudes, maintained the veto.

Some American officials disagreed. The *apertura a sinistra*, they thought, would both isolate the Communists and move the Italian government toward necessary and beneficial reforms, thereby undermining the basis of the Communist appeal. The debate over the opening to the Left began in the U.S. Embassy in Rome, and we are lucky indeed to have with us today a hero of this struggle, George Lister, who came to Rome in late 1957 as a first secretary. Lister's prior experience in Eastern Europe and the Soviet Union had instructed him in the vast differences between democratic socialism and totalitarian communism. He now proposed that he be permitted to talk to Socialists, and, with Zellerbach's approval, Lister developed a widening circle of contacts. He was soon reporting encouraging evidence of Socialist responsiveness to this dialogue. William Colby, the CIA station chief (and later CIA director), also saw the *apertura* as a means of splitting the Left and argued for subventions that would replace funds the PSI had received from Communist sources.

However, as I have described in *A Thousand Days*, the arrival in 1959 of Outerbridge Horsey as deputy chief of mission brought about a reversion to the Luce hard line. Horsey was a self-righteous fellow of exceedingly rigid right-wing views. He feared a center-left coalition as "a dangerous trap" that would lead ineluctably to the neutralization of Italy; the thing to do with the Socialists, he thought, was to "drive them back" into the arms of the Communists. Of course that is exactly what Moscow would have wanted. Horsey exerted severe pressure on Lister to cease his efforts with the Socialists; but Lister continued the meetings and, once when

Horsey was on vacation, carried his case, with his immediate superior's approval, to Zellerbach, for which Horsey never forgave him.

In January 1961 Kennedy became president. I joined the administration as one of his special assistants. Interest in Italian affairs was hardly high in the White House, but I soon learned that a member of McGeorge Bundy's National Security Council staff, Robert W. Komer, was also advocating a change in our policy toward the *apertura*. Komer, who had come to the White House from the CIA, was a very bright man, a witty memorandum writer and a relentless goad to action; he later served ably as ambassador to Turkey and undersecretary of defense for policy. He and I at once became allies in the determination to lift the Eisenhower veto on the PSI. Discussions when I went to Italy in April 1961 confirmed my sense that the time was overdue for this change in U.S. policy.

As Komer and I were discovering each other in Washington, Averell Harriman, Kennedy's newly appointed roving ambassador, visited Rome. George Lister, who served as interpreter in some of his meetings with political leaders, alerted Harriman to the embassy's hangup about the PSI and its unrelenting opposition to the center-left. Harriman, whose political instincts were generally unerring (except when it came to his native state of New York), got the Italian situation at once, was much irritated by the pontifical Horsey and, on his return to Washington, pronounced Lister the only officer in the Rome Embassy who understood the Communist problem.

A lot of good this did Lister, however; on his rotation back from Rome, where he received the department's top rating for his job performance, he was informed that the annual Promotion Panel had recommended him for "selection out" of the Foreign Service. Harriman rescued Lister and enabled him to continue to play a key role in changing U.S. Italian policy in the department, though at considerable cost to his personal career. In recent years George Lister has made notable contributions to the development and institutionalization of human rights as a major theme in American foreign policy and as a permanent bureau in the State Department. As for Outerbridge Horsey, the State Department, in the fashion of that day, rewarded him for being wrong by promoting him to become ambassador to Czechoslovakia.

As one who has worked with professional diplomats on a multitude of occasions for more than half a century, I hold the career foreign service in the highest respect—a corps of intelligent, devoted, and brave men and women. But the department that Kennedy inherited from Eisenhower hardly represented professional diplomacy at its best. Under John Foster Dulles and his conception of "positive loyalty," the department had been effectively disciplined and purged. Independent and liberal spirits had a rough time in those Dulles years. The time-servers and reactionaries who prospered under Dulles regarded the new administration as a collection of meddling and soft-headed amateurs.   I knew nothing of it at the time and find it hard to believe even now; but the researches of Alan Platt and Spencer Di Scala reveal that in November 1961 some officers in the Rome Embassy, led, according to Italian sources, by Vernon Walters, the military attaché and a man of extreme right-wing views (later Ronald Reagan's ambassador to the United Nations and George Bush's to West Germany), actually recommended U.S. military intervention if necessary to stop a center-left government. So harebrained an idea would not have got far in the Kennedy administration, but the mere discussion shows the intensity of official resistance to the *apertura*. There is no doubt that Italian opponents of the *apertura*, among them such wily politicians as Giulio Andreotti, eagerly worked on their allies in the U.S. Embassy.

In Washington, despite Averell Harriman's visit to Rome, the department's Italian desk continued to insist on the Eisenhower veto and to oppose any Italian government that would be dependent even on outside support by the PSI. The argument now was that lifting the veto would constitute impermissible intervention in internal Italian politics—a most peculiar argument, since it was the veto itself that constituted the intervention, and lifting it would leave the Italians free to make their own decisions and permit Italian politics to take its natural course.

The new U.S. ambassador in Rome, G. Frederick Reinhardt, was an urbane and likable man of conventional views, who continued, though with much less conviction than Horsey, to oppose the *apertura*. While Freddy Reinhardt supposed that the center-left development was probably inevitable at some point, he wondered what the great hurry was. I had known him in earlier times, and he was always courteous when we met. But he not unreasonably disliked White House amateurs poaching on his turf, and he complained to Kennedy (and later in his oral-history memoirs) about my meddling in Italian affairs.

Of course before getting involved at all, I had talked to Kennedy, as Bob Komer had talked to Bundy. Both the president and his special assistant for national security had no doubt in their minds that it was time for the American veto on the PSI to go. Prime Minister Fanfani's visit to Washington in June 1961 provided an opportunity to signal the change in policy. The *apertura* was not on the State Department's agenda for the talks, but Kennedy told Fanfani privately that, if the Italian prime minister thought the center-left a good idea, we would watch developments with sympathy.

This should have ended the matter, but it did not. The embassy in Rome and the Italian desk in Foggy Bottom both continued their tactics of obstruction. Why did not Kennedy and Bundy simply order a reversal of policy? To answer this question, one must appreciate the murkiness of bureaucratic politics. Both men were preoccupied with questions of far greater urgency. Nineteen sixty-one, after all, was the year of the Bay of Pigs, the trouble in Laos, the Kennedy-Khrushchev meeting, the Berlin Crisis, the Soviet resumption of nuclear testing. Kennedy and Bundy were having arguments with the department on fronts they considered a good deal more consequential than Italy. In effect they gave Schlesinger and Komer hunting licenses, but did not choose to expend their own ammunition on so low-priority an issue. I should add that Kennedy never at any point told me to stop what he well knew I was doing on the Italian front.

Komer and I had allies inside and outside the government. In the department not only Harriman but George Ball, the undersecretary, Roger Hilsman, the chief of intelligence and research, William R. Tyler, assistant secretary for European affairs, and Richard N. Gardner, deputy assistant secretary for international organization affairs (and later a distinguished ambassador to Italy) were with us. Robert Kennedy, the attorney general; Arthur Goldberg, the influential Secretary of Labor; and the wing of the AFL-CIO led by Walter and Victor Reuther of the United Auto Workers were all on our side. As usual, no one knew where Secretary of State Dean Rusk stood.

Still, with top officials otherwise engaged, the anti-*apertura* officers who commanded the direct line of action were able to conduct a dogged rearguard fight. I speculated on their motives in *A Thousand Days:* "It was partly, I imagine, the chronic difficulty of changing established policies; partly the patriotic conviction on the part of certain Foreign Service officers that they owned American foreign policy and, in any case, knew better than the White House [what it should be]; partly an innate Foreign Service preference for conservatives over progressives along with a traditional weakness for the Roman aristocracy. Whatever the motives, the sages of State's Italian desk spent 1961 predicting that the opening to the left would not come for years. Then, as the *apertura* gathered momentum, they produced an alternative argument: that it was coming anyway and therefore did not require our blessing. The pervading attitude was that in no case should we encourage a development which would constitute a crushing blow to communism in Italy and throughout Europe; rather Nenni and his party must meet a series of purity tests before they could qualify for American approval."

I visited Rome again in February 1962. I had then a long talk with Nenni at Tullia Zevi's house. I pressed him on the implications of the *apertura* for foreign affairs. Nenni in his charming and candid way emphasized his dislike of the Communists, his support for the Common Market and his acceptance of NATO on a de facto basis. His party's traditional neutralism, he said, meant the preservation of the existing European equilibrium; such an action, he argued with a certain Jesuitical relish, would clearly be not neutral, so the PSI was against it.

But in May 1962 the State Department Italianists were still declaring that the Nenni Socialists were "not anti-Communist" and that their success would strengthen anti-NATO sentiment in Italy. The absorption of the top people in high-priority items permitted midlevel officials on the Italian desk to continue their obstruction, which they did with impressive assiduity. As I wrote in *A Thousand Days*, "It was an endless struggle. Meetings would be called, decisions reached, cables sent; then the next meeting would begin with the same old arguments. One felt entrapped as in a Kafka novel."

In October 1962, sixteen months after Kennedy's talk with Fanfani, I sent an exasperated memorandum to Bundy. It began: "As you will recall, the White House has been engaged for about fifty years in an effort to persuade the Department of State that an air of sympathy toward the Nenni Socialists would advance the interests of the United States and of Western democracy.... During this period, practically *all* the evidence has supported our view that the Nenni Socialists have split irrevocably from the Communists and are determined to bring their party into the democratic orbit.... During this period, however, State at every step along the way has resisted proposals to hasten the integration of the Socialists into the democratic camp."

Six weeks later State came up with a new and even more far-fetched theory: that, if the Socialists entered the Italian government, the Russians might take it as a proof of U.S. weakness and miscalculate the West's determination—as if Khrushchev based his assessment of American will on the composition of the Italian government. By this time the possibility was arising that, if the opponents of the *apertura* prevailed, this might encourage the Christian Democrats to move right rather than left in broadening the government's base and bring into power a right-wing government with neofascist support, like the disastrous Tambroni government of 1960. In January 1963 Bob Komer and I sent Kennedy a memorandum recalling his Italian directives, describing our frustrations and concluding: "Lest you think you run the United States Government, the matter is still under debate."

However, our campaign was not altogether in vain. The center-left enthusiasts in Rome appreciated efforts and were used to foot-dragging in foreign offices. In February 1963 Anthony Sampson reported to the *London Observer* from Rome, "Nenni, the old firebrand Socialist, cannot now contain his praise for Kennedy.... There is hardly a word of anti-Americanism, except on the far right." In April, Harriman, who had been assistant secretary for the Far East, returned to European affairs as undersecretary for political affairs. The old crocodile was skilled and definitive in the uses of power and rapidly brought the bureaucracy under control.

In July 1963, when Kennedy himself visited Rome, he took Nenni aside at a garden party at the Quirinale Palace and engaged him in a conspicuously long conversation. Opposition to the center-left now vanished in Washington. In November 1963 the Nenni Socialists entered the government. The center-left government was at last in existence.

If only one could say that the center-left victory fulfilled our hopes of thirty years ago! But the failure of the center-left to regenerate Italian politics, to purify the administration of government, to produce economic and social reforms, and to realize Gaetano Salvemini's dream of progressive Italian democracy is another story, and one that many at this conference are far more competent than I am to tell.

As a lover of Italy, I am still waiting—and hoping.

20

POLITICAL LESSONS: ITALY AND CHILE

George Lister

I thought that presentation was vintage Schlesinger. It was very good to hear directly from the man who played the leading role in changing Washington policy regarding the Italian center-left. I was particularly fascinated by Arthur's account of how he became involved in Italian affairs. Those of us who love Italy and are concerned with its past, present, and future are very glad indeed that he did become involved. I wish that I had known Koestler; his books influenced me greatly in my youth. And as I read the opening pages of Arthur's remarks to us this morning, I recalled once again what I consider to be one of the best observations by Karl Marx: "We are all accidents of history." That is the way I see myself and everyone else. So I suppose it was only natural that Arthur Schlesinger's account would cause me to reflect on how I became involved with Italy.

Many years ago I was an undergraduate at CCNY (where Arthur now presides at the Graduate School). Growing up on the sidewalks of New York, I went to CCNY because it was free, and I attended the Evening Session because during the day I was working full-time as a bank teller. CCNY was then one of the more radical colleges in this country. Every night you could find three groups of students arguing and debating in the basement: the Socialists, the Stalinists and the Trotskyites. I did not have much time, but occasionally I would ask questions, moving from one group to another. Looking back on my life you might say this was Operation Head Start. After seven years of night school, I received my degree.

Soon after passing the Foreign Service exams and joining the career diplomatic service, I was assigned to Warsaw as third secretary. Poland was a great university for me. Under the Soviet-imposed dictatorship there, practically everyone was strongly anti-Communist, including most of the government people I met. And Poland was the most pro-American country I have ever known, more pro-American than the United States. Poles saw themselves as caught between Germany and Russia, while we were protected by the Atlantic and Pacific Oceans. Talk about accidents of history! There was a Polish joke that "God watches out for little babies, drunks, and the United States of America." Another Polish joke explained the difference between capitalism and socialism: "Capitalism is the exploitation of man by man. And socialism is vice versa." I left Warsaw feeling that if there ever was a collapse of the Soviet empire it would start in Poland. I was right on that one.

After Poland, I attended a year of Russian-language training at Columbia University, then served two years in Moscow, followed by four years on the Polish desk, back in Washington. By that time I was requesting an assignment in the free world, preferably in a country with a large Communist party. I was very lucky to be sent to Rome as first secretary. And that is how I became involved in Italy.

As Arthur has already said, when I arrived in Rome in late 1957, our embassy shunned contact with the PSI. I had expressed a special interest in covering the Italian Left, and I proposed that I talk with the Socialists (along with the left-of-center Christian Democrats, Social Democrats, and Republicans, of course). Among other things I pointed out that the combined Communist-Socialist vote was growing, and that it might soon begin to approach a majority. I also said I was sure the Communists did not want us to develop a dialogue with the Socialists. My request was granted. So, in February 1958, I called Riccardo Lombardi to seek an appointment. We met for coffee at the Parliament, where Lombardi was a deputy. After some polite exchanges, Lombardi asked whether my visit reflected a change in U.S. policy. I replied that I had just arrived in Rome and was trying to meet as many Italians as possible. Many years later following his death, friends of Lombardi told me that, at the time of this first encounter, he had suspected that I was with the CIA. I was not, and never have been. In any event, our friendship flourished and we had many conversations, which I carefully reported to Washington.

Then my relations with the PSI expanded rapidly, although of course not all Socialists were responsive. Two of my main contacts were Paolo Vittorelli and Giovanni Pieraccini. I debated day and night with my new

Socialist friends, arguing that if they were sincere about helping Italian democracy and the working class they should distance themselves from the Communist party and enter the democratic area of Italian politics. I promised that by so doing they would greatly influence State Department policy and contribute significantly to the development of Italian democracy.

Fortunately my wife, Aleta, and I, along with my mother, had a conveniently located apartment in Rome, and it soon came to be an open house for advocates of the center-left. There was very encouraging progress in Socialist public statements and actions. I even began to receive phone calls (sometimes late at night) from Nenni's friends, asking my opinion of public statements they were thinking of recommending for him. Of course they did not automatically accept views. Occasionally it was suggested that I should meet with Nenni. I would have welcomed that, but I was under embassy orders not to do so, and so I politely declined.

Frankly, one of the greatest surprises in my relations with the Nenni Socialists was their ignorance of the United States. I did not know one PSI leader who had been here, and some of their questions about this country were startling. Let me give you an example. At one point I felt the progress in our relations was so encouraging that it would be useful to invite a leading Socialist for a visit to the United States, as a guest of our government. I suggested Vittorelli. That was no problem for our embassy or the department, and Paolo was certainly enthusiastic. But the day after I invited him he returned to my office, rather concerned, and said that Nenni had ruled he could go to the United States on two conditions: (1) that if he were invited to speak in the United States, he could accept; and, (2) that if he wanted to criticize the United States upon his return to Italy he could do so. I stared at Vittorelli for a moment and then replied that both conditions were fine with us, and that if he would like reliable details about some of the problems and defects in U.S. daily life, I would be glad to supply them before his departure. Vittorelli thought his visit to the United States was a great success, and so did I. Then we invited more Socialists, and they came—without negotiating prior conditions.

Of course, as many of you know, these were difficult times in Italian domestic politics. I will never forget one afternoon during the Tambroni government of 1960, when the Christian Democrats were dependent on MSI support in Parliament. The Communists were hoping to split Italy between the Right and the Left, with the conservatives, neofascists, and the United States on one side, and the democratic Left, the Socialists, and the Communists, supported by the USSR, on the other. On this occasion the Communists had organized a massive rally against the government, and they slowly moved forward toward the police lines, singing and shouting. Suddenly there were shots, and the police cars charged. The demonstrators fled but, after an instant of panic, I thought it best to just stand alone in the street. As the police came hurtling past, I could see what had sounded like shots was the police banging their sticks on the sides of their cars. There were fights and arrests, of course, but I was lucky and walked away unharmed. Those were exciting days.

As Arthur had indicated, this was also a hard time in the embassy, and sometimes I felt isolated. But it helped to know there was some support back in Washington. One of the most dependable Washington advocates of the center-left in those days is here with us today, Dorothy Zaring, along with her husband, Joe Zaring. Dorothy was in the research side of CIA, and an articulate proponent of dialogue with the Socialists.

When my four-year tour of duty in Rome ran out, I was transferred back to the department, where I soon met Arthur Schlesinger, a major step forward for me. Once Averell Harriman had saved me from being "selected out," it was possible to cooperate with Arthur, even though I was no longer officially involved with Italian affairs. We were in close contact; my Italian center-left friends kept coming to Washington, I would take them to the White House to meet Schlesinger, and the dialogue flourished. Arthur continued to play the key role in Washington. Kennedy talked with Nenni in July 1963, and in November 1963 the Socialists entered the government, in large measure thanks to the efforts of Arthur Schlesinger.

Are there any lessons to be learned from all of this? Well, before I try to answer that, let me tell you briefly of a sequel to my Italian experience. Soon after returning to the department, I was assigned to Latin American affairs, where I had begun my career. One of the first countries that caught my attention was Chile, where the Socialist party was in close alliance with the Communists and, once again, there was no Socialist contact with us. I urged that we initiate a dialogue with the Socialists, but to no avail. Eduardo Frei of the Christian Democrats was elected president in 1964 and the Communists and Socialists remained in opposition. Then in 1970, Salvador Allende won a fair election and the Socialists and Communists came to power. In 1973 Allende was overthrown by a military coup, and thousands of Chilean refugees came to the United States. I was soon immersed in the Chilean exile community, including Socialists of various viewpoints. Meanwhile, we were making progress in the department in recommending a higher priority for human rights in our foreign policy, and our Human Rights Bureau was created. The human rights issue was a major factor in our support for Chilean democracy, while distancing ourselves from the Pinochet dictatorship and improving our relations and dialogue with the Chilean democratic opposition. I was convinced that there would be no transition to democracy in Chile without the cooperation of the democratic wing of the Socialist party. And I pushed my Socialist friends hard, urging them to reject Leninism and to take an honest and consistent position in favor of democracy and human rights in their visits to the State Department. When they did that it had a very favorable impact, not only in Chile but also in the United States. Chile returned to democratic rule in 1989 and the Socialists are now in the government.

The stories of Italy and Chile are far from identical, of course, but the similarities are startling. Could the Chilean tragedy have been avoided if there had been a dialogue with the Socialists? What would have happened in Italy if there had been no dialogue with the Socialists? We will never know. But I think both the Italian and Chilean stories call attention to the importance of dialogue and distinguishing between the democratic and the antidemocratic left. I emphasized both of those themes during my visit to Santiago, Chile, as a guest of the Chilean government, and certainly both themes are relevant here today.

Well, with those comments, and in that perspective, perhaps it is best for me to simply conclude by saying that, considering everything, including what *might* have happened in Italy thirty years ago, we were all lucky to have had Arthur Schlesinger in Washington as the defender of Italian democracy.

Thank you, Arthur.

PART 3

IS THERE A FUTURE?

21

A HISTORIAN'S PERSPECTIVE

Giorgio Spini

It seems to me that we are living today at a turning point, a decisive turn on a planetary scale. Indeed, the 1989 revolution, the downfall of the Soviet Union and the end of the Communist governments, are but the most conspicuous aspect of the change we are undergoing. But we must not forget that in the years before the 1989 revolution we had the downfall of all of the last fascist governments and military dictatorships in Latin America. We also must not undervalue the importance of the change wrought in the United States by the end of the Reagan and Bush periods and the beginning of the new Clinton administration. And so it would be odd if only Italy were to escape this revolutionary wave and if the course of Italian Socialism were not to be influenced deeply by the end of the cold war.

But perhaps what now is closing is not only the forty-year period of the cold war; we are probably at the end of an age that began more than seventy years ago. The beginning was with the mass murders, with the horrors of the First World War, when all the most advanced and civilized countries used the instruments of civilization, the most perfect tools of science and progress, for a mass extermination such as the world had never seen before. This was a sort of mortal sin of Western civilization, in fact a horrible civil war among civilized countries. This mortal sin of Western civilization was paid for bitterly with more than seventy years of convulsions. The First World War looked as if it confirmed Lenin's doctrine on imperialism. Remember Lenin and the last stage of capitalism, which led inevitably to imperialistic wars? And so the Leninist revolution was made irresistible. Later the counter-revolution, the Fascist counter-revolution, came, and then Nazism, the Second World War, the Holocaust, and the cold war, but the origin of it all was in 1914. We are now at the closing of this era of blood and of horrors. Seventy years—it's a biblical number, isn't it? It has a certain fascination. Probably, we are at the end of the seventy years' captivity. We may hope that the punishment of Western civilization is at an end and that a new age is opening before us.

Change in Italy in this last year assumed aspects that look less clear than in other countries and that surely leave us disoriented and fearful. It is entirely clear in the United States that there is nothing particularly tragic in passing from Republican administrations to a Democratic one. Relatively clear is a passage in France from the Mitterand era to a time probably dominated by center-right parties. And in case one day England should pass from the Conservative party to the Labour party, it wouldn't be anything surprising. But in Italy a wide section of the citizens looks as if it had a new motto: "abasso la partitocrazia," or "down with the parties." The change arrives with a dark cloud of financial and political scandals, which have hit especially the Christian Democratic party and the Italian Socialist party. The changes are surrounded by a cloud of confusion. Until now our country has been governed by a coalition that proclaimed that it was in power in order to repel the Communists (or perhaps the Fascists); at the same time these parties pretended that they were engaged in ironing out the traditional differences between the rich north and the poor south of the peninsula. It is understandable, if disquieting, that today heirs of Communism and heirs of Fascism or more simply the founders of the traditional privilege of the north, present themselves as the rising forces, the rising stars of Italian politics. And it is also understandable, if disquieting, that they raise that battle cry "down with the parties"—which was, after all, you remember, the same battle cry of Mussolini's fascists. The problem now is what is or what can become the course of the Italian Socialists in this new and highly preoccupying situation.

I arrived here after I attended the last session of the so-called party assembly in Rome. And it seems to me that there are other members of this audience who were with me at that meeting; and I would be glad to listen to their comments or their objections. It seemed to me that the will of the Italian Socialists first of all to put their own house in order was clear, even though there were differences of opinion between a faction more preoccupied with continuity (led by party secretary Giorgio Benenuto), and a current more preoccupied with a break with the past. Led by

Valdo Spini, this latter group believes that it was not only a question of cleaning house but a question of party reorganization. The parties are going to have a period of reorganization that will lead to a new national congress, probably before this year ends.

And at the same time all of the instruments of Italian politics are changing because we all expect a new electoral law that should change the rules of the game. It is suspected that the present system of many parties will be replaced by a system of two or three parties at the most; from the proportional system of voting we will go toward something more like the French or the German system. So the Italian Socialist party will have a congress and prepare itself for a new stage of political history in Italy with a new organization and new instruments. But not only that; I felt the desire for a new program, and this quest was embodied by both the most prominent men in the radical wing of Valdo [Spini] and the moderate wing of Benvenuto. Everyone agrees on the need for a reexamination of the whole program, especially from the point of view of economic, fiscal, and social programs: health, education, and so on. Because we cannot enter into a new world, into a new period of history, with an old baggage of ideas and the same commonplaces that were repeated twenty to thirty years ago, there will probably be a need not for a mobilization of the bodies but of the brains. A mobilization of talents, and probably not those talents that could be found inside the ranks of the party but outside.

Here we are in front of an audience of historians, students of history. Let me advise you, keep your eye on *that* side of the Italian question. It is inevitable that the press and the mass media tend to fill our eyes and ears with stories of corruption, former ministers who have to undergo a trial and so on. That is true, that is important, but it is not all! The change of the political personnel of the party's leadership is important but not only for the future history of Italian Socialism. Let me say frankly the whole history of Italy will be decided by bright new ideas if it is possible, the bright new ideas that will mature during these next months.

We are living in a time of terrible confusion (and not only in Italy); we have a desperate need of clearer ideas and of a new perspective. That shall be the central work and the main course of Italian Socialism in the months and years ahead of us. At least, that is my personal conviction, but, of course, I am not infallible. It would be very nice to have a Methodist pope but I have not been elected, and do not have the privilege of infallibility.

22

ITALIAN POLITICS AFTER "KICKBACK CITY"

Francesco Gozzano

In February 1992, a hurricane hit Italy that overwhelmed the political and economic system. Important governmental, parliamentary, and business exponents, managers of public and private industry, and high functionaries of the state have been involved in the greatest scandal that the country has ever known. The old power structure, tested by a half-century of democratic practice, has been upset and overturned because of an initiative of the magistracy, which has assumed the role of the great "moralizer" of public life and which has provoked a wave of public consensus. Riding this wave have been new political forces, uncompromised by the old government, that have presented themselves on stage with the intention of sweeping away a system judged corrupt.

What has surprised and struck both domestic and international public opinion has been not so much the revelation of the scandals of the past decades as the fact that their discovery has actually touched off a process of liberation, even though a significant section of the public was involved (including that part which declared itself estranged from or hostile to power). If so-called Kickback City has revealed how deep and rooted was the criminal interchange between the political class, the world of business, and high state officials, it has also emerged that benefiting from this perverse exchange was not only a small, corrupt minority but a large slice of the public, with different degrees of responsibility.

Begun as a judicial investigation to unmask existing corruption in the municipal administration of a great city like Milan—once a traditional example of good Socialist government—the judiciary's investigation has not only uncovered the wrongdoings of the politicians but also those of the business class, which until the day before had counterpoised itself to the corrupt political caste and identified itself as an example of the healthy and productive part of the country. And both of these groups have been involved and overwhelmed. The representative institutions and the major parties (DC, PSI, PSDI, PRI, PLI) that in the last decades have governed the country have lost credibility, as have the entrepreneurial class of the largest private (from Fiat to Montedison, from Ferruzzi to Olivetti) and public companies (from IRI to ENI, from ENEL to ANAS [the state holding company, the state hydrocarbon company, the state electric company and the state road-building entity]). The most immediate consequences were the secretaries of the above-mentioned parties losing their positions, the loss of consensus in the last elections, the beginning of an electoral reform, and, most worrying, uncertainty about the country's future. These developments raise a series of questions.

Nor have the repercussions in the business world been less significant. There have been a series of resignations, of a new beginning for the hierarchies of firms, of tragic deaths of industrialists and state company managers, from Gardini to Cagliari, of a profound crisis and consequent paralysis in productive activity, especially with regard to public contracts. Finally, the magistracy has been identified (but unsettling cases of corruption have emerged even among the judges) as the benefactor of humanity, as savior of the country, with the assumption of a protagonist's role in public life over and above the specific tasks of the judiciary power. The consequent confusion of roles has significantly marked Italian political debate.

But we shall examine all of this in greater detail when we discuss Italy's prospects. For the moment, in tracing the events of the last few months, we cannot neglect one question: Why all of this now? Did there not exist before now a system of wide corruption that always enjoyed impunity at all levels? Was the discovery of "Kickback City" the fruit only of a single judge's—Antonio Di Pietro's—actions, or was it also a consequence, even if indirect, of the fall of the Berlin Wall, which has opened up visible cracks in the system of *omertà* and connivance that reigned in Italian society? Probably it was a combination of all these elements. At any rate, it is obvious that in Italy before the discovery of "Kickback City" that there existed as in other Western democracies a subtle corruption at different levels that assumed the form of recommendations, of payoffs, of exchanges of favors, of perquisites, to which almost everybody had tacitly adapted themselves even though every so often some scandal emerged. In the majority of cases, these scandals were ignored by an obliging magistracy.

Among the most notorious episodes to have come to public knowledge were the scandal regarding the banana importations of the 1950s, which involved the then Finance Minister Trabucchi (later acquitted); and the one involving sales of land where, at the end of the decade, Fiumicino airport would be built, and other public works for the Rome Olympic games. We cannot forget that the president of ENI, Enrico Mattei, was considered the originator of the policy of exchanging favors with political parties (which, twenty years later, would produce the so-called petroleum scandal). It was on that occasion that Parliament decided to approve legislation for the public financing of parties in the hope (or the illusion) of thereby breaking the illicit business ties between private interests and the political world. But only two years after the approval of that law the Lockheed scandal exploded. This affair resulted not only in the condemnation of a minister but wounded the president of the republic and forced him to resign.

The singular characteristic of those years was the practically exclusive involvement of Christian Democratic exponents. While it is true that this party had the major responsibility in managing power, it is also true that the DC shared power with the exponents of other parties (PLI, PRI, and PSDI until 1964, then also the PSI) who were only marginally involved in the scandals before the 1980s (the major responsibilities were shared with the Social Democrats, three of whose secretaries were involved or found guilty to different degrees: Tanassi, Longo, and Nicolazzi). It is also singular that almost all the DC exponents emerged undamaged from this involvement in scandals, which did not happen for the PSDI secretaries. Was this because of collaboration with large sectors of the magistracy, above all Roman? Whatever the reason, everything seemed to proceed as usual: a lot of talk and suspicion, but few convictions. The "system" embraced everything, the special forum from which parliamentarians benefited easily acquitted them, and civil society suffered these episodes of corruption seeking in its turn to draw marginal benefits at the expense of the state, which was "robbed" with impunity and which got even by robbing the citizens.

But all this could not protract itself to infinity, and when the degeneration of power assumed clamorous aspects the relationship of *omerta* that had been established between corruptor and corrupted, and the relationship of consensus between majority and opposition, cracked.

What disturbed the subtle web of interests that had consolidated itself within the country and that saw Christian Democrats and Communists joined together—even if on opposite ideological shores—was the arrival of Bettino Craxi as PSI secretary and the explosive role he assumed in Italian political life. Up to then, the Socialists did not effectively condition the hegemonic power of the DC, even though they had entered the governing coalition about a decade earlier. It is true that they had succeeded in imposing upon the government several important points of their program such as the nationalization of the electric industry or a new "workers' constitution," but the Christian Democrats solidly held the reins of command in their own hands. In short, the Socialists were junior partners in the ruling coalition and their weight was not sufficient to modify effective command.

All of this threatened to change when Craxi erupted onto the political scene. On the one hand, he attempted to escape the subordinate role the Socialists had vis-à-vis the DC; on the other, he rebelled against the obsequious attitude a large part of the PSI assumed with regard to the Communists. He tried to modify the power ratio with the PCI, hoping to head a movement that would be an alternative to the DC while at the same time continuing governmental collaboration with this party. In simple terms, Craxi challenged the consociative model upon which Italy had been based until then and which saw the DC and PCI in the roles of majority and opposition; there was no hope of a real alternative, given the international veto against the Communists. The new Socialist secretary immediately upset the apple cart. In the Moro kidnapping he adopted an attitude contrary to the line of firmness backed by the DC and the PCI. With regard to governing the country, he asked and obtained from the DC equality in the division of governmental and subcabinet positions, giving rise to a scientific "occupation" of power according to which the most important jobs were no longer to be the exclusive province of the DC but were to be split among the ruling parties: IRI to the DC, ENI to the PSI, an equitable division of RAI (Italian state television), and so on.

But the story did not end with the sharing of benefits. It also invested the more exclusively political aspects of power with the PSI demand for greater prestige, reflecting the "centrality" in politics the Socialists hoped to tear away from the DC in order to become the pilaster of public life. This policy had unpleasant implications and formal aspects. Craxi's brusque and arbitrary manners (considered arrogance typical of the newcomer to power) gave rise to two reactions. On the one hand, new people attempting to insert themselves into the leader's court emerged; on the other, those who criticized his methods distanced themselves from his politics. There appeared a real dichotomy: Craxi was a new personality of undoubted political acumen who attempted to free Italy from the suffocating embrace (the "historic compromise") of Communists and Christian Democrats and to insert the country into the mainstream of modern European social democracies; he was also a person who did not shrink from arrogance in order to affirm himself on the political stage.

This laceration of Craxi's personality could not but have repercussions on his politics. Thus he sought to attain the leadership of the Left, following the example of Mitterand in France, by requesting an act of submission from the Communists; he also, however, refused to break with the DC, cultivating instead ever more convenient alliances with them in a competition that did not assume the shape of a political alternative (because the numbers were not there) but of collusion. Thus the weight and the pressure of the Socialists on the Italian political and economic scene frequently assumed very unpleasant forms. Where political and ideological appeals for a consensus were insufficient, the lack was made up by a web of interests and favors that united administrators and entrepreneurs and that would eventually lead to that degeneration called *Tangentopoli*, or "Kickback City."

But the picture would not be complete if we did not include other contributory elements. The custom of seeking favors indispensable to the maintenance of power had become generalized (and here there was no distinction between majority and opposition). Everyone profited from this atmosphere of corruption, even if marginally, so that the few voices that denounced it did not find sympathetic ears.

Another element emerged with greater clarity during Craxi's four years in power that induced people not to modify their general line of conduct: the undoubted progress on the domestic and the international planes. These were years of economic growth, of reduced internal conflict, of increased international weight (the firm response to the Americans at Sigonella, the entrance into G7): in short, internal stability never before achieved. The game seemed perfect and everyone took advantage of a situation that seemed optimal and destined to last forever (the slogan of the time was: the ship sails). However . . .

The latent dissatisfaction in that part of the public which considered itself excluded from the benefits of the prevailing consociative political situation manifested itself in the regional elections of 1990, especially in the north. In this region a new party, Umberto Bossi's Lombard League, achieved an extraordinary success and affirmed itself as the largest party in Lombardy by overturning, in this and in other regions, the traditional Christian Democratic domination and eroding as well the positions of the other parties. That vote sounded the alarm; it was a symptom of the country's dissatisfaction with the manner in which political power was managed and of the DC's loss of its capacity for interdiction on which it had depended and prospered for forty years. The effects of bad government and the end of the Communist peril unleashed forces that had remained until then unexpressed and repressed. These exposed the precarious nature of the existing political equilibrium and thus also of the governmental formula known as the center-left.

In this way, new political tendencies within the ruling parties gained strength and produced the referendum movement led by Christian Democrat Mario Segni, as well as determining the passage of La Malfa's PRI to the opposition. These movements had their culminating moment in the spring 1991 referendum modifying the electoral law for the Chamber and the substitution of only one preference for the multiple preferences that had existed before. This was not a mere technicality but the first concrete attempt to break the old incrustation and the *omertà* within and among the parties that had resulted, among other things, in the practice of splitting jobs (the so-called *lottizzazione*) and the division of illicit profits that derived from percentage payments on the value of public contracts (the "kickbacks")—the corruption phenomenon that was to explode during the next year. The innovative and explosive charge of that proposal was not fully comprehended by many politicians, beginning with Craxi, who tried to make Segni's initiative look ridiculous by inviting voters to go to the sea rather than to the polling places. This invitation was summarily rejected by the great majority of Italians and the political defeat suffered on that occasion by Craxi signaled the start of his decline and the beginning of the end of consensus within the PSI. It demonstrated that Craxi had committed a grave political error and that he no longer had his finger on the political pulse of the nation. Vice versa, the success of the referendum movement touched off a mechanism that, if not properly alternative to the existing governmental system, strongly conditioned the country's future. Contributing to this development was the end of the PCI, the birth of the PDS and *Rifondazione comunista*, which illustrated how the effects of the fall of the Berlin Wall had reverberations on Italian political life.

During the following months, up to the national elections of 1992, there began a contest between the supporters of the old and tested center-left coalition (first a five-party, and then a four-party alliance) and the innovators who advocated a new but as yet indistinct and contradictory alternative. These innovators had different protagonists—Segni's, referendum supporters, the Republicans now in the opposition, PDS neo-Communists, the hybrid *Rete*, Bossi's League. These were diverse formations but united in opposition to the center-left majority. It was basically between these two coalitions (the one organic, the other profoundly divided) that the 1992 elections were fought. The results were a significant political defeat of the old four-party coalition, which, however, retained enough of its parliamentary majority to produce a government and to elect its candidate as president of the republic (this despite the fact that, during the previous months, and during the electoral campaign, the *Tangentopoli* affair had exploded with the arrest of Mario Chiesa and the Milan city assessors). But the development had not yet assumed the overwhelming dimensions and impetus it was to have in the following months with the request to indict many authoritative Socialists and Christian Democrats (from Craxi to Forlani, from Andreotti to De Michelis). In fact, despite their having been the first ones cited for "Kickback City" the Socialists retained a certain power of interdiction. Even if Craxi personally had to abandon his hope of being elected president of the republic or head of the government, he was still able to make his candidate prime minister, the Socialist Giuliano Amato, who had been a member of his previous government. It thus appeared that the hope that the referendum of the previous year would produce significant election results was in vain. Even if new formations such as the *Rete* and the League had obtained notable results and the DC had retreated, the old four-party coalition was not decisively defeated; in fact, it succeeded in conserving its position of power.

But the power base was vacillating, as the investigation conducted by the Milanese magistrates (baptized "Clean Hands") would soon demonstrate. When, in August 1992, Bettino Craxi on the pages of *Avanti!* attacked the judges, accusing them of having constructed a conspiracy against him, persecuting him without real proof, and neglecting the fact that the illicit financing of parties was a well-worn practice and involved everyone (as Craxi had already maintained in the Chamber in July), he was immediately denounced as attempting to intimidate the judges, of defending a corrupt and illegal system, of supporting corruption, and of himself being corrupt. With Craxi the entire Socialist party was subjected to public scorn, seen as the personification of the evil, and considered part of a system to be overthrown without pity. The effects were seen in the local elections of spring 1993, which witnessed a collapse of the Socialists in their traditional Milanese fortress and in the other great cities of the north—and this despite Craxi's abandonment in February of the PSI secretary's position and his practical exile from political life.

The events of the past year and a half have been amply covered by the international press, so it is not necessary to review them. The crisis that invested the system established by the old political parties also produced the hope of profound change in political and industrial relationships. But what shape will such changes assume? A first indication has been the voting law. After a referendum modifying the method of electing senators, legislation has been adopted making analogous changes in the election of the Chamber, passing from proportional representation to single-member districts. New national elections under this system were held in the spring of 1994.

But a fundamental question dominates the political scene. Will the new electoral law be enough to modify substantially and in depth the relationship between citizen and state and the way politics is practiced in Italy? An innovation occurred with the formation of the Ciampi cabinet, the first that has not been headed by a political exponent and whose ministers have been chosen because of their technical qualities and not as party representatives. This government has been indirectly supported also by groups of the traditional opposition (like the League and the PDS) in return for an explicit pledge to resign and to hold early elections immediately after approval of the new electoral law and of the budget. But this temporary measure has not completely satisfied the supporters of a new system, who are represented both inside and outside of the parties. A debate has thus been touched off regarding the real and effective depth of the change that should occur and that has also invested the old political parties.

The first to move in this direction was the Christian Democratic party. It was the first organization to change its secretary (from Forlani to Martinazzoli) and its name (from DC to the Popular Party), to initiate a profound internal restructuring, to modify some rules of its constitution (instituting the rule that its adherents elected to Parliament could not be members of the government), and to react with substantial unity to the loss of credibility provoked by Tangentopoli. It also resisted the flattering innovativeness of Segni and of new local leaders demonstrating, despite the harsh attacks unleashed by the Lombard League, that it remained a vital, if ailing, party that still has a role to play despite having been struck in some of its most representative leaders such as Andreotti. In sum, it has resisted the winds of change and electoral defeats to such an extent that not even its worst enemies can trace future scenarios that do not consider its presence and participation. This is all the more significant if it is remembered that the DC had the burden of power for more than forty years, that the wave of desecration that has hit Italy has obviously invested this party above all others, and that it can no longer invoke its indispensability as an anti-Communist bulwark, given the disappearance or attenuation of the Communist threat.

Giving the lie to those who considered it an obsolete and useless party destined to disappear once its role in the center of the political lineup ended, the DC aimed to present itself as the pole of aggregation of a new centrism in opposition to the League competing with a PDS seeking a similar aggregating function. There is within its ranks, however, a strong current that hopes to reach an agreement with Occhetto's people precisely with a view to fighting the League. The struggle within the party, therefore, is between these two lines, and it is interesting to observe how Mario Segni's defection and the birth of Alleanza Democratica (AD), inspired by him and uniting lay and leftist exponents (PDS members, autonomous Socialists, Republicans), not only has not provoked mass desertions of Christian Democrats toward the new movement, but has not even occasioned formation of a large group oriented toward AD, except in support of a new centrism. The unrest within the PDS touched off by the dialogue opened with AD has been attributed to the DC's new centrism. We may also observe that the failure of exponents who have left the traditional organizations to make converts is not characteristic only of the DC; neither Martelli nor Ingrao, charismatic personalities of the PSI and the PDS, carried many people with them when they left their respective parties. The phenomenon is rather one of abandoning political life, of a disengagement from direct activity, which seems to characterize many personalities once heavily involved in the elaboration and implementation of a particular political line.

This illness seems to have struck the Socialists above all. Craxi's resignation after sixteen years at the party's head and the practical end of internal debate and all internal opposition constituted a trauma for many Socialists. For some, Craxi's resignation meant liberation from a nightmare, from excessive submission to a master; in others it provoked a period of uncertainty and crisis that has caused many defections, especially among the voters. Many of these people were shocked by revelations of crimes committed by Socialist exponents of various levels and in all regions, and the involvement of important personalities who for years had held power on the local and national planes. These revelations had effects in the electoral arena, especially in the large cities, and in the collapse of support within public opinion, already critical of the lifestyle and behavior of many managers.

The dispersal and loss of support at the popular level could not but reflect itself upon the ruling group. Long years of control by Craxi had practically excluded the possibility of an internal opposition capable of assuming party responsibilities once the old secretary and the persons close to him had been ousted. Thus it was not an accident that, Craxi having left, two former union leaders succeeded him within a few months. Giorgio Benvenuto and Ottaviano Del Turco had no responsibility for determining party policy or for managing the organization precisely because of their positions—the first was head of the UIL; the second, the CGIL—and thus no fault for the terrible image the Socialists had in the country.

But for the new PSI heads, the problem was not only that of recouping the party's image but that of elaborating an alternative political line that would be credible compared to the one that failed during Craxi's last days. On the one hand, there reemerged the old push for a rapprochement with a PDS purified of its Leninist and Stalinist incrustations and the rejection of a renewed alliance with the DC and the centrist parties; on the other, there reappeared the jealousy and the traditional rivalry with the ex-Communists. Above all there was the knowledge that by renewing the old "Front" ties with the PDS (which had also been received into the family of the Socialist International) the PSI would have been the junior partner in a leftist coalition while the PDS would have the hegemony; that is, the opposite of Craxi's goal. There was a tendency toward a revival of the relationship with a renovated DC, but at the same time an attentive evaluation of the new situation represented by AD and Mario Segni. The hope was to resuscitate a "different" center-left capable of being an alternative to the PDS embrace.

Pushing the Socialists in the center-left direction was also the PDS's own ambiguity. Claiming to be the only old party immune from "Kickback City" (but this proud claim was contested by the magistrates), the PDS presented itself as the guiding party of a renovated Italian democracy, an alternative to the DC and the League. But two lines also coexisted within the PDS. These were represented by (1) the supporters of unity of the Left, which presupposed a close alliance with *Rifondazione comunista* and the *Rete;* and (2) those who instead remained attentive to the old center in the hope or the illusion of assuming the central role in Italian political life (which had been the boast of the DC and an ambition of the PSI). It was the old division, characteristic of almost all Italian parties, between a soul that wished to be centrist and one that wished to be a political alternative. This is the origin of the unclear relationship between PDS and AD, the PDS's refusal to dissolve the party within a democratic alliance whose programmatic shape was still indistinct, a proud claim of the "diversity" directly linked to the old Communists. If the old axiom of political scientists is true, that all countries are ruled from the center, the PDS had to turn its attention beyond its own Left to a renovated DC, an attention accepted by part of the new Popular Party. In short, the fear raised by the League "wind" encouraged organizations to overcome old ideological divisions and to seek unusual alliances.

The organization that did not seem to have preoccupations of this type was precisely the League. Unlike all the other political parties—which in response to necessities imposed by the new electoral law were already researching possible alliances with a view toward creation of a new coalition government—the League is the only political force that intends to fight its battle alone, even recognizing that its electorate is limited to the north and the center; the South belongs to others. According to the latest prophecies of Umberto Bossi, the League is destined by parthenogenesis to split between a Right and a Left, giving rise within itself to a dialectic typical of democracies but with a "totalizing" vision. In his judgment, the struggle will be between the demands of federalists, who will express what is new, and the "statists" represented by the DC and the PDS, which characterize the "old."

The conflict between old and new is certainly not an unheard-of histori-cal event; would it have erupted anyway had there never been a Tangento-poli? With their Milanese colleagues in the lead, have the magistrates performed a beneficial task for Italian society by injecting into the political world that desire for moral cleanliness that seems to have pervaded the entire country? It is difficult to give a definitive answer to questions that presume others, but what is certain is that a machine has been put into motion. Beginning from judicial investigations this mechanism has turned the political and economic world on its ear, eliminating pockets of corrup-tion that had flourished in the underbrush of Italian politics for decades. This liberating function of the magistracy has been exalted by all as a kind of democratic revolution. But observers have also seen in this substitution of one political power for the others the seeds of confusion among the three traditional orders that support modern democracies.

Perhaps the real problem is something else. Recognizing the necessity of overturning the former system, is there not the risk that in this icono-clastic fury some fundamental values—such as those which relate to human rights—will be swept away? In the end, might not everything be resolved by a new oligarchy substituting the old in the name of the new? Is there not perhaps the danger of encouraging chameleonlike behavior, a reigning hypocrisy in which all degrade themselves in order to keep their positions? Or is there the danger that the craze for newness might allow adventurers and demagogues to triumph, overwhelming democratic insti-tutions and opening the way for hidden authoritarian solutions?

For Italy a future full of political, economic, and moral unknowns has opened. It will be necessary to follow developments attentively and to be vigilant in order to prevent the perpetuation of old systems and protago-nists—and to ensure that dark horizons and forerunners of the most dispa-rate and desperate adventurers do not appear.

23

IS A "SECOND REPUBLIC" NECESSARY?

Elisa Carrillo

Because of international Communism's collapse and the cold war's end, there have been major changes in the manner in which the Italians are facing major scandals shaking the republic. Let us look at the past. If we consider Mafia penetration of the political process and the attempt of the P-2 Masonic Lodge to substitute its power for that of the state; if we focus on three episodes of the 1980s—the Mafia assassination of General Carlo Alberto Dalla Chiesa in Palermo, the mysterious suicide of the financier Roberto Calvi under Blackfriars' Bridge in London, and the equally non-suicidal suicide by poison in an Italian prison of another notorious financier, Michele Sindona—it might seem that they are interconnected and symptomatic of structural flaws in Italian democracy.

This allegation may have some merit for the past, but can we maintain that it holds up today? Scandals are no longer ignored or tolerated, if one may judge from the current wave of arrests of prominent politicians and businessmen, the resignation of cabinet members, and the strong support given by the general public to "Operation Clean Hands." All the major parties have been implicated in the kickback scandals, which have involved bribes to politicians for government contracts for everything from the presidencies of state agencies to cleaning hospitals. During recent weeks alone, three cabinet ministers have resigned, and the head of ENI, the giant state-owned energy agency, has been arrested.

Although it is true that power has not alternated since the republic's formation in 1946, it would be well to remember that alternation depends on the will of the electorate, and for whatever reason(s), the electorate chose to give the Christian Democratic party a plurality of votes. But does this fact, which has been the root cause of past scandals, reflect structural flaws in Italian democracy? One may legitimately speculate on whether the defects in the constitution and political process that have permitted scandals can be remedied without structural changes. There have been some promising developments in this sense:

First, while not tampering with Italy's basic social welfare system, the Amato government succeeded in obtaining an austerity budget that for the first time in decades made a real effort at self-discipline. The reduction of the cabinet from thirty to twenty-four members reduced the swollen government bureaucracy and the opportunities for political patronage.

Second, tough measures against organized crime and especially the Mafia have been adopted. These give more power to the police and judges. The assassination of top Sicilian magistrates Falcone and Borsellino in 1992 incensed Italians in general, not merely the Sicilians.

Third, important steps have been initiated to privatize the enormous state holdings, which represent a far larger share of the national economy than in any other member of the European Community and which, more important, constitute juicy plums for thousands of political appointees.

Fourth, the system of proportional representation has been modified. The republic's founders, in a reaction against Fascism, designed the system to give expression to as many political opinions as possible. This goal was obtained, but, almost as a corollary, it produced political gridlock, the avoidance of accountability, and coalition government based not so much on shared values as on a distribution of patronage.

Fifth and finally—and this is the cause for the greatest optimism— there is a revival of civic consciousness among Italians. Perhaps many Italians were willing to put up with corruption in the government when a Communist threat was perceived, but with the erosion of this threat, they no longer see their personal fates tied to specific parties. To dishonesty, corruption, and violence, the average Italian is now saying, "basta," and the republic's fundamental institutions are sound.

24

THE FUTURE OF THE LEFT: EUROPE AND ITALY

Gino Giugni

Much speculation took place after the collapse of the Berlin Wall concerning the destiny of the Left in Europe. This essay will be based upon the assumption that the political Left, although it is not a concept belonging to the category of logical necessity, is a necessary element of modern democracy.

This is a very easy finding. The real question, however, is, What is the Left? Or better, What is the Left, now? What is or will be Left in Italy?

Up to the collapse of the Wall in Western Europe an almost thorough correspondence between the Left and democratic socialism would have been easily found out. Throughout the century the area of the Left in Europe had been the prevailing domain of Socialist movements in their manifold varieties. In addition, toward the end of the century an epochal event had taken place: the end of the Communist schism. Furthermore the impoverishment of 1968-born leftist gauchism, notably in its Marxian components, had deprived the Left of another wing, this one situated on its antisystem side. From all that, we may infer that at the end of 1989 the area of the left in Europe had been dominated in a uniform and almost hegemonic way by socialism in its reformist or gradualist version (i.e., social democracy). The only challenge, though a marginal one with reference to the whole, was offered by the Green parties, or by the social and opinion movements, (i.e., "single issue" movements).

On the European scale the outlook was clear-cut. Within the area of the free, democratic, and industrial West the only exception to social democratic hegemony was the United States—an exception whose roots have been studied and explored for decades. Three years after the collapse of the Wall, social democratic hegemony is faced with a hard challenge, and the danger of a collapse should not be underestimated.

Social democracy draws its identity mainly from socialist reformism as opposed to revolutionary socialism. A reformist version of socialism has long prevailed within the social democratic area since revolutionary expectations collapsed. But socialist reformism in its long history has taken many different forms.

The classic variety of reformism, of Marxist derivation (mainly, Kautsky, Jaurès, Turati, the Austro-Marxians), which defined itself in contrast to the revolutionary strategy, considers reform as a step toward the creation of a new society. In opposition to petty or piecemeal reformism, it advocates structural reforms. Compared to structural reformism, piecemeal reformism refers mainly to social legislation of low profile not intended to affect the economic system as a whole. One of the latest expressions of structural reformism may be found in the "common program" of the PS and the PCF, or in the so-called revolutionary reformism (Riccardo Lombardi, Gilles Martinet, etc.). Even the earlier version of reformism as "good administration of capitalism" (1936 Front Populaire) is not foreign to this construction insofar as the "good administration" of power is taken itself as a transitory step toward the final, radical transformation of society. The very Italian experiment of the center-left in the 1960s was often carried out within this frame of reference.

Reforms were conceived as tools and targets to stir the masses. Changes are not an end in themselves, but rather a means to trigger and support social movements, thus providing them with a political outlet, in an endless motion toward more advanced reforms. This version of reformism found fertile soil in the Socialist movements in the Southern European countries and had wide acceptance also among nonorthodox Communist intellectual circles. In contrast, trade-off reformism, connected with political patronage, might be classified as a minor expression, if not a degenerate one, of socialist reformism. It never became a doctrine, but it was largely practiced by Socialist parties when and where they exerted or shared power.

In light of these questions we might ask: What is social democracy? A comparative analysis of the values and goals common to the official programs of the Social Democratic parties conducted two years ago discovered that the idea of socialism as a road toward a New Society, a realm of

Utopia, or, to put it gently, a new but predictable structure of the economy and society, had been abandoned.

In other words socialism as an ultimate end, or even as the end of history, passed away. It has been replaced by the ideal of progress as a process of trials and errors. Pragmatism, experimentalism, and an "open society" won the match. Popper has defeated Marx. After one hundred years, we are witnessing the triumph of Bernstein's revisionism combined with the Fabian approach. As far as the spiritual roots of socialism are concerned, the SPD program mentions "Christendom . . . humanist philosophy . . . the Enlightenment . . . Marx's historical and sociological doctrine . . . the experience of the workers' movement," and women's liberation.

This syncretistic philosophy is common to all the European Socialist parties. One may wonder whether a difference still exists with liberalism or at least with the more creative projects of American liberalism. Even the definition of liberal socialism in Europe is enjoying a mounting success. But the question itself does not make much sense: first, because it might be found that European social democracy absorbed like a sponge most such creative projects; second, because at its very end socialism is as European as liberalism in its New Deal, Fair Deal, New Frontier varieties is American. If there is no such ultimate end, the common ground lies in the common values. Their *differentia specifica*, beyond the generally accepted values of freedom and democracy, seem to be solidarity and equality: these values obviously have more appeal in the countries where they have been opposed to a revival of Darwinist individualism. But equality is no longer conceived as uniformity. In the Second International era the word *Kollektivismus* had been among the most commonly employed in the language of Socialist doctrines; nowadays, however, equality is conceived as equal opportunity (*Selbstbehauptung* [self-maintenance] is one of the values emphasized in the SPD program). In turn, solidarity generates loyalty to the social or welfare state, but with two important developments. First, the welfare state is built upon the readiness of the "stronger" social layer to share with the weaker, but without worsening permanently its standard of living, therefore remaining "strong." Neither impoverishment and pauperism nor austerity would belong to the "Socialist way of life." Second, the state should provide guidance to individual and/or group self-help, instead of relieving them of responsibility for themselves.

As we go through the specific demands listed in the rather lengthy Socialist programs, we find, for instance, that traditional demands such as worker participation seem to have lost priority, while the cognate idea of economic democracy often seems to be a container of vagueness. On the contrary, there has been an unforeseeable reversal in the hierarchy of topics, and prominence has been gained by the issues relating to civil, political, and social rights.

The conversion to market-economy philosophy is complete, but some basic ideas as public spending in a Keynesian policy framework still hold on. The same applies to public property; although more than a dogma it still appears to be considered a workable tool—with decreasing importance, however—aimed at improving the environmental context of the market itself. Nationalization is no longer the mythical aim it used to be; its appeal ended with the implementation of the Common Program by the Mauroy government in 1981.

A new aspect lies in the social basis of Socialist movements, one sought after everywhere, far beyond the boundaries of the working class, with keen attention being paid to consumers and the self-employed. Social democracy is no longer the political arm of the trade unions as it had been defined until recently. Organized labor still plays an important political role in some countries (e.g., Germany and the United Kingdom). But it can no longer be identified as the main support for the once almost exclusive workers' party. Social democracy is not even an organized "social block," but rather a multiclass, an opinion, or even a catchall party. The new but intense attention being paid to ecology (or, even more recently, to bioethics) calls for a social consensus widely larger than that achievable through wage earners (who on these issues can at times be found on the wrong side) or anyway though a permanent alliance among social classes.

Such was the reality of social democracy in its peak of expansion at the end of the 1980s. The picture has changed, mainly in the Latin or Southern European countries, where socialism is facing dramatic crises. It may be a symptom of a historical decline, but to answer the question as to whether social democracy would be swept away by a revival of revolutionary expectations, or replaced or integrated into left liberal democratic movements, is for the time being more a matter for prophecy than for rational prediction. It should be emphasized that in recent decades most Socialist parties had been called to rule their countries (and, of foremost importance, local governments) and that the exercise of power usually displays a corrosive effect mainly on public morality. A loss of electoral appeal in Spain, Sweden, Greece, or even France—where postelection prospects look for now the worst—might be a sheer physiological effect of an exercise of power that has lasted too long. One can hardly state, on the contrary, that this decline is affecting the SPD or even the Labour party. Although the latter party has been out of power for almost fifteen years, after suffering from splits and defeats, it still seems to exert an unchallenged leadership of the opposition.

Historical decline or temporary setback, preservation of identity or confluence into a newborn Left—all of these dilemmas at present cannot find an answer that would not be written in water. In spite of all, experience shows that social democracy (or liberal socialism) in Western Europe still maintains a dominant role within the Left, and sometimes is identifiable with the Left itself. It is in the process of losing power in government, but it still would lead the opposition. Even in France, the foreseen challenge of the Greens did not materialize.

The case of Italian Socialism is the most dramatic. The forecast of a possible historical decline should be coupled with the more drastic one of a possible collapse, affecting at least its older branch, the Italian Socialist party, and even the heir of the Communist party, now transformed into the much weaker, uncertain, and divided Democratic Party of the Left (PDS).

The PSI's breakdown is the effect of an unfortunate combination of many factors, including:

- the secondary role played by it within the Left since the fall of Fascism, which was balanced only by the practice of power allotment masterly carried on by the former leader, Craxi, through the use of unbiased power of interdiction or power of coalition. This power derived mainly from a strict proportional representation system. This method of power sharing is now collapsing under the impact of the "clean hands" judicial prosecution;
- the disruption of Craxi's personal, charismatic leadership following the impact of a defeat in the 1992 elections and later the explosion of the "moral question" involving him;
- the above-mentioned judicial, and extensive prosecution of corruption, which is leading to a breakdown of the whole political system, but which hit the PSI and its ruling group, its top and middle leadership harder than other parties;
- the loss of creative initiative in political action, with the practical decline of proposals endowed with a potential appeal, like presidential government;

- the arrogant rejection of the referendum on electoral reform (which greatly appealed instead to public opinion) as a strong symbol of change;
- the stubborn indifference shown toward the process of change taking place in the Communist party after 1989, following the ambitious project to gather into the PSI the right (the governmental) wing of the former PCI. Furthermore, such an attitude, in the present perspective of a modification of the electoral system from proportional representation to single-member constituencies can no longer stand.

Taking the PDS as part of the socialist area (both parties are affiliated with the European Socialist party and belong to the same group in the European Community) one finds a situation that could hardly be considered healthier. The moral question hit this party too, although with remarkably less intensity. The imperative choice between a government program to endorse and a policy inspired by a primary concern with mass action is tackled through the method of avoidance and postponements. The growing competition of the reborn Communist party and other leftist groupings strengthen this practice of wait and see. Its electoral appeal is running around a mere 15%. The search for a new set of principles shows a deep cleavage—partly generational—among "reformist socialists," old Marxists, and a newly shaped layer of leadership leaning toward American liberalism and now, of course, fascinated by Clinton and Clintonism. The latter attitude presents an ambiguous look, where a respectable search for new political horizons stands side by side with an opportunistic attempt to bypass the problem of unity between the two parties, PSI and PDS, that share a common origin and whose members still address one another as "comrade."

The Western European Left, as stated before, by and large still keeps its prevailingly Socialist feature, even though the current decade will show if the trend will be one of decline or consolidation. In Italy, however, the forecast might be darker. Either the Socialist party, in strict cooperation with its historical mate is reborn, or what is left of its immense historical wealth will have to be delivered to a non-Socialist Left. The final outcome might be beneficial, but such a process might be long, and painful, and perhaps full of dangers and traps for democracy itself.

SELECT BIBLIOGRAPHY

Archives

Archivio Centrale dello Stato (Rome)
  Casellario Politico Centrale
  Ministero Interno, Direzione Pubblica Sicurezza
  Partito Socialista Italiano—Affari Generali
  Verbali del Consiglio dei Ministri
Archivio Lelio Basso (Rome)
Archivio Storico della Resistenza in Toscana (Florence)
International Institute for Social History (Amsterdam)
Istituto Giangiacomo Feltrinelli (Milan)
Istituto Socialista di Studi Storici "Filippo Turati" (Florence)
Archivio del Socialismo Italiano (Florence)
John F. Kennedy Library (Boston)
  Arthur M. Schlesinger, Jr., Papers
  National Security Council, Countries File
  Oral Interviews
  President's Office Files

Printed Primary Sources

Anzi, Felice. *Il movimento operaio socialista italiano (1882–1894)*. Rome, 1946.
Atti Parlamentari. Chamber of Deputies and Senate. Rome, various years.
Avanguardia Socialista: Periodico settimanale di propaganda e di polemica. Milan.
Avanti! Rome and Milan.
Baldini, Nullo, and Antonio Verganini. *Cooperazione e socialismo: Relazione al XI Congresso Nazionale*. Reggio Emilia, 1910.
Barbato, Nicola. *Anarchici e socialisti*. Bologna, 1896.
———. *Il socialismo difeso al tribunale di guerra*. Turin, 1896.
Bartalini, Ezio. *Il Partito socialista italiano e l'agitazione antimilitarista*. Imola, 1904.

Benvenuto, Giorgio, et al. *Strategia riformista e sindacato.* Milan, n.d.

Bernaroli, E. *Manuale per la costituzione e il funzionamento delle Leghe dei contadini.* Rome, 1902.

Bissolati, Leonida. *La politica estera dell'Italia dal 1897 al 1920.* Milan, 1923.

———. *Relazione sull'Avanti!* Modena, 1900.

———. *Socialismo e governi: Relazione al VII Congresso Nazionale.* Imola, 1904.

Bollettino della Direzione del Partito Socialista Italiano (Rome).

Bonavita, F. *Questioni al congresso: Ferri o Turati?* Castrecoro, 1902.

Bonomi, Ivanoe. *L'azione politica del Partito socialista e i suoi rapporti con l'azione parlamentare.* Imola, 1902.

———. *Leonida Bissolati e il movimento socialista in Italia.* Milan, 1929.

———. *Le vie nuove del socialismo.* Rome, 1944.

Bosio, Gianni, ed. *Karl Marx-Friedrich Engels: Scritti italiani.* Milan, 1955.

Bussi, Armando. *Socialismo e anticlericalismo: Relazione al X Congresso Nazionale.* Alfonsine, 1908.

Cabrini, Angiolo. *La legislazione sociale, 1859–1913.* Rome, 1913.

Cabrini, Angiolo, and Giuseppe Canepa. *Proposte di assicurazioni sociali in Italia: Relazione pel VII Congresso Nazionale delle società di resistenza.* Turin, 1908.

Centro Economico per la Costituente. *Convegno sui consigli di gestione.* Milan, 1946.

Colajanni, Napoleone. *Gli avvenimenti in Sicilia e le loro cause.* Palermo, 1895.

Congresso operaio italiano tenutosi in Milano nei giorni 2–3 agosto 1891. *Riassunto delle discussioni e deliberazioni.* Milan, n.d.

Cortesi, Luigi. *L'Italia nel 1898: Tumulti e reazione.* Milan, 1951.

———, ed. *Turati Giovane: Scapigliatura, positivismo, marxismo.* Milan, 1962.

Craxi, Bettino. *Costruire il futuro.* Milan, 1977.

———. *Relazione al Comitato Centrale, Roma 15–17 novembre 1976.* Rome, 1976.

———. *Le tesi per il 42 Congresso. Palermo 22–26 aprile 1981.* Milan, 1981.

———. *Tre anni.* Milan, 1983.

Critica Sociale. Milan.

Croce, Benedetto. *Materialismo storico ed economia marxista.* Milan, 1900.

Della Seta, Alceste. *Il Partito socialista e le questioni dell'antimilitarismo: Relazione al XI Congresso Nazionale.* Rome, 1910.

Dinale, Ottavio. *Il movimento dei contadini e il Partito socialista.* Florence, 1902.

Egemonia e democrazia. Gramsci e la questione comunista nel dibattito di Mondoperaio. Supplement to *Mondoperaio,* no. 718 (July-August 1977). Rome.

Ente per la storia del socialismo e del movimento operaio italiano [Opere di G. E. Modigliani]. Attività parlamentare dei socialisti italiani. Rome, 1967.

Giolitti, Giovanni. *Memorie della mia vita.* Milan, 1967.

"Il Governo Craxi." Special edition of *Vita Italiana* 33, nos. 7–8 (July-August 1983).

Gramsci, Antonio. *Opere di Antonio Gramsci.* 5 vols. Turin, 1966.

Graziadei, Antonio. *La produzione capitalistica.* Turin, 1899.

———. *Memorie di trent'anni.* Rome, 1950.

Istituto Giangiacomo Feltrinelli. *Documenti inediti dell'archivio Angelo Tasca: La rinascita del socialismo italiano e la lotta contro il fascismo dal 1934 al 1939.* Introduzione e documenti a cura di Stefano Merli. Milan, 1963.

Kuliscioff, Anna. *Lettere d'amore a Andrea Costa, 1880–1909.* Milan, 1976.

———. *Proletariato femminile e Partito Socialista: Relazione al XI Congresso Nazionale.* Milan, 1910.

Kuliscioff, Anna, in memoria: a Lei, agli intimi, a me. Milan, 1926.

Labriola, Antonio. *Lettere a Engels.* Rome, 1949.

Labriola, Arturo. *La guerra di Tripoli e l'opinione socialista.* Naples, 1912.

———. *Ministero e socialismo: Risposta a Filippo Turati.* Florence, 1901.

———. *Riforme e rivoluzione sociale.* 2d ed. Lugano, 1906.

Lazzari, Costantino. *I principii e i metodi del Partito Socialista Italiano.* Milan, 1911.

Lerda, Giovanni. *Appoggio a indirizzi di governo: Relazione al XI Congresso Nazionale.* Rome, 1910.

Libertini, Lucio, ed. *La sinistra e il controllo operaio.* Milan, 1969.

Lizzadri, Oreste. *Il socialismo italiano dal frontismo all centro-sinistra.* Rome, 1974.

Lotta di Classe: Giornale dei lavoratori italiani (Milan).

Manacorda, Gastone, ed. *Il socialismo italiano nella storia dell'Italia.* Bari, 1966.

Marchetti, Luciana, ed. *La Confederazione Generale del Lavoro negli atti, nei documenti, nei congressi, 1906–1926.* Milan, 1962.

Martelli, Claudio. *Alle radici del terrorismo.* Rome, n.d.

Michels, Roberto. *Il proletariato e la borghesia nel movimento socialista italiano.* Turin, 1908.

———. *Storia del marxismo in Italia.* Rome, 1910.

Mondo Operaio (later *Mondoperaio*). (Rome).

Morandi, Rodolfo. *Opere di Rodolfo Morandi.* Turin, 1961.

Nenni, Pietro. *Gli anni del centro-sinistra: Diari, 1957–1960.* Milan, 1982.

———. *La battaglia socialista per la svolta a sinistra nella terza legislatura, 1958–1963.* Rome, 1963.

———. *I conti con la storia: Diari, 1967–1971.* Milan, 1983.

———. *Intervista sul socialismo italiano.* Bari, 1977.

———. *La lutte de classes en Italie.* Paris, 1930.

———. *Le prospettive del socialismo dopo la destalinizzazione.* 2d ed. Turin, 1962.

———. *Rodolfo Morandi: Una vita, una dottrina, una politica.* Rome, 1955.

———. *Socialisti e comunisti.* Rome, 1944.

———. *Storia di quattro anni, 1919–1922.* Milan, 1976.

———. *Tempo di guerra fredda: Diari, 1943–1956.* Milan, 1981.

Occhetto, Achille. *Il sentimento e la ragione.* Milan, 1993.

Olivetti, A. O. *Questioni contemporanee.* Naples, 1913.

Panzieri, Raniero. *La ripresa del marxismo in Italia.* Milan, 1972.

Partito Socialista Italiano. Stenographic Reports of Congresses, varying years and cities.

Prampolini, Camillo. *L'insurrezione e il Partito socialista.* Milan, 1899.

Progetto Socialista. Bari, 1976.

Rigola, Rinaldo. *Il Partito socialista e il movimento operaio: Relazione al XI Congresso Nazionale.* Rome, 1908.

Romita, Giuseppe. *Dalla monarchia alla repubblica.* Milan, 1966.

Rosselli, Carlo. *Liberal Socialism.* Edited and with an introduction by Nadia Urbinati. Princeton, 1994.

———. *Socialismo liberale.* Turin, 1973.

Salvemini, Gaetano. *Italian Fascist Activities in the United States.* Edited and with an introduction by Philip V. Cannistraro. New York, 1977.

———. *Opere.* Milan, 1960–66.

Schiavi, Alessandro. *Filippo Turati attraverso le lettere dei corrispondenti.* Bari, 1947.

La Soffitta: Organo della Frazione Rivoluzionaria intransigente (Rome).

Treves, Claudio. *Un socialista: Filippo Turati.* Milan, n.d.

Turati, Filippo. *Discorsi parlamentari.* 3 vols. Rome, 1950.

———. *Il Partito socialista e l'attuale momento politico.* Milan, 1901.

———. *Le vie maestre del socialismo.* 2d ed. Naples, 1966.

Turati, Filippo, and Anna Kuliscioff. *Carteggio.* Turin, 1949–78.

Vecchietti, Tullio. *I socialisti per la svolta a sinistra.* Rome, 1962.

Secondary Sources

Agosti, Aldo. *Rodolfo Morandi: il pensiero e l'azione politica.* Bari, 1972.

Amato, Giuliano, and Luciano Cafagna. *Duello a sinistra: Socialisti e comunisti nei lunghi anni '70.* Bologna, 1982.

Amato, Pasquale. *Il PSI tra frontismo e autonomia, 1948–1954.* Cosenza, 1978.

Anna Kuliscioff e l'età del riformismo. Rome, 1977.

Aquarone, Alberto. *L'Italia giolittiana (1896–1915).* Bologna, 1981.

———. *Tre capitoli sull'Italia giolittiana.* Bologna, 1987.

Arfé, Gaetano. *Storia dell'Avanti!* 2 vols. Milan, 1956.

———. *Storia del socialismo italiano.* Turin, 1965.

Averardi, Giuseppe. *Storia dei socialisti democratici da Palazzo Barberini alla scissione del 4 luglio 1969.* Milan, 1977.

Banfi, Arialdo, et al. *Storia del partito socialista.* 3 vols. Venice, 1979.

Barese, Orazio. *Mancini.* Milan, 1976.

Basso, Lelio. *Il Partito Socialista Italiano*. Milan, 1958.

Battalgia, Roberto. *Storia della Resistenza*. Turin, 1953.

Benzoni, Alberto. *Il Partito socialista dalla Resistenza a oggi*. Venice, 1980.

Bocca, Giorgio. *Il terrorismo italiano 1970–1978*. Milan, 1979.

Cafagna, Luciano. *La grande slavina: L'Italia verso la crisi della democrazia*. Venice, 1993.

Cammett, John M. *Antonio Gramsci and the Origins of Italian Communism*. Stanford, 1967.

Candeloro, Giorgio. *Il movimento cattolico in Italia*. Rome, 1953.

Cannistraro, Philip V. *La fabbrica del consenso*. Bari, 1975.

Carrillo, Elisa. *De Gasperi: The Long Apprenticeship*. Notre Dame, 1965.

Cartiglia, Carlo. *Rinaldo Rigola e il sindacalismo riformista in Italia*. Milan, 1976.

Catalano, Franco. *Filippo Turati*. Milan, 1957.

Cazzola, Franco. *Carisma e democrazia nel socialismo italiano: Struttura e funzione della direzione del PSI*. Rome, 1967.

———. *Governo e opposizione nel parlamento italiano: Dal centrismo al Centro-Sinistra*. Milan, 1974.

———. *Il partito come organizzazione: Studio di un caso, il PSI*. Rome, 1970.

Ciufolletti, Zefiro, Maurizio Degl'Innocenti, and Giovanni Sabbatucci. *Storia del PSI*. 2 vols. Bari, 1992–93.

Clark, Martin. *Antonio Gramsci and the Revolution That Failed*. New Haven, 1977.

Colapietra, Raffaele. *Leonida Bissolati*. Milan, 1958.

Colarizi, Simona. *Classe operaia e ceti medi: La strategia delle alleanze nel dibattito socialista degli anni trenta*. Venice, 1976.

Colliva, Paolo. *Camillo Prampolini e i lavoratori reggiani*. Rome, 1958.

Cortesi, Luigi. *La costituzione del Partito socialista italiano*. Milan, 1962.

D'Angelo Bigelli, Maria Grazia. *Pietro Nenni dalle barricate a palazzo Madama*. Rome, 1970.

De Felice, Renzo. *Mussolini il fascista: La conquista del potere*. Turin, 1966.

———. *Mussolini il rivoluzionario*. Turin, 1965.

Degl'Innocenti, Maurizio. *Il socialismo italiano e la guerra di Libia*. Rome, 1976.

De Grand, Alexander. *In Stalin's Shadow: Angelo Tasca and the Crisis of the Left in Italy and France, 1910–1945*. Dekalb, Ill., 1986.

———. *The Italian Left in the Twentieth Century: A History of the Socialist and Communist Parties*. Bloomington, Ind., 1989.

Delzell, Charles. *Mussolini's Enemies: The Italian Antifascist Resistance*. Princeton, 1961.

Diamante, Ilvo. *La Lega. Geografia, storia e sociologia di un nuovo soggetto politico*. Rome, 1993.

Di Scala, Spencer. *Dilemmas of Italian Socialism: The Politics of Filippo Turati*. Amherst, 1980.

————. *Renewing Italian Socialism: Nenni to Craxi.* New York, 1988.

Drake, Richard. *The Revolutionary Mystique and Terrorism in Contemporary Italy.* Bloomington, Ind., 1989.

Emiliani, Paolo. *Dieci anni perduti: Cronache del Partito Socialista Italiano dal 1943 a oggi.* Pisa, 1953.

Fedele, Santi. *Fronte popolare: La sinistra e le elezioni del 18 aprile 1948.* Milan, 1976.

————. *Storia della concentrazione antifascista, 1927–1934.* Milan, 1976.

Finetti, Ugo. *Libro bianco sulla crisi socialista: Tre anni, 1969–1972.* Milan, 1972.

Finzi, Roberto. *L'unità operaia contro il fascismo: gli scioperi del marzo 1943.* Bologna, 1974.

Fondazione Pietro Nenni. *Nenni dieci anni dopo.* Rome, 1990.

Fonzi, Fausto. *Crispi e lo "Stato di Milano."* Milan, 1965.

Galli, Giancarlo. *Benedetto Bettino.* Milan, 1982.

Galli, Giorgio. *Il bipartismo imperfetto: Comunisti e democristiani in Italia.* 2d ed. Bologna, 1967.

Garosci, Aldo. *Storia dei fuorusciti.* Bari, 1953.

————. *Vita di Carlo Rosselli.* Florence, 1973.

Gerosa, Guido. *Craxi: Il potere e la stampa.* Milan, 1984.

————. *Nenni.* Milan, 1972.

Gilbert, Mark. *The Italian Revolution: The Ignominous End of Politics, Italian Style.* Boulder, Colo., 1994.

Giovine, Umberto, and Paolo Pilliteri. *Europa socialista.* Milan, 1979.

Grimaldi, Ugoberto Alfassio, and Gherardo Bozzetti. *Bissolati.* Milan, 1983.

Hellman, Steven. *Italian Communism in Transition: The Rise and Fall of the Historic Compromise in Turin, 1975–1980.* New York, 1988.

Hostetter, Richard. *The Italian Socialist Movement: Origins, 1860–1882.* Princeton, 1958.

Istituto socialista di studi storici. *L'emigrazione socialista nella lotta contro il fascismo (1926–1939).* Florence, 1962.

Landolfi, Antonio. *Il socialismo italiano: Strutture comportamenti valori.* Rev. ed. Cosenza, 1977.

————. *Storia del PSI.* Milan, 1990.

Lange, Peter, George Ross, and Maurizio Vannicelli. *Unions, Change and Crisis: French and Italian Union Strategy and the Poltical Economy, 1945–1980.* London, 1982.

La Palombara, Joseph. *The Italian Labor Movement: Problems and Prospects.* Ithaca, N.Y., 1957.

Lepre, Aurelio. *Storia della svolta di Salerno.* Rome, 1966.

Levra, Umberto. *Il colpo di stato della borghesia: La crisi politica di fine secolo, 1896–1898.* Milan, 1975.

Lindemann, Albert S. *The "Red Years."* Berkeley and Los Angeles, 1974.

Lyttelton, Adrian. *The Seizure of Power: Fascism in Italy, 1919-1929.* New York, 1973.

Mafai, Miriam. *Lombardi.* Milan, 1976.

Maier, Charles S. *Recasting Bourgeois Europe.* Princeton, 1975.

Mammarella, Giuseppe. *Riformisti e rivoluzionari nel Partito socialista italiano.* Padua, 1969.

Manacorda, Gastone. *Il movimento operaio italiano attraverso i suoi congressi (1853–1892).* Rome, 1953.

———. *Storiografia e socialismo.* Padua, 1967.

———, et al. *I fasci siciliani.* 2 vols. Bari, 1975.

Marucco, Dora. *Arturo Labriola e il sindacalismo rivoluzionario in Italia.* Turin, 1970.

Merkel, Wolfgang. *Prima e dopo Craxi: Le trasformazioni del PSI.* Padua, 1987.

Merli, Stefano. *Il "partito nuovo" di Lelio Basso.* Venice, 1981.

Mershon, Carol, and Gianfranco Pasquino. *Italian Politics: Ending the First Republic.* Boulder, Colo., 1994.

Miller, James. *From Elite to Mass Politics: Italian Socialism in the Giolittian Era, 1900-1914.* Kent, Ohio, 1990.

Moretti, Paolo. *I due socialismi: La scissione di Palazzo Barberini e la nascita della socialdemocrazia.* Milan, 1975.

Napolitano, Giorgio, and Eric Hobsbawm. *The Italian Road to Socialism.* Westport, 1977.

Pansa, Gianpaolo. *L'anno dei barbari. Diario cattivo di come la crisi dei partiti ci ha regalato l'incognito leghista.* Milan, 1993.

Pasquino, Gianfranco, and Patrick McCarthy, eds. *The End of Postwar Politics in Italy: The Landmark 1992 Elections.* Boulder, Colo., 1994.

Pedone, Franco, ed. *Il Partito Socialista Italiano nei suoi congressi.* 4 vols. Milan, 1959–63.

Pellicani, Luciano. *Gramsci e la questione comunista.* Florence, 1976.

———. *Miseria del Marxismo: Da Marx al Gulag.* Milan, 1984.

———. *I rivoluzionari di professione.* Florence, 1975.

Pepe, Adolfo. *Storia della Confederazione Generale del Lavoro dalla fondazione alla guerra di Libia, 1905-1911.* Bari, 1972.

Pernicone, Nunzio. *Italian Anarchism, 1864-1892.* Princeton, 1993.

Piccone, Paul. *Italian Marxism.* Berkeley and Los Angeles, 1983.

Punzo, Maurizio. *Dalla Liberazione a Palazzo Barberini: Storia del Partito Socialista Italiano dalla ricostruzione alla scissione del 1947.* Milan, 1973.

Ragionieri, Ernesto. *Socialdemocrazia tedesca e socialisti italiani, 1875-1895.* Milan, 1961.

Riosa, Alceo. *Il Partito Socialista Italiano dal 1892 al 1918.* Rocca San Casciano, 1969.

———. *Il sindacalismo rivoluzionario in Italia.* Bari, 1976.

Roberts, David D. *The Syndicalist Tradition and Italian Fascism*. Chapel Hill, N.C., 1979.

Romano, Sergio. *L'Italia scappata di mano*. Milan, 1993.

Rosengarten, Frank. *The Italian Anti-Fascist Press (1919–1945)*. Cleveland, Ohio, 1968.

Saba, Marina Addis. *Anna Kuliscioff: Vita privata e passione politica*. Milan, 1993.

Sabbatucci, Giovanni, ed. *Storia del socialismo italiano*. 6 vols. Palermo, 1979–81.

Salomone, A. William. *Italy in the Giolittian Era: Italian Democracy in the Making, 1900–1914*. Philadelphia, 1960.

Salvadori, Massimo L. *Egemonia e pluralismo: Il dibattito sul rapporto fra socialismo e democrazia*. Venice, 1977.

Santarelli, Enzo. *La revisione del marxismo in Italia*. Milan, 1964.

Sartori, Giovanni. *Teoria dei partiti e caso italiano*. Milan, 1982.

Scalfari, Eugenio. *L'anno di Craxi (o di Berlinguer?)*. Milan, 1984.

Schiavi, Alessandro. *Anna Kuliscioff*. Rome, 1955.

———. *Esilio e morte di Filippo Turati*. Rome, 1956.

———. *Filippo Turati*. Rome, 1955.

———, ed. *Omaggio a Turati nel centenario della nascita, 1857–1957*. Rome, 1957.

Settembrini, Domenico. *Socialismo al bivio*. Milan, 1978.

———. *Socialismo e rivoluzione dopo Marx*. Naples, 1975.

Spadolini, Giovanni. *L'opposizione cattolica da Porta Pia al '98*. Florence, 1961.

Spini, Valdo. *I socialisti e la politica di piano (1945–1964)*. Florence, 1982.

———, and Sergio Mattana, eds. *I quadri del PSI*. Florence, 1982.

Spriano, Paolo. *Storia del Partito Comunista Italiano*. 5 vols. Turin, 1967–75.

Sylos Labini, Paolo. *Le classi sociali negli anni '80*. Bari, 1986.

Tamburrano, Giuseppe. *Pietro Nenni*. Bari, 1986.

———. *Storia e cronaca del centro-sinistra*. Milan, 1990.

Tamburrano, Giuseppe, and Antonio Padellaro. *Processo a Craxi*. Milan, 1993.

Tasca, Angelo. *Nascita e avvento del fascismo*. 2 vols. Bari, 1965.

Trent'anni di politica socialista (1946–1976): Atti del convegno di Parma. Rome, 1977.

Ullrich, Hartmut. *La classe politica nella crisi di partecipazione dell'Italia giolittiana, 1909–1913*, 3 vols. Rome, 1979.

Valiani, Leo. *Questioni di storia del socialismo*. Turin, 1958.

Vigezzi, Brunello. *Giolitti e Turati: Un incontro mancato*. 2 vols. Milan and Naples, 1976.

———. *Il PSI, le riforme e la rivoluzione (1898–1915)*. Florence, 1981.

Wollemborg, Leo J. *Stelle, Strisce e tricolore: Trent'anni di vicende politiche fra Roma e Washington*. Milan, 1983.

CONTRIBUTORS

JOHN ALCORN teaches history at Trinity College in Hartford, Connecticut. He also specializes in Italian literature. His publications include "I fasci siciliani ed il primo grande sciopero contadino dell'Italia liberale (1893)," *Nuove Prospettive Meridionali* 3, nos. 5–7 (1993).

JOEL BLATT teaches history at the University of Connecticut-Stamford. His specialties are the interwar histories of France and Italy, French responses to Italian Fascism, and French policies toward Italian political emigrés. He has long researched the Rosselli murders in Italian and French archives, turning up significant documents, writing articles, and presenting papers on Carlo Rosselli, his relationship to Italian Socialism, and his opposition to Fascism.

PHILIP CANNISTRARO, Distinguished Professor of Italian American Studies, Queens College, City University of New York, has published widely in the cultural history of Italian Fascism, including work on Fascist propaganda and on Italian-American emigration and a biography of Margherita Sarfatti. Besides his books on fascism, he edited and published a work written by Gaetano Salvemini, *Italian Fascist Activities in the United States.*

ELISA CARRILLO, professor of History at Marymount College, Tarrytown, New York, is best known for a biography of Alcide De Gasperi. She has also published widely in the history of Italian Catholicism.

SIMONA COLARIZI, University of Naples, has published widely in the field of Italian Socialism and, most recently, fascism. She has edited the political writings of Riccardo Lombardi in two volumes, and her books include *Classe operaia e ceti medi.*

ALEXANDER DE GRAND, professor of history at North Carolina State University, specializes on fascism and the history of the Left. Besides his books on fascism, he is the author of a book on Angelo Tasca's role in France and Italy and of a parallel history of the Socialist and Communist parties, *The Italian Left in the Twentieth Century.*

SPENCER M. DI SCALA, organizer of the international symposium that gave rise to this book, has published books on PSI founder Filippo Turati and on Italian socialism from 1926 to 1987, as well as numerous articles on Italy. His most recent book is *Italy: From Revolution to Republic, 1700 to the Present.* He is professor of History at the University of Massachusetts at Boston.

GINO GIUGNI, former president of the Socialist party, served as chair of the Senate's labor committee and as minister of labor. He was instrumental in drafting the major piece of labor legislation during the republic (the "Brodolini law"), has published widely in the field of labor relations, and has close contacts with top American labor experts. He is a contributor to *La Repubblica,* and other major publications and was an influential member of the Mondoperaio group. At the time of Tangentopoli, he was deeply involved in trying to establish a new political force on the Left.

FRANCESCO GOZZANO is a respected journalist with a long and diverse experience. He has specialized in Italian and American political affairs and was most recently editor of *Avanti!*

ANTONIO LANDOLFI is a former senator and principal adviser to former Socialist party Secretary Giacomo Mancini; he was also an intimate of Pietro Nenni and participated in many of the important decisions made within the Italian Left in the postwar period. Landolfi is a professor at the Free University of the Social Sciences at Rome (LUISS) and is the author of numerous books such as *Storia del PSI* and, more recently, *Il socialismo,* and of countless articles and reviews. He has written for *Avanti!* and other newspapers and journals and appears regularly on Italian television. He is one of the best-informed commentators on the Italian political system.

GEORGE LISTER served as a U.S. career diplomat for many years, specializing in Eastern European and Latin American affairs, including assignments to Moscow and Warsaw. He was first secretary in the Rome

Embassy during 1957–61. In early 1958, after obtaining embassy approval, he initiated the first official U.S. contact with the Italian Socialist party (at that time closely aligned with the Communists). Mr. Lister's objective was to persuade the Socialists to distance themselves from the Communists and to enter the democratic area of Italian politics. His efforts proved extraordinarily successful and the Socialists eventually joined in the formation of center-left governments, thereby isolating the Communists. However, the Rome Embassy's deputy chief of mission actively opposed these endeavors; as a result Mr. Lister was not only passed over for promotion but was also recommended for dismissal from the diplomatic service. He was saved by the intervention of Averell Harriman, then with the State Department, as described in Arthur Schlesinger's book on the Kennedy Administration, *A Thousand Days*. Mr. Lister currently serves as senior policy advisor in the State Department Bureau of Democracy, Human Rights and Labor. In November 1992, the government of Chile invited him to Santiago as a guest to thank him for his work on behalf of democracy and human rights there. In May 1994, the Kim Dae Jung Peace Foundation invited him to South Korea to speak on U.S. human rights policy.

BORDEN PAINTER is professor of history, director of Italian programs, and interim acting president of Trinity College (Hartford, Connecticut). He teaches courses in early modern Europe and modern Italy and concentrates his current research on Italian Fascism. His most recent articles are "Renzo De Felice and the Historiography of Italian Fascism," in the *American Historical Review* (April 1990) and "American Films in Fascist Propaganda: The Case of the Exhibition of the Fascist Revolution, 1942–43," in *Film and History* (September, 1992).

LUCIANO PELLICANI is a political scientist, sociologist and professor at the Free University of the Social Sciences in Rome (LUISS). Pellicani contributes regularly to Italian newspapers on current politics and was the editor of the Socialist party's ideological review *Mondoperaio*. He is the author of major works such as *Rivoluzionari di professione* and has published books ranging from Marxist philosophy to Ortega y Gasset to the history of India. Pellicani advised Craxi on ideology and ghostwrote the Socialist secretary's famous "Il vangelo socialista" (*L'Espresso*, 27 August 1978). He immediately turned against Craxi during the early phases of Tangentopoli and organized a national symposium of Socialist intellectuals to confront the issue head-on. As a member of the Socialist party's top organs, including the Directorate and the National Assembly, Pellicani was in a unique position to analyze and criticize the party's policies.

MARGHERITA REPETTO-ALAIA is currently director of the Italian Cultural Institute in Washington, D.C. Her publications include a work on the UDI (Union of Italian Women) and a co-edited book on the foundation of the Italian republic.

THOMAS ROW is assistant professor of history at the Johns Hopkins University, Bologna Center.

GIOVANNI SABBATUCCI teaches contemporary history at the University of Macerata. He has published widely on post-World War I Italy. He has also edited a massive six-volume work on the history of Italian Socialism from its beginnings and a short volume on Socialist reformism.

ARTHUR SCHLESINGER JR. became interested in Italy in his youth and has followed Italian affairs ever since. As special adviser to President John F. Kennedy, he led the movement within the administration favoring participation of the Socialists in the government—which produced the center-left. Famous for his books on American history and a regular political commentator for the American press and television, he is the Albert Schweitzer Professor Emeritus at the Graduate School and University Center of the City University of New York.

DOMENICO SETTEMBRINI, professor of history at the University of Pisa, has written extensively on fascism and communism and has published the wide-ranging *Storia dell'idea antiborghese in Italia, 1860–1989*. He is a regular commentator on current Italian politics for major Italian periodicals.

CARLA SODINI teaches history at the University of Florence. She has published widely in the field of Renaissance and Reformation history but also writes on the history of socialism and current developments in Italian politics.

GIORGIO SPINI is one of Italy's top historians. He has taught at the University of Florence in Italy and at Harvard, the University of Wisconsin, and the University of California-Berkeley. His research works span from Italy, France, and Spain to Great Britain, the United States and North Africa. He is known especially for his books on seventeenth-century European and American history, on the Medici, and on the Italian Risorgimento. A Methodist lay preacher, he is author of a largely diffused history of the Italian Protestants. His last book is a survey of the origins of socialism from More's Utopia to the early nineteenth century. He was decorated with the War Cross for his participation in the Resistance. He is the chairman of the Istituto Socialista di Studi Storici and co-editor of the *Rivista Storica Italiana*.

GIUSEPPE TAMBURRANO, professor at the University of Catania, has published several major books, including *Storia e cronaca del centro sinistra*, and works on Antonio Gramsci, the Christian Democrats, and the relationship between Socialists and Communists. A counsellor to Pietro Nenni, he edited some of his diaries, published a long interview with Nenni, and is currently head of the Nenni Foundation in Rome. He contributes to publications such as *La Repubblica, Il Corriere della Sera,* and *L'Espresso* and regularly appears on Italian television. One of the PSI's most authoritative and critical members, Tamburrano disagreed with Craxi's policies and is co-author of *Processo a Craxi,* an analysis of Craxi's rise and fall from power.

CARLO VALLAURI, professor at the University of Siena, contributes regularly to major Italian periodicals and is an expert and widely published author on the history of socialism and of fascism. His books include *Le radici del corporativismo*, a fundamental examination of Fascist labor policy.

INDEX